Learning Tableau Made Easy

By Indera E. Murphy

Tolana Publishing
Teaneck, New Jersey

Learning Tableau Made Easy

Tolana Publishing
PO Box 719
Teaneck, NJ 07666 USA

Find us online at www.tolanapublishing.com
Inquiries may be sent to the publisher: tolanapub@yahoo.com

Our books are available online at www.barnesandnoble.com. They can also be ordered from Ingram.

ISBN-13: 978-1-935208-37-2
ISBN-10: 1-935208-37-3

Library of Congress Control Number: 2017914132

Printed and bound in the United States Of America

Notice of Liability
The information in this book is distributed on as "as is" basis, without warranty. Every effort has been made to ensure that this book contains accurate and current information. However, the publisher and author shall not be liable to any person or entity with respect to any loss or damage caused or alleged to be caused directly or indirectly, as a result of any information contained herein or by the computer software and hardware products described in it.

Trademarks
All companies and product names are trademarks or registered trademarks of their respective companies. They are used in this book in an editorial fashion only. No use of any trademark is intended to convey endorsement or other affiliation with this book.

v1.0

About The Tools And Techniques Series

Learning Tableau Made Easy, is part of a growing series of computer software books that will cover a variety of software tools that provide the ability to create a variety of reports and visualizations, to aid in the analysis and decision making process. This book has been designed to be used as a self-paced learning tool, in a classroom setting or in an online class. All of the books contain an abundance of step-by-step instructions and screen shots to help reduce the "stress" often associated with learning new software. Some of the titles are shown below.

ISBN: 978-1-935208-36-5

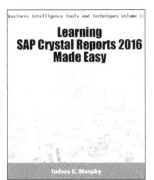

ISBN: 978-1-935208-35-8

ISBN: 978-1-935208-18-1

ISBN: 978-1-935208-34-1

ISBN: 978-1-935208-29-7

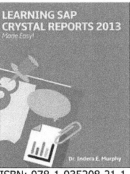

ISBN: 978-1-935208-21-1

ISBN: 978-1-935208-28-0

ISBN: 978-1-935208-22-8

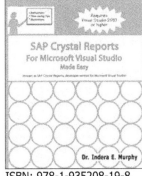

ISBN: 978-1-935208-19-8

ISBN: 978-1-935208-27-3

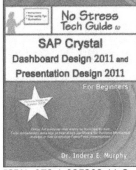

ISBN: 978-1-935208-11-2

ISBN: 978-1-935208-26-6

Visit us online at www.tolanapublishing.com for more titles and information

Why A Book On Tableau?

I felt that readers, especially people new to Tableau, would prefer to have more assistance in learning how to get the most out of the software. As a professor and author, I do not feel that flipping between a web site and the software's help file is the most ideal way to learn how to use the software.

In general, there are very few books with hands-on exercises for this complex software. I know that many books claim to have "step-by-step instructions". If you have tried to follow books that make this claim and you got lost or could not complete a task as instructed, it may not have been your fault. When I decided to write computer books, I vowed to really have step-by-step instructions that actually included every step. This includes steps like which file to open, which menu option to select and more. In my opinion, it is this level of detail that makes a computer book easy to follow. I hope that you feel the same way.

Over the years, I have come to realize that many people only use a small percent of the features that software has to offer. One of my goals in all of the books that I write, is to point out as many features as possible. My theory is that if more people knew about more than 10% of the features that a software package has, at the very least, they would try a few of them.

About The Author

Dr. Indera E. Murphy is an author, educator and IT professional that has over 25 years of experience in the Information Technology field. She has held a variety of positions including technical writer, programmer, consultant, web designer, course developer and project leader. Indera has designed and developed software applications and web sites, as well as, manage technology driven projects in several industries. In addition to being an Executive Director and consultant, as an online adjunct professor, she has taught courses in a variety of areas including project management, technical writing, information processing, Access, HTML, Windows, Excel, Dreamweaver and critical thinking.

Thank you for purchasing this book!

CONTENTS

GETTING STARTED WITH TABLEAU **1-1**
Welcome To Tableau! 1-2
How This Book Is Organized 1-3
Conventions Used In This Book 1-4
Tableau Software Editions 1-5
Self-Service Business Intelligence 1-6
What Can Tableau Do? 1-7
    Step 1: Find The Data 1-7
    Step 2: Connect To And Prepare The Data 1-7
    Step 3: Create The Reports Or Dashboards 1-7
    Step 4: Share The Data 1-7
Tableau Installation Options 1-8
Data Concepts 1-8
Tableau File Types 1-10
Start Page 1-12
My Tableau Repository 1-13
Exercise 1.1: Viewing A Sample Workbook 1-14
Exercise 1.2: Create A Basic Visualization 1-16
    Create The Visualization 1-16
    Create Another Chart 1-18
Data Is Data, Right? 1-19

CONNECTING TO DATA SOURCES **2-1**
Data Types 2-2
Exercise 2.1: Create A Folder For Your Files 2-3
Exercise 2.2: Connect To A CSV File 2-3
    How To Create A New Workbook 2-3
Data Source Tab Workspace 2-5
    Left Pane 2-5
    Canvas Section 2-7
    Grid Section 2-7
    Menu Options 2-10
    Data Source Tab Toolbar 2-13
Exercise 2.3: Create A Connection To A TXT File 2-14
    Changing The Data Type 2-15
Exercise 2.4: Create A Connection To An Access Database 2-15
Exercise 2.5: Change The Location Of The Data Source 2-16
Connecting To SQL Server Databases 2-16
Using Data In A PDF File 2-18
Exercise 2.6: Create A Connection To A PDF File 2-18
Use Some Of The Data Menu Options 2-19
Exercise 2.7: Replace A Relational Data Source 2-19
    Select The Replacement File 2-20
    How To Change The Field Reference 2-21
Exercise 2.8: Paste Data As A Data Source 2-22
Exercise 2.9: Export Data To A CSV File 2-22
    Export Data From The Data Source Tab 2-23
    Export Data From The Sheet Tab 2-23
Exercise 2.10: Import A Workbook 2-23

PREPARING DATA FOR ANALYSIS **3-1**
Is The Data Ready For Visualizations? 3-2
Report Design Process 3-2
Exercise 3.1: Learn About The Data Interpreter 3-6
Is The Data Interpreter Always Available? 3-6

Data Cleansing Options...3-7
    Built-In Data Cleansing Options...3-8
    Built-In Data Transformation Options...3-9
Exercise 3.2: Split Data In A Column...3-10
Filters 3-11
Exercise 3.3: Create Filters For A Live Connection 3-11
    Create The Sales Rep Filter...3-12
    Create The Order Year Filter...3-12
Data Extracts...3-14
Exercise 3.4: Create A Filter For An Extract Connection...3-14
Exercise 3.5: Add Another Data Source To A Workbook...3-15
Exercise 3.6: Working With Pivot Data 3-16
    Pivot Fields..3-17
What Is A Relationship?...3-17
Relational Databases 3-17
Understanding Joins 3-19
What Is The Star Schema?...3-22
Exercise 3.7: Create The Data Sets For The Charts That Will Be Created In This Book 3-23
    Create A Data Set That Has Joins 3-23
    Hiding Columns 3-24
    Renaming A Data Set 3-24
    Add Another Data Source To The Workbook 3-25
Creating Other File Types...3-25
Exercise 3.8: Create A Data Source File 3-26
Exercise 3.9: Create A Packaged Workbook File 3-26
Blending Data 3-26
    Using The Edit Relationship Dialog Box For Data Blending...3-26
Order Of Operations In Tableau...3-27

CREATING CHARTS...4-1
Sheet Tab Workspace..4-2
    Menus 4-2
What Is A Shelf?...4-10
    Columns Shelf...4-10
    Rows Shelf..4-10
Dimensions And Measures..4-12
Continuous And Discrete...4-13
Exercise 4.1: Create A Bar Chart...4-15
How To Create A Vertical Bar Chart 4-16
Data Pane 4-17
Aggregate Functions...4-20
Show Me Button 4-21
Exercise 4.2: Create A Text Table 4-24
Creating And Using A Combined Field 4-24
The Marks Card..4-25
Exercise 4.3: Use The Marks Card Color Option Button 4-27
Exercise 4.4: Create A Highlight Table...4-27
    Change The Highlight Background Color 4-27
Exercise 4.5: Create A Pie Chart..4-28
Exercise 4.6: Create A Side-By-Side Bar Chart...4-29
Exercise 4.7: Create A Stacked Bar Chart...4-30
Exercise 4.8: Create A Continuous Line Chart...4-30
Exercise 4.9: Create A Discrete Line Chart 4-31
Exercise 4.10: Use The Measure Generated Fields 4-32
Exercise 4.11: Separate The Legend 4-33
Organizing Worksheets...4-33
Organizing The Data Pane...4-35
Analytics Pane 4-36

SORT, FILTER AND GROUP DATA **5-1**
    Sorting Data 5-2
        Manual Sorting 5-2
        Computed Sorting 5-2
    Exercise 5.1: Sort Data In Descending Order 5-2
    Exercise 5.2: Sorting Data On A Text Table 5-3
    Sort By Using Drop And Drag 5-3
    Exercise 5.3: Create A Custom Sort Order 5-3
    Exercise 5.4: Sort Data Using The Legend 5-3
    Changing The Default Sort Order For A Field 5-4
    Exercise 5.5: Sort On A Field Not Displayed On The Chart 5-5
    Creating A Hierarchy 5-5
    Filters 5-6
    Filters Shelf 5-6
    Exercise 5.6: Create A Filter For A Date Field 5-7
    Exercise 5.7: Create A Filter For A Category Field 5-8
    Date Field Hierarchy 5-9
    Exercise 5.8: Filter Data By The Order Amount 5-9
    Exercise 5.9: Create Top 10 Filter Criteria 5-10
    Exercise 5.10: Use The Show Filter Option 5-11
    Exercise 5.11: Customize Filters On The Chart 5-12
    Slicing Filters 5-13
    Exercise 5.12: Create A Territory Slicing Filter 5-13
    Exercise 5.13: Create Year And Quarter Slicing Filters 5-13
    Context Filters 5-14
    Exercise 5.14: Create A Context Filter For The Year 5-14
    Pages Shelf 5-14
    Exercise 5.15: Use The Pages Shelf 5-15
    Grouping Data 5-16
    Exercise 5.16: Create A Group By Selecting Category Members 5-16
    Create A Group By Selecting Marks On A Chart 5-17
    Exercise 5.17: Create A Group From The Data Pane 5-18
    Understanding The Include Other Option 5-19
    Sets 5-19
    Exercise 5.18: Create A Constant Set 5-20
    Exercise 5.19: Create A Computed (Dynamic) Set 5-21
        Create The Chart 5-21
    Exercise 5.20: Create a Set From A Filter 5-21
    Viewing Data 5-22
    Exercise 5.21: Create A Bookmark File 5-23
    Exercise 5.22: Copy Sheets To A Different Workbook 5-24

CREATING CALCULATED FIELDS **6-1**
    Types Of Calculations 6-2
    Calculated Fields 6-3
        Options For Creating A Calculated Field 6-3
    If...Then...Else Statements 6-5
    Exercise 6.1: Use The ATTR Function To Calculate The Order Amount By Territory 6-6
    Exercise 6.2: Calculate The Line Item Total 6-7
    Exercise 6.3: Combine String Field Values 6-7
    Exercise 6.4: Use The CONTAINS String Function 6-8
    Date Functions 6-8
    Exercise 6.5: Create A Date Formula To Calculate The Order Processing Time 6-8
    Exercise 6.6: Create Ad-Hoc Calculations 6-10
        Create The Rep Name Ad-Hoc Calculation 6-10
        Create The Line Item Ad-Hoc Calculation 6-11
        Add An Ad-Hoc Calculation To A Chart 6-11
    Table Calculation Types 6-11
    Understanding Data Granularity 6-12
    Quick Table Calculations 6-12
    Exercise 6.7: Create A Running Total Calculation 6-13
    Exercise 6.8: Create A Percent Of Total Calculation 6-13

Apply A Quick Table Calculation To A Chart 6-14
Exercise 6.9: Create A YTD Total Calculation 6-15
Table Calculations 6-15
Exercise 6.10: Use The Add Table Calculation Option 6-15
Modifying A Table Calculation 6-17
Adding Totals 6-17
Exercise 6.11: Add Grand Totals To A Table 6-17
Drill Down On Grand Total Calculations 6-18
Exercise 6.12: Add Subtotals To A Table 6-18
Adding Percents 6-19
Exercise 6.13: Rank Customer Order Totals By State In 2016 6-19
What Is A Parameter? 6-20
Exercise 6.14: Create A Parameter For A Top N Filter 6-21
Exercise 6.15: Create A Parameter For A Calculated Field 6-22
    Create The Parameter 6-22
    Create The Calculated Field 6-23
    Create The Chart 6-23

ADVANCED CHARTS **7-1**
Exercise 7.1: Create A Heat Map 7-2
Geography Maps 7-2
Exercise 7.2: Create A Symbol Map 7-2
Exercise 7.3: Create A Tree Map Chart 7-3
Exercise 7.4: Create A Circle View Chart 7-4
Exercise 7.5: Create A Side By Side Circle Chart 7-4
Exercise 7.6: Create A Dual Line Chart 7-5
Exercise 7.7: Create A Discrete Area Chart 7-6
Exercise 7.8: Create A Combination Chart 7-7
Exercise 7.9: Create A Dual Combination Chart 7-8
Exercise 7.10: Create A Scatter Plot Chart 7-8
Changing The Shape Of The Symbols Displayed On The Chart 7-9
Exercise 7.11: Create A Box And Whisker Plot Chart 7-9

DASHBOARDS AND STORIES **8-1**
Dashboard Workspace 8-2
Exercise 8.1: Create A Sales By State And Category Dashboard 8-4
    Prepare The Sheets For The Dashboard 8-4
    Customize The Dashboard 8-5
Exercise 8.2: Use Two Filters In A Dashboard 8-7
    Modify The Sales By Sub Category Chart 8-7
    Create The Dashboard 8-7
Layout Pane 8-8
What Are Actions? 8-10
Exercise 8.3: Create A Link To Another Dashboard 8-11
Creating Stories 8-12
Story Workspace 8-12
Exercise 8.4: Create A Story 8-13

GETTING STARTED WITH TABLEAU

After reading this chapter and completing the exercises you will:

- ☑ Know about the different editions of Tableau
- ☑ Know how to connect to an Excel workbook
- ☑ Be able to create a basic visualization

CHAPTER 1

Welcome To Tableau!

Tableau is Business Intelligence software that is known for being a tool that is used to create visualizations and dashboards. Almost all businesses today that maintain data, have a need to display and share data to help them get their job done and to make business decisions. Often, businesses have data in a variety of data sources and need a way to pull data from several data sources to create a variety of reports and dashboards, for analysis, presentation and proprietary business requirements.

Reports allow one to be able to read and make sense of large amounts of data, that is most often stored in a database. Some databases have limited reporting capabilities and only allow reports to be created in that "type" of database. If you need to create a report that has data (information) in both Oracle and Microsoft SQL Server databases for example, you could use Tableau to create dashboards using data from both of these databases. In addition to the large scale databases mentioned above, Tableau also supports the following file types: Excel, Access, PDF and text, to name a few.

The primary goal of Tableau is to allow a wide range of users to have the ability to work with the raw data in databases and other file formats to be able to create visualizations that allow data to be interpreted and analyzed. You can also create complex charts that include calculated fields and parameters.

Tableau is a tool that is used to create dashboards that display analytic data visually. What makes it popular, is its ability to take enterprise analysis reporting functionality and make it available in an interface that new users can understand. The fact that Tableau can connect to a large number of data sources, also makes it a popular tool.

Tableau primarily displays data graphically. The benefit that the right visualization provides for analysis, is that they make it easier to see important details and values that are outside of the expected range. A key component of displaying data visually is to make sure that the data does not display too much detail or too much summary data.

Why Aren't More People Using Tools Like Tableau?

There are several reasons that keep people from using BI tools, including the following:

- ☑ Cost.
- ☑ Some tools are very difficult to learn how to use.
- ☑ Little or no technical expertise, in terms of creating reports, paper based or graphical.
- ☑ Some tools are lacking one or more of the features discussed in the next section.

While all of the above are valid reasons for not using BI tools, there are tools that are available that can get you up and running without needing a PhD, to use them. The one skill that I think will make learning Tableau or any other BI tool easier to learn, is if you know and understand the data that you need to use, to create the reports. In my opinion, users that know their data, are better equipped to create reports, then some IT people are.

What Tableau Brings To Visual Analytics

Tableau is used to visually present data in an easy to understand format. Tableau has the ability to display data at a detail level (using the Text Table visualization) or at a summarized level (using a chart visualization). In addition to that, Tableau offers the following and more.

- ☑ Ability to handle and process large amounts of data.
- ☑ Ability to connect to a variety of data sources.
- ☑ Relatively easy for non IT people to learn.
- ☑ A growing array of discovery and ad-hoc analysis options.

Who This Book Is For

This book is geared towards people that are new to Tableau, that need to learn how to create dashboards or presentations, usually for data analysis.

A hands-on approach is usually the best way to learn most things in life. This book is a visual guide that shows you how to create or modify over 55 visualizations. There are over 340 illustrations that practically eliminate the guesswork and let you know that you are completing the steps correctly. As you work through the exercises in this book, my hope is that you start to visualize how you can take some of the topics covered and apply them to the visualizations that you need to create on your own.

The good thing is that you have taken a great first step towards learning Tableau, by purchasing this book. Now, all you have to do is use this book to learn how to overcome the hurdles. From time to time, I will point out functionality that may not work as expected. When I do this, I am not complaining, merely pointing out things that I think you should be aware of.

This book is written from the end user perspective, meaning there is not a lot of in-depth "theory behind the theory", if you know what I mean. I am aware that you have other things to do and that reading and completing the exercises in this book needs to be helpful, but not time consuming, at the same time. I also know from experience that people learning new software want to know why some topics are important. I hope that this book meets your expectations.

It is my sincere hope that whatever your current skill level is with Tableau, that you will learn more about features that you are already familiar with as you go through this book, and that you learn about features that you did not know existed. I also hope that you find that this book gets you up to speed quickly, as time is money! Learning new tips and shortcuts will let you work faster and smarter. The more you know about Tableau, the easier your day to day visual design experiences will be.

So sit back and lets get started!

How This Book Is Organized

Topics and exercises in one chapter build on ones covered in previous chapters. To get the most out of this book, it is not advised that you skip around. The first reason is because some of the workbooks used in later chapters are created in exercises earlier in the book. The other reason is that a topic or option may have been covered in more detail earlier in the book. If you decide to skip around and cannot complete an exercise because there is something that you do not understand, you will have to go back and find the section that covers the topic that you have a question about. Below is an overview of what is covered in each chapter.

Chapter 1, Getting Started With Tableau provides an overview of Tableau, including the editions, file types that can be created, viewing a sample workbook and creating a basic visualization. Software installation options are also covered.

Chapter 2, Connecting To Data Sources covers options on the Data Source tab and how to connect to a variety of data source types.

Chapter 3, Preparing Data For Analysis picks up where the previous chapter left off. More options on the Data Source tab are covered, including creating filters, extracts, joins and blends.

Chapter 4, Creating Charts provides an overview of the workspace used to create charts. This chapter also introduces many of the chart types that are available. And yes, this chapter also covers creating charts.

Chapter 5, Sort, Filter And Group Data covers features that are used to change how the data is displayed on a visualization. This includes creating filters for different data types, understanding the various sort options, and grouping data so that it can be displayed in a specific order on a chart.

Chapter 6, Creating Calculated Fields covers creating formulas that combine string fields, creating calculated fields and using the DateDiff function. Creating parameters is also covered.

Chapter 7, Advanced Charts picks up where Chapter 4 left off. You will learn how to create the following chart types: Tree map, Symbol map, Side-by-side circle, Circles view, Dual line, Discrete area, Dual combination and Scatter.

Chapter 8, Dashboards And Stories covers creating dashboards, creating a link in a dashboard to another dashboard and creating a story.

Objectives Of This Book

This book is written to accommodate self-paced, classroom and online training. While there are no required prerequisites to successfully complete the exercises in this book, having a general knowledge of any of the following would be helpful.

- ☑ Prior version of Tableau Desktop or Tableau Public
- ☑ Database structures

- ☑ Creating filters and sorting data
- ☑ Creating charts

Step-by-step instructions are included throughout this book. This book takes a hands-on, performance based approach to teaching you how to use Tableau and provides the skills required to create charts efficiently. You will get the most from this book if you are sitting in front of your computer and work on the exercises. After completing the exercises in this book, you will be able to perform the following tasks and more:

- ☑ Create connections to several types of data sources
- ☑ Utilize visualization design and planning techniques
- ☑ Understand database concepts
- ☑ Filter, sort and group data
- ☑ Create and customize charts
- ☑ Create calculated fields and use functions
- ☑ Create parameters
- ☑ Create dashboards and stories
- ☑ Export data

Conventions Used In This Book

I designed the following conventions to make it easier for you to follow the instructions in this book.

- ☑ The Courier font is used to indicate what you should type.
- ☑ SMALL CAPS are used to indicate an option to click on or to bring something to your attention.
- ☑ This icon indicates a shortcut or another way to complete the task that is being discussed. It can also indicate a tip or additional information about the topic that is being discussed.
- ☑ This icon indicates a warning, like a feature that has been removed or information that you need to be aware of. This icon can also represent what I call a quirk, meaning a feature that did not work, as I expected it to.
- ☑ This icon indicates that some of the screen shot/figure is not displayed, because it does not provide any value.
- ☑ Many of the options in the software are available in more than one place. I only explain them once. The entries in the index reference where the option is explained or demonstrated.
- ☑ [Text in brackets] references a section, table or figure, that has more information about the topic being discussed. If the reference is in a different chapter, the chapter number is included in the reference, like this: [See Chapter 2, Update Options]
- ☑ When you see "YOU SHOULD HAVE THE OPTIONS SHOWN IN FIGURE X-X", or something similar in the exercises, check to make sure that your screen does look like the figure. If it does, continue with the next set of instructions. If your screen does not look like the figure, redo the steps that you just completed so that your screen does match the figure. Not doing so may cause you problems when trying to complete exercises later in the book.
- ☑ The section heading EXERCISE X.Y: (X equals the chapter number and Y equals the exercise number) represents exercises that have step-by-step instructions that you should complete. You will also see sections that have step-by-step instructions that are not an exercise. Completing them as you go through the book is optional.
- ☑ Some dialog boxes in Tableau have OK and Cancel buttons. Viewing these buttons on all of the figures adds no value, so for the most part, they are not shown.
- ☑ "Save the My practice file as" means to open the My practice file and save it with the new file name specified in the instruction. The reason that I have you do this is to keep the files that you create intact, as some files are used more than once, as the starting point for other exercises.
- ☑ "E2.1 File Name" is the naming convention for exercises that you will create. E2.1 stands for Chapter 2, Exercise 1. You may consider some of the file names long. I did this on purpose, so that it is easier to know what topic the exercise covers. If you do not like to type or do not want to type the full exercise name, you can just type the first part as the file name. That way, when you have to use an exercise to complete another exercise, you will be able to find the correct exercise. For example, if the exercise name is E5.5 Orders shipped between 4-1-2016 and 6-30-2016, you can type E5.5, as the file name for the exercise.
- ☑ DATA ⇒ TABLEAU_DATA ⇒ EDIT DATA SOURCES means to open the DATA menu, select the option (in this case, select the file Tableau_Data), then select the option EDIT DATA SOURCE, as shown in Figure 1-1.

Options that have an ellipsis (...) after the option name (like Refresh All Extracts), opens a dialog box.

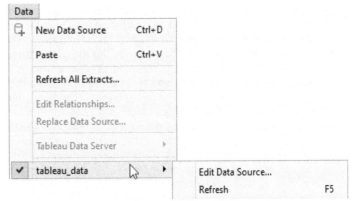

Figure 1-1 Menu navigation technique shown

Assumptions

Yes, I know one should never assume anything, but the following assumptions have been made. It is assumed that . . .

- ☑ You have Tableau version 10.3 or higher installed.
- ☑ You know that the operating system used to write this book is Windows 8.1. If you are using a different version of Windows, any or all of the following can apply:
  ① Some of the screen shots may have a slightly different look.
  ② Some of the instructions for the Windows tasks may be different.
  ③ The path to folders and files (for the software) on your computer may be different then the paths listed in this book.
- ☑ You know that this book only covers the Windows version of Tableau. This book has not been tested using the MAC version of Tableau. (1)
- ☑ You have access to the Internet to download the files needed to complete the exercises in this book and to download any updates to Tableau, that are available.
- ☑ You know to click OK or the appropriate button to close a dialog box and know to save the changes to the workbook or file, before going to the next exercise.
- ☑ You know that when I use the word **REPORT**, that it includes any format that displays data, including visualizations and charts.
- ☑ You know that I am not perfect and sadly, you may find minor mistakes in this book. It is not intentional and I apologize for any inconvenience.
- ☑ You know that the words "field" and "column" are used interchangeably.
- ☑ You know that when you see <smile>, that signifies my attempt of adding humor to the learning process.
- ☑ You understand that there will be options on dialog boxes that will not be referenced in the step-by-step instructions. When that is the case, accept the default value.

(1)
💡 **MAC Version Differences**
I am not a MAC user, but after snooping around, below are the minor differences that I have read about.
1. The keyboard shortcuts are different. The Help file in Tableau, has a table of keyboard shortcuts for both MAC and Windows.
2. The MAC edition has fewer data connectors. The most notable that are not available are MS Access, Analysis Services (SSAS), Power Pivot and ODBC.

Tableau Software Editions

There are several Tableau software editions, as explained below.

- ☑ **TABLEAU DESKTOP** has two versions: Personal and Professional. Besides the cost difference, the biggest difference is the number of data sources that you can connect to. To view a list of the data sources for each version, see www.tableau.com/products/desktop#data-sources-personal.

  The **PERSONAL EDITION** can connect to data sources that are stored on your computers hard drive, opposed to a data source that is stored on a server. Examples that can be used in this edition are Access databases, Tableau Data Extract files, Excel files and .csv files. You can also connect to a few online data sources. This edition can only share and publish files to the Tableau Public server. (2)

The **PROFESSIONAL EDITION** can connect to all of the data sources that Tableau supports. In particular, this edition can connect to more relational databases, including NoSQL databases, Microsoft Analysis Services (SSAS) and web service API's. This edition can publish workbooks to Tableau Public Server and Tableau Online. (2)

☑ **TABLEAU DESKTOP PUBLIC** This edition is free. For the most part, it has the same functionality that Tableau Desktop has. Tableau Desktop Public is an app, meaning all of your work is saved online. The biggest differences are that it supports a limited number of data sources and the workbooks that are created cannot be saved on your computers hard drive. They have to be saved online. This means that other Tableau Public users can search and view your workbooks. For the purposes of learning Tableau, that is fine because you can delete the files when you are done. Keep in mind that data stored on the Tableau Public Server is owned by Tableau. For a list of supported data sources, see www.public.tableau.com/en-us/s/download.

☑ **TABLEAU ONLINE** As its name indicates, this edition is accessed online. Files are created and saved online. The benefit that this edition has over Tableau Public, is that files published online (in the cloud) can only be accessed by people that you authorize. This edition is not covered in this book. For more information, see www.tableau.com/products/cloud-bi. (2)

☑ **TABLEAU READER** This edition is free. It does not allow workbooks to be created. Workbooks created in Tableau Desktop that are saved as a packaged workbook (.twbx), can be opened and interacted with (use functionality like drill-down, filters and discover) in this edition. This is helpful if you do not store the files (.twbs) on a Tableau server, they can be viewed using Tableau Reader. For more information, see www.tableau.com/products/reader.

(2) There is a monthly fee to use this edition.

Getting Help With Tableau

Below are ways to get help if you have a question on how to use a feature or option in Tableau.

① **Read this book** from cover to cover and complete the exercises. Many of the basic questions that you may have are probably covered in this book.
② **Forum** You can post questions and learn how other people are using the software. The forum is also a great way to keep current on the latest trends and for getting ideas on how to enhance the reports that you create. It can be an invaluable resource. You will have to create an account to be able to post and answer questions. There is a link for the forum on the right side of the Start Page in Tableau. [See Figure 1-2]
③ **Read the PDF Help file** This file is the PDF version of the online help file. In the version drop-down list, select the version of Tableau that you have installed, then download the file.
See www.tableau.com/support/help

Tableau Software Updates

Many software companies have changed to a faster update release schedule for some of their software titles. Tableau falls into this category. The core functionality of the software does not change frequently. A large portion of the updates are new features, modifications to existing functionality or name changes of existing options.

One of my favorite features of Tableau is that an updated version (interface changes, new features and bug fixes) is released at least quarterly. For users, that is great. For authors that write books about the software, the frequent updating presents a problem. By the time you read this book, or any book on Tableau for that matter, some parts of the book will be out of date. Sadly, there isn't anything that I can do about this, other then what I am doing right now, and that is to be up front about the situation.

Self-Service Business Intelligence

Business Intelligence, is often called BI for short. BI can also stand for Business Information. Both terms have the same meaning. Even though the concept of business intelligence has been around for over a decade, there are still different schools of thought in the business community on what it is, what it isn't and how it should be implemented. BI is the first topic discussed in this book because it is a primary reason that people use tools like Power Pivot, Tableau and Power BI Desktop. All of these tools allow you to perform some, if not all, of the analysis needed to make business decisions.

BI, in the broad sense, is a collection of technology and applications that are used to gather, store, access and analyze data, often in an enterprise environment. Generally speaking, business intelligence is the process of analyzing data, raw or otherwise and converting the analysis into knowledge. This process is usually used to make business decisions or track business trends and changes. This decision making process requires the raw data to be transformed, so that it can be presented accurately and usually the data is presented in real-time. The typical business intelligence process includes querying, forecasting, data mining, statistical analysis and reporting.

During my corporate IT career, business intelligence solutions were designed and developed by IT people like me. These solutions took months, sometimes years to complete and were often complex. And lets not talk about the cost <smile>. Things are changing, especially for ad-hoc reporting and analysis needs. Self service business intelligence tools are making it possible for business people to create their own reports, often with very little or no help from the IT department.

These tools are often used with what is known as "big data" (a process that companies use to store massive amounts of information electronically). Data Scientists, go through the data using these tools to find business insights (also known as discovering data), to find additional services, products and programs to offer their customers.

BI, especially self-service or personal (do it yourself) business intelligence, is gaining a lot of momentum because companies are looking to bring more decision making tools to their employees. One goal of BI solutions is to bring data from all over the company and place it in what came to be known as a "data warehouse". This repository of data, should be accurate and not redundant. This allows employees at several levels in the company to gain access to data that will help them make more accurate business decisions in a timely manner. And yes, a major goal is to make a company more profitable.

Who Will Benefit From Using Tableau?

There are several categories of people that can benefit from using Tableau, as explained below.

DATA ANALYSTS While people that fall into this category may not have this job title, they will use the software to import data, prepare the data for analysis, create calculated fields, create reports and dashboards, either for their own use or for other people to use.

END USERS often benefit from the work of Data Analysts. They tend not to create the reports or dashboards that they use in their decision making process. At most, some end users will create reports, but not import or prepare the data for analysis. People that often fall into this category are managers and executives in a company. People in this group may be able to use Tableau Reader, instead of Tableau Desktop, if cost is an issue.

DEVELOPERS create Enterprise BI solutions. People in this category usually work in the IT department. They understand concepts like data warehouses, data models, big data and cubes. People in this category know how to design and create the infrastructure needed to support and maintain the BI initiatives. They can also create any new databases that may be needed. Job titles that are in the category are Programmer and Data Architect.

What Can Tableau Do?

The goal of this section is to explain Tableau functionality. You can use this section as a pseudo project plan for each visualization that you need to create.

Step 1: Find The Data

Each visualization needs data. In this step you need to find, connect to, clean and transform the data as needed. If you know that the data is clean and in the right layout, you may be able to skip parts of this step.

Step 2: Connect To And Prepare The Data

The data should be clean by the time you get to this step. The goal of this step is to get the data ready for the creation of the visualization. Calculations that are needed for the visualization (charts or maps for example) are created in this step.

Step 3: Create The Reports Or Dashboards

Tableau offers a wide variety of visualization options that can be used to create and enhance a report, including charts, maps and parameters.

Step 4: Share The Data

Depending on the environment, this step may or may not be needed. This step can be used to load the visualization to the cloud or to a server, so that other people can view and use it. In Tableau, this functionality is known as PUBLISHING A DATA SOURCE. Tableau also has file types that can be used to share the visualizations that you create, without needing a server.

> **What Is The Difference Between The 32 And 64-Bit Versions Of Tableau?**
> ① If you know that you will be working with large data sets (millions of records in tables), you should consider installing the 64-bit version of Tableau.
> ② The 32 bit version can be installed on a computer that has a 64-bit operating system.

> **Which Version Of Tableau Should You Install, The 32 Or 64 Bit Version?**
> If you will use a lot of files created in Excel or Access and you have Microsoft Office installed, select the same bit version of Tableau that your version of Microsoft Office is. [See Chapter 2, Microsoft Excel And Access Driver Requirements] I read a blog post that said that starting with version 10.5, the Windows version of Tableau Desktop, Tableau Reader and Tableau Public, will only run on computers that have a 64-bit operating system.

Tableau Installation Options

If you have not already installed the software, you can use one of the following options, listed below.

Option 1: Install The Trial Version Of Tableau Desktop

The trial version only works for 14 days. I have not used the trial version, but from what I have read, it only allows connections to local files, like text, Excel and Access. You should install the software when you are ready to use it.

1. To download the trial version, go to this web page. www.tableau.com/products/desktop

2. Click on one of the following buttons on the web page. Both buttons point to the same page to download the trial version.
   ☑ Try Now
   ☑ Try it for free

3. Type in your email address ⇒ Click the Download button. I recommend saving the file (TableauDesktop. . .exe), to your desktop, to make it easier to find, but you can save the file wherever you want.

4. When the download is complete, right-click on the file that you just downloaded and select Run, to install the trial version.

Option 2: Install The Tableau Public App

The Tableau Public app requires Microsoft Windows 7 or higher and Internet Explorer 8 or higher. The majority of exercises in this book can be completed using this edition. The exercises that cannot be completed are indicated.

1. Go to this web page. https://public.tableau.com/en-us/s/download

2. Type in your email address ⇒ Click the Download button ⇒ Click the **DOWNLOAD THE APP** button ⇒ Save the file to your desktop.

3. When the download is complete, right-click on the Tableau Public Desktop.exe file and select Run as administrator.

4. Accept the license agreement ⇒ Click the Customize button ⇒ Select at least one of the shortcut options and the Check for Tableau product updates option ⇒ Click the Install button. When finished, Tableau Public will open.

Option 3: Academic Option

If you are a K to 12 teacher, a college student or instructor, this option enables you to get Tableau Desktop for free. I believe that this license is good for one year. Go to www.tableau.com/academic for information and to complete the form.

Data Concepts

Before you go any further, there are some terms that you need to understand to get a better idea of how visualizations created in Tableau can aid in the decision making process, display trends in data and much more. This section explains terms and concepts that you need to understand to be able to use Tableau effectively. These terms will also help you start to understand how powerful Tableau is. You may have heard of some of these terms before, but are not exactly sure what they mean.

These concepts have been around long before Tableau was developed. In some cases, I explain how the concept works in general, then explain what part of the concept Tableau implements or supports. The goal of this section is to briefly explain them and their relationship to Tableau. Think of this section as a mini glossary. Yes, I know that a glossary usually goes at the end of a book, but I believe that these are terms and concepts that you need to understand, or at least be aware of **before** you start to learn how to use Tableau.

Aggregation Is a way to summarize or group data values. This is accomplished by using AGGREGATE FUNCTIONS, like SUM and COUNT.

Dashboards The intended goal is to display large amounts of data in a clear, consolidated and meaningful way. Dashboards usually contain two or more visuals on the same page. A dashboard should allow the person viewing it to see the information at a glance. Sadly, out in the workplace, you will see dashboards that have animation and gauges that are hard to figure out what the data represents. Try not to join the group of people that create this type of dashboard. <smile>. In Tableau, a dashboard is a sheet/view in a workbook that displays visualizations from charts that were created in the workbook.

Data Refresh This feature is used to copy (re-import) the most recent version of data into Tableau, from the original data source.

Data Source A data source is what the data is stored in. Examples of data sources are databases, text files, OLAP cubes and spreadsheets.

Data Source Connection Contains instructions that Tableau uses to connect to a data source, so that the data can be imported into Tableau.

Data Warehouse is a repository that primarily stores enterprise data. The data is stored in relational databases. A data warehouse is often a core component of Business Intelligence, because it has the data that is used for analysis and reporting.

Direct Connection is the same as a LIVE CONNECTION in Tableau. It uses the data source opposed to an EXTRACT CONNECTION (which Tableau supports). An extract creates a copy of the data and saves it with the workbook. Usually, data in an extract file is not current.

ETL is the process of selecting data, loading data, rearranging or deleting columns, joining columns from different tables and creating calculated fields, which are all part of getting the data ready to be analyzed. The IT world refers to this process as EXTRACT TRANSFORM LOAD (ETL for short). Many Excel users have been completing these tasks manually for years, without knowing what its called.

It is very possible that you will need to repeat many of the ETL steps several times to get the data the way that you need it. It took me hours and hours to create the practice files for this book. I remember spending six hours creating and loading data into a database, then realized that I had some fields in the wrong table. In Tableau, ETL is the process of cleaning data.

JSON is a data file format that was originally created in Java Script. This file type can be used in Tableau.

Metadata in Tableau contains the following: changes you make in the workbook, including aliases, joins, connection information, field type changes, groups and sets. Metadata can be saved to a Tableau data source (.tds) file.

ODBC is a generic driver that is used to connect to a Windows based database, that the software (in this case Tableau) does not provide a connector for. An example that comes to mind is a FileMaker database.

Structured Query Language (SQL) is the programming language that is most used to interact with databases. It is used to create and populate tables with data, modify data and retrieve data from a database. This is also known as a QUERY. Before you start to frown, the answer is no, you do not have to write SQL code to retrieve the data that you need for the exercises in this book. At some point, you may have the need for functionality that Tableau cannot provide, in terms of retrieving data to import. If that is the case, you will have to write code to get the data that you need or get someone in the IT department to write the code to get the data for you. In Tableau, you can use SQL, with databases that support it. For example, SQL Server databases, use T-SQL, which is a version of SQL specifically for SQL Server databases. Using SQL, is beyond the scope of this book.

Union A union is a connection between two tables. It is how two or more tables are joined (linked). Tables can be joined when they have at least one field in each table, that has the same value. Tables can have more than one relationship. For example, an invoice table can be joined to a products table because each invoice will have at least one item from the products table. The invoice table could also be joined to a sales rep table if the invoices have a sales rep number. When that is the case, usually the sales reps name is displayed on the invoice. You may know this concept as a **RELATIONSHIP**.

Visualization A visualization is a graphical representation, like a table or chart, that is used to display data. One way that visualizations created in Tableau are different from traditional reports is that they do not have report headers, footers or page numbers, probably because visualizations are usually not printed, like traditional paper based reports are. The Sheets tab is used to create a visualization and customize how the data is displayed. I don't know about you, but I prefer to say "chart" instead of visualization. In Tableau, a visualization or view, is the equivalent to a report and often referred to as a **DATA VISUALIZATION**.

Workbook This is the term that Tableau uses for the files that you create. Tableau uses the term workbook to reference the file that it saves, that has the data, charts, dashboards and stories. I suspect this is because the Tableau workbook has tabs at the bottom, like Excel workbooks have.

Tableau File Types

You can save files that you create in several formats. Some of the file types are used to share the workbooks (and data) that you create, with other people. Tableau has the file types explained below. The extension is in parenthesis. By default, in Tableau Desktop, these files are saved in the **MY TABLEAU REPOSITORY** folder, but you can save them in a different location or you can change the repository location.

 The majority of these file types are not supported in Tableau Public.

- ☑ **WORKBOOKS (.TWB)** This is the default file type when a workbook is saved. This is the most used file type because it is the one that is used to connect to data, create the charts, dashboards and stories. Workbook files can also store any or all of the following: Calculations, renamed fields and aliases. This file type is used to create all of the other file types explained below. (3) (4) (5) (6)
- ☑ **PACKAGED WORKBOOKS (.TWBX)** This file type saves the workbook (.twb) file and background image files. This file type can be viewed using Tableau Reader. (3) (6) (7) (8)
- ☑ **BOOKMARKS (.TBM)** This file type saves one worksheet (one sheet tab in a workbook), that you want to share, in its own workbook. This file can be accessed from any workbook. When this file is opened, a sheet is added to the workbook that is currently open, to display the bookmark file. Filters for the visualization are saved in this file. This file does not include the **PAGES SHELF CURRENT PAGE SETTING** or **PARAMETERS**. The data does not update automatically in this file type. If this file type is not stored in the Bookmarks folder in the repository, it will not appear on the Window menu ⇒ Bookmark submenu. The file can still be accessed, if it is saved in another location. (3) (7)
- ☑ **DATA SOURCE (.TDS)** This file type contains a shortcut to the original data source connection information. It also contains changes made to the data source, including added groups, changed default properties and calculated fields. This file type is helpful when you need to connect to a data source on a regular basis, because using this file reduces the amount of time needed to connect to the data source. Information about the data source is hidden in this file type. (4) (5) (9)
- ☑ **PACKAGED DATA SOURCE (.TDSX)** This file type saves the data source (.tds) file discussed above and data extract file (.tde), as one file. (7) (8) (9)
- ☑ **DATA EXTRACT (.TDE)** This file type is used when you want to share all or a subset of the data. This file has a local copy of the data. The file type is created from an extract connection. Worksheets and dashboards are not saved in this file. This file type allows you to work offline. (7) (8)
- ☑ **MAP SOURCE (.TMS)** This file type is used to save map images from a **WEB MAP SERVICE (WMS)** server or a **MAPBOX MAP**, so that it can be shared. The map can be imported into another workbook or this file can be used to create a new map chart.
- ☑ **PREFERENCE (.TPS)** This file stores a custom color palette that you create.

(3) The connection information is also saved with this file type.
(4) Metadata is also saved with this file type.
(5) This file type does not store the actual data. This keeps the file size small.
(6) By default, this file type is saved in the Workbooks folder, but it can be stored in another location.
(7) This file type is used to share the workbook with people that do not have Tableau Desktop installed or do not have access to the data source.
(8) This file type is saved in a zip file, which also contains local data source files (like Excel and Access files).

(9) By default, this file type is saved in the Data Sources folder.

Sharing Data
Keep in mind that while creating workbooks that can be distributed to others or used without a live connection, that the data may be sensitive. By that I mean that you need to make sure that the people the data will be shared with, have the appropriate security clearance or rights, to view the data.

Tableau Data Sharing Options

The options discussed below are the servers that you can place workbooks and data sources on, so that they can be shared.

☑ **TABLEAU SERVER** This software is installed on a network server. This option is not covered in this book. There is a free 14 day trial version that you can install. For more information, see www.tableau.com/products/server. (10)

☑ **TABLEAU ONLINE** is a hosted (by Tableau) version of Tableau Server discussed above. It requires the data to be in a Data Extract file (.tde) or the data source has to be stored in the cloud. (10)

☑ **TABLEAU PUBLIC** is a free server and hosted by Tableau. Files are placed on this server in the cloud and can be searched for and viewed by anyone that has a Tableau Public account. Files on this server can be viewed using the Tableau Public free app.

(10) There is a monthly fee for this hosting. Files published to this server have to be created in Tableau Desktop Professional.

Opening Tableau

When you first open Tableau, you will see the window shown in Figure 1-2, if you are using Tableau Desktop. This is the **START PAGE**. Figure 1-3 shows the Start Page for Tableau Public.

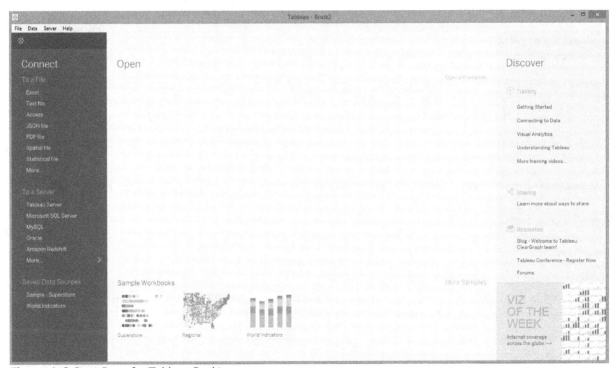

Figure 1-2 Start Page for Tableau Desktop

Clicking the Logo button below the File menu, shown in Figure 1-2, displays the last workspace that you viewed.

Figure 1-3 Start Page for Tableau Public

Start Page

The Start Page has three panes, as explained below.

The **CONNECT PANE** on the left, lists the data source types that you can connect to. The data sources that you see, depend on the edition of Tableau that you have installed. You will see fewer options in this section, if you are not using Tableau Desktop Professional. The sections are explained in the Connect Pane Sections, section below.

The **OPEN PANE** displays workbooks that you have recently opened. As you will see, this section will fill up quickly. At the bottom of this section are sample workbooks that you can use, to get some ideas from. Tableau Public does not come with the sample workbooks.

Clicking the **MORE SAMPLES LINK** opens a web page on Tableau's web site that has more sample workbooks that you can download. They can help you learn more about Tableau.

The **DISCOVER PANE**, on the right, has links for training videos and other learning resources, like the blog and forum.

Connect Pane Sections

The options in the To A File and To A Server sections are used to connect to a data source that you have not already saved a connection for.

To A File The options in this section are for connecting to file that is often stored on your computers hard drive. Select the **MORE** option if you want to select a file created in Tableau that has data that you want to import into the workbook that is currently open, or to use as the starting point for a new workbook.

To A Server The options in this section are primarily used to connect to a data source that is on a server or the web. An exception is connecting to a Power Pivot file, which can be on your computers hard drive. The options displayed in this section will change, depending on the databases that you connect to the most.

If you have server software installed on your computer, you should be able to connect to a local database. For example, I have SQL Server installed on my laptop and can connect to a SQL Server database that is stored on my laptops hard drive, in Tableau.

Selecting the **MORE** option displays the panel, on the right side of Figure 1-4. You will see the database types that you can connect to, based on the edition of Tableau that you have installed.

Saved Data Sources The files in this section are the data sources that have been saved. The ones shown in Figure 1-4 are for the sample workbooks, that come with Tableau.

Connections in this section come from connections that you save in the My Tableau Repository folder. Saving connections to this folder is particularly helpful for data sources that you have to log into, to connect to.

This will save you time because you create the connection once, with the login and security information.

Then when you need to use the same data source in another workbook, select the connection from here. The same connection file can be used by an unlimited number of workbooks.

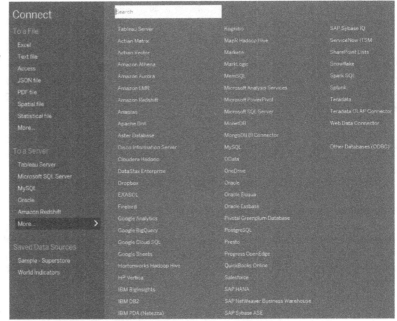

Figure 1-4 Database types that you can connect to

Another benefit of saving connections that require login information is that if the login information or location of the data source changes, you only have to make the changes in the connection file, opposed to having to change several workbook files. Think of a saved data source as a template for a connection.

The Folder Structures In Tableau

When Tableau is installed, two folder structures are created. The Tableau folder structure, shown in Figure 1-5, is in the Program Files folder, on your computers hard drive. It contains the files needed to create workbooks and visualizations. The majority of folders shown in the figure are used to create a repository, as you will see in the next section.

Each software update the you install, creates the folder structure shown in the figure. As shown, I have folder structures for versions 10.2 and 10.3. This means that even though you install an update, you can still run a previous version of Tableau, that you have installed.

Figure 1-5 Tableau folder structure

My Tableau Repository

Folders are created for different file types that you can create. This folder structure is named **MY TABLEAU REPOSITORY**, as shown in Figure 1-6.

The path to these folders is C:\Users\YourUserAccount\Documents.

By default, workbooks that you create in Tableau Desktop are saved to the My Tableau Repository folder.

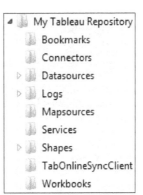

Figure 1-6 My Tableau Repository folder structure

If you want to create your own repository, in a different location, you can, by creating a folder where you want to create the repository, then change the location of the default repository in Tableau. When you do this, the folders shown in Figure 1-6 are copied to the new repository location.

One reason to have more than one repository set of folders is to keep all of the files for each project separate. For example, this year you may create dashboards for the real estate division and next year you create charts and dashboards for the finance department. More than likely, you do not want the real estate dashboards mixed in with financial dashboards.

You can name your repository folder whatever you want, as long as the name meets the Windows naming convention requirements. Changing the location of the repository does not move the files in the original repository.

The contents of the folders that you may have a need to use are explained below.

Bookmarks stores the BOOKMARK (.TBM) files that you create.

Datasources stores data sources, data extracts and a sample Excel file, for the sample workbooks that came with the software. You can copy files to this folder that will be used as a data source. The files that you would copy to this folder are local files. Doing this is optional. If the file that you need is somewhere on your hard drive, you can leave it where it is and still be able to use it in Tableau.

Logs stores the log files that are automatically created. Log files are created when you have a problem in Tableau, make certain changes to the options in Tableau, or run the Data Interpreter.

Mapsources stores the map source (.tms) files that you create.

Shapes contains a copy of the shapes that come with Tableau. You can add shapes that you create to this folder.

Workbooks stores the workbook (.twb) and packaged workbook (.twbx) files that you create.

The **Preference.tps** file is a template file that is used to create and add custom color palettes.

Exercise 1.1: Viewing A Sample Workbook

 This exercise cannot be completed using Tableau Public. You should read through the exercise to get familiar with the workspace.

If you have not already done so, this exercise will show you how to view a sample workbook.

1. Open Tableau.

2. On the Start Page, click on the Superstore sample workbook. You will see the sheet shown in Figure 1-7. This is a dashboard that has three charts. Figure 1-8 shows a sheet (also referred to as a worksheet) that displays data in a text table layout. As you can see, Tableau can display data in a variety of layouts. As shown in the figures, you can see that Tableau has a lot of options.

3. Click the **SHOW START PAGE BUTTON** (the icon, in the upper left corner, with the Tableau logo, below the File menu), to return to the Start Page. You should see the superstore workbook in the Open section of the window.

 Pinning A Workbook To The Open Section Of The Start Page
Over time, you will probably create or open a lot of workbooks. This section can display at least 18 workbooks (at least on my laptop). If there are workbooks that you always want displayed in this section, you can pin them. To pin a workbook, hold the mouse pointer over the icon for the workbook, then click the push pin icon, in the upper left corner, as shown in Figure 1-9. The button for the workbook will display the push pin icon. You will see that pinned workbooks are moved to the beginning of this section.

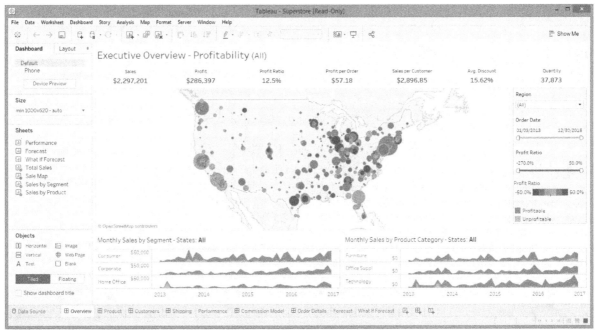

Figure 1-7 Dashboard in the sample workbook

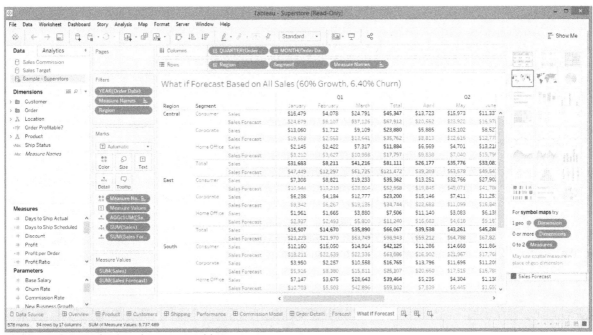

Figure 1-8 Data displayed in a text table

To unpin the workbook, click the push pin button again.

Figure 1-9 Option to pin a workbook

How To Remove A Workbook From The Open Section
Removing a workbook from the Open section does not delete it. It is just removed from the Open section. To remove a workbook, click on the X, in the upper right corner, as shown above in Figure 1-9.

Tableau can connect to Excel **.XLS** and **.XLSX** files, that are created in Excel 2007 or higher.

Exercise 1.2: Create A Basic Visualization

I am sure that you are anxious to see what Tableau has to offer. In this exercise, you will connect to a sample workbook and create a bar chart.

If you are using Tableau Public, complete Chapter 2, Exercise 2.1, then come back here and complete this exercise.

1. Open Tableau, if it is not already open ⇒ On the Start Page, in the Connect pane, click on the Excel link.

2. On the Open dialog box, double-click on the Sample-superstore.xls file. If you do not see this file, navigate to the My Tableau Repository Datasources folder (shown earlier in Figure 1-6) ⇒ Click on the folder for the version of Tableau that you have installed ⇒ Click on the folder for the language that you have installed. The Data Source tab shown in Figure 1-10 should be displayed.

    As shown, the data source (in this exercise, an Excel workbook) has three sheets. The next task is to select the sheet, that has the data needed to create the visualization.

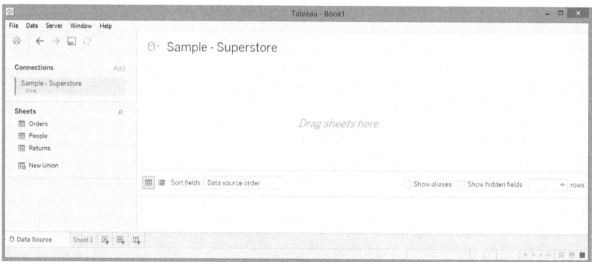

Figure 1-10 Data Source tab

3. Drag the Orders sheet to the **DRAG SHEETS HERE** section, shown above in Figure 1-10.
    Notice in the lower left corner of the window, that a tooltip lets you know what the next step is. In this exercise, none of the data source features, like sorting or filtering the data, will be used.

4. Click on the Sheet 1 tab.

Create The Visualization

The window shown in Figure 1-11 is used to create the visualization. On the left side of the window, on the **DATA TAB**, notice that the data source is listed at the top. If the workbook is connected to more than one data source, all of the available data sources will be listed here. On the right side of the window, you may see the **SHOW ME TAB**. It is not displayed in the figure. It will be displayed when fields are added to the canvas.

1. On the Data tab, in the **MEASURES SECTION**, drag the Sales field to the **COLUMNS SHELF**, as illustrated in Figure 1-12. Notice that part of a chart has been created.

2. On the Data tab, in the **DIMENSIONS SECTION**, drag the State field to the **ROWS SHELF**.
    Notice that several visualization types are enabled on the Show Me tab. You could change the chart type to any of the options that are enabled.

3. Click the Show Me button, to close the tab. The chart should look like the one shown in Figure 1-13. It displays the total sales amount per state.

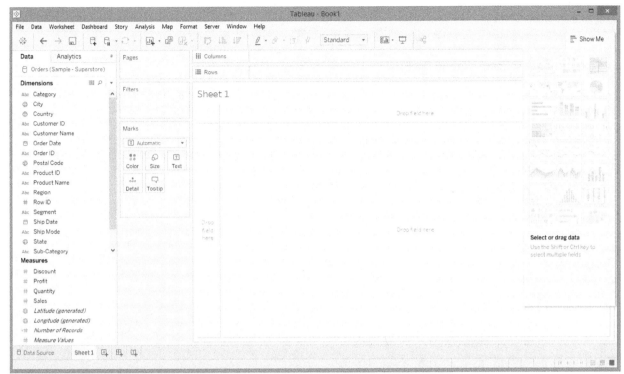

Figure 1-11 Sheet tab

Figure 1-12 Field added to the Columns shelf

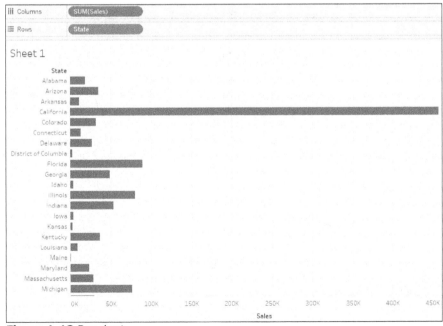

Figure 1-13 Bar chart

Create Another Chart

In this part of the exercise, you will duplicate the chart that you just created and add another field to the chart.

1. Right-click on the Sheet 1 tab ⇒ Duplicate.

2. On the Sheet 2 tab, add the Ship Mode field to the Rows shelf. The chart shown in Figure 1-14 shows the total sales amount by state and by ship mode (how each order was shipped).

    Notice that the states are automatically displayed in alphabetical order. Not bad for adding three fields to the canvas, to create a chart, especially considering that I have not explained what most of the options on the workspace are used for <smile>.

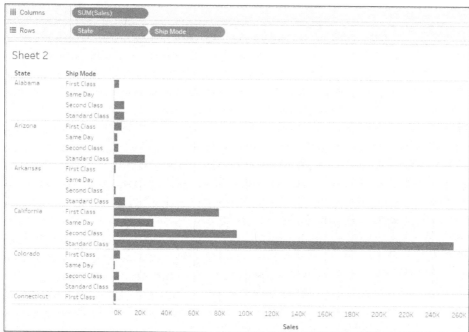

Figure 1-14 Bar chart created using three fields

Save The Workbook

In Tableau Public, read the Publish Files and Connect To The Tableau Server sections in the PDF file, to complete this part of the exercise.

1. File ⇒ Save As.

    The path shown at the top of the dialog box shown in Figure 1-15, is the default location where workbooks are saved. You can save files in another folder.

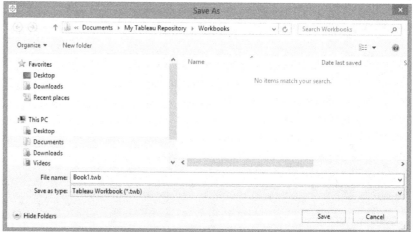

Figure 1-15 Save As dialog box

2. In the File name field, type E1.2 Basic charts ⇒ Click the Save button.

3. Display the Start Page. You will see your workbook in the Open section.

Data Is Data, Right?

The answer to this question is yes and no. That is because there is data that you know about, data that you need to know about and data that you do not know about. Each of these types of data is presented differently, even though they are all used for decision making. These concepts are explained below.

Data That You Know About This type of data is probably the one that you are most familiar with. Reports created from this type of data are used to monitor existing processes. Examples include weekly status reports for monitoring inventory levels or a monthly sales report. Data for this type of report is usually displayed in rows and columns in a table layout.

Data That You Need To Know About Reports created with this type of data is used to try and answer a question, to help determine why something is or is not occurring or why there are values outside of the expected range. An example of this type of report is a sales report by region and product. The report will let you see which products are selling the best in each region. A Top 10 sales rep report by state is another example.

Data That You Do Not Know About The goal of this data concept is to see if there are many patterns in the data. This is known as **DATA DISCOVERY**. This type of report is usually visual. Reasons for creating this type of report includes "What If" analysis and looking for opportunities. Opportunities include ways to improve production, reduce costs or increase sales.

Opening Workbooks Created In Earlier Versions Of Tableau

When you open a workbook that was created in an earlier version of Tableau, you will see the dialog box shown in Figure 1-16.

If you do not want to upgrade the workbook, close it when you are finished viewing it. If prompted to save the changes, click No.

Figure 1-16 Upgrade workbook warning

If you want to make changes to the workbook **AND** need to keep the original workbook intact, open the workbook and save it with a different file name or save it in a different folder with the same file name before making any changes to the file.

CONNECTING TO DATA SOURCES

After reading this chapter and completing the exercises you will:

☑ Know how to connect to several different types of data sources
☑ Know what the options on the Data Source tab are used for
☑ Be able to use options on the Data menu

CHAPTER 2

Overview

As you learned in the previous chapter, Tableau can connect to a variety of data sources. The edition and version of Tableau that you have installed, determines the data sources that you can connect to. New connectors are included, added or updated in the software upgrades. This chapter will show you how to connect to some of the data sources, as well as, how to use the options on the Data Sources tab.

Data Types

Each field in the data source must have a data type. The data type determines what type of information can be stored in the field. Table 2-1 explains the data types that are supported in Tableau. The second column shows the icon displayed in Tableau, that represents the data type. The data types listed in the table, are available in most databases. If the fields in the data source have a data type, Tableau will use that data type. If the fields in the data source do not have a data type, or have a data type that Tableau does not support, Tableau will give the field one of the data types in the table.

Data Type	Icon	Description
String	Abc	The string data type is also known as the **TEXT DATA TYPE**. This data type primarily stores text (non numerical) data. This data type can also store numbers, spaces and other special characters. Numeric data that is stored in a string field is treated like text. This is done when there is no need to use the numeric data in any type of calculation. An example of numeric data that is often stored as a text field, is zip codes.
Numerical	#	This data type can only contain numbers and decimal points. This includes currency values and integers. This data type can be used in a calculation like addition and multiplication. This is the same as the **NUMBER DATA TYPE** that you may already be familiar with.
Date		This data type stores the month, day and year in one field.
Date Time		This data type stores the month, day, year, hour, minutes, and seconds in one field. Often, the time portion of this data type is not displayed on reports.
Boolean	T|F	Boolean fields (relational only) set a logical value to true/false, yes/no or 1/0.
Geographic		This data type is most often used to display data on a map, as a geographical reference. The data in the field can contain an address, city, state or some entity, like longitude or latitude coordinates, which points to a specific location on a map.

Table 2-1 Data types explained

 The numerical and date data types can be formatted to change how they are displayed.

 There may be times when Tableau does not select the correct data type. When that is the case, you can change the data type on the Data Source tab or on a Sheet tab.

 Calculated Fields
In addition to the icons shown above in Table 2-1, calculated fields have an equal sign in front of the data type, as shown at the top of Figure 2-1. Also notice that instead of displaying the table name that the field is in, the word "Calculation" is displayed.

Figure 2-1 Calculated field icon

What Is A Connection?

A connection is Tableau's terminology for attaching and logging in, if necessary, to a data source and importing (or loading) data. Tableau workbooks have their own data engine. The data is imported into this data engine. If you have used Excel, the data engine in Tableau is like the Power Pivot data model/database in Excel.

Why Do I Have To Connect To A Data Source?

First, I should explain what a data source is. A data source contains the underlying data for the report that you will create or modify. The most common data source is a database. The connection lets Tableau know where the database is located. Every Tableau workbook has to have at least one data source. As you will see, a data source can be used by all of the visualizations in the workbook. Connecting to data will remind you of importing or loading data.

Exercise 2.1: Create A Folder For Your Files

In this exercise you will create a folder to store the practice files in, for this book. It is a good idea to store all of the files in the same folder on your computers hard drive so that you can find them easily. I will refer to this folder as "your folder" throughout the book. The instructions below show you how to create the folder at the root of the C drive.

1. Open Windows Explorer ⇒ Right-click on the C drive ⇒ New ⇒ Folder.

2. Type `Tableau Book Files` as the folder name, then press Enter.

3. Files needed for some of the exercises in this book are in a zip file. To have the link for the zip file sent to you, send an email to tableaufiles@tolanapublishing.com. If you do not receive an email in a few minutes with the subject line Tableau Book Files, check the spam folder in your email software.

4. Download the zip file to the folder that you just created ⇒ Open Windows Explorer ⇒ Right-click on the zip file and select the option to extract the files. Use the zip software that you currently use or you can use the compressed folder tool in Windows Explorer ⇒ Confirm that you see the More Data folder in the Tableau Book Files folder.

5. **TABLEAU PUBLIC ONLY**, Read the Using Tableau Public.pdf file, and complete the Create A Tableau Public Account section.

Data Source Options

As you saw in Chapter 1, there are a lot of different file and database types that you can connect to. The connection exercises in this chapter cover file types and databases that you may use the most. Because connecting to databases, usually requires that you have other software installed, only two database types are covered in this book.

CSV Files

CSV files are text files because they do not contain any formatting, even though they are usually used and saved in Excel. Having the ability to import data into Tableau from CSV files, opens up a lot of possibilities, especially if you do not have direct access to data that is stored in an enterprise database, or if you are using Tableau Desktop Personal or Tableau Public. You can get the IT department to export the data from an enterprise system and save it in a CSV file for you.

CSV File Tips
To use a CSV file, it must meet certain criteria, in addition to having the CSV file extension. On your own, if you are having trouble using a CSV file, open the file in Note Pad or another text editor and confirm the following:
① The file does not have anything other than a header row and the rows of data. If used, the header row has to be the first row in the file.
② If column headings are used, the first row must contain a heading for every field. The remaining rows can have fewer fields then the first row, but not more fields. For example, most addresses have a zip code field, but there are a few records that do not. The first row must have a zip code field heading.
③ Commas or double quotes need to separate each field, including fields that do not have data. This will create place holders for the empty fields to keep the data in the other fields after it, lined up correctly.
④ Each row must end with a line feed or carriage return (the equivalent of pressing Enter).

Exercise 2.2: Connect To A CSV File

In this exercise, you will learn how to connect to a .csv file.

How To Create A New Workbook

A new workbook can be created from any open window in an existing workbook. The steps below show you how.

Connecting To Data Sources

1. File ⇒ New.

   You can display the Start Page to connect to a
   data source or in the workbook, on the Sheet tab,
   click the **CONNECT TO DATA** option, illustrated in
   Figure 2-2 or click the **NEW DATA SOURCE** button.

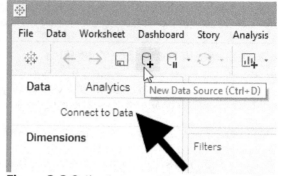

Figure 2-2 Option to connect to a data source illustrated

2. On the Connect panel shown in
   Figure 2-3, click on the **TEXT FILE** option.

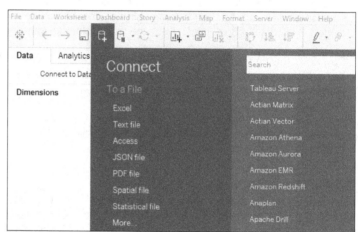

Figure 2-3 Connect panel on the Sheet tab

3. Navigate to your folder ⇒ Double-click on the Import Orders.csv file.

   Notice in Figure 2-4 that even though you only selected the CSV file to connect to, that the .txt file is also
   displayed on the Data Source tab, in the Files section. That is because both files are in the same folder and
   Tableau will automatically display all text files in the folder. Also notice that the Import Orders.csv file is the
   only one listed in the Connections section. This is how you know that currently, there is no connection to the
   Fact Sales.txt file.

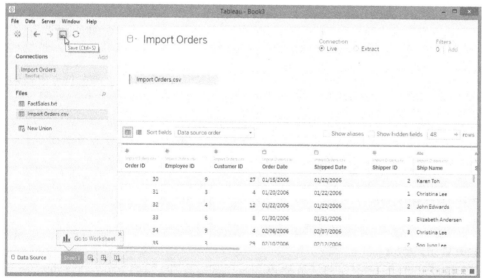

Figure 2-4 Connection to the csv file

4. Click the Save button, shown above in Figure 2-4 ⇒ Type `E2.2 Connect to CSV file`, as the file name.

Data Source Tab Workspace

This section explains options on the Data Source tab. This tab is the interface that is used to view and make changes to the data. This includes connecting to data sources, creating filters for the data, creating data extracts, rename the data source connection, preview data, join tables and more.

This page is automatically displayed when the initial connection to the data source is made, or once the workbook is connected to a data source and saved. When the workbook is opened from then on, a Sheet tab is automatically displayed, instead of the Data Source tab.

At the bottom of this tab, in the lower left corner, you will see five buttons, starting with the Data Source button. More than likely, the only button that you will use from this view is the Sheet 1 button. It is used to create a visualization. The remaining buttons are explained in Chapter 4.

In the lower right corner of the workspace, are three buttons. Until the workbook has two or more sheets, these buttons really do not provide any value. These buttons are explained in Chapter 4.

 Clicking the logo button below the File menu, shown in Figure 2-5, displays the Start Page.

The Data Source tab has the following sections: Left Pane, Canvas and Grid, as illustrated in Figure 2-5. The sections are explained below.

 Resizing The Left Pane
This section, as illustrated in Figure 2-5, can be resized. To resize the pane, place the mouse pointer to the right of the pane and drag the pane in the direction (left or right) that you want to resize it to.

Left Pane

This section displays information about the data retrieved from the connection. The options in this section are explained below.

Connections Section The options displayed in this section are slightly different, depending on the type of data source. For example, Figure 2-4 above, shows the options for a text data source. Figure 2-5 shows the options for an SQL Server database.

The **ADD** link is used to create a connection to another data source.

The data source name can be renamed, by selecting the **RENAME** option, shown in Figure 2-6.

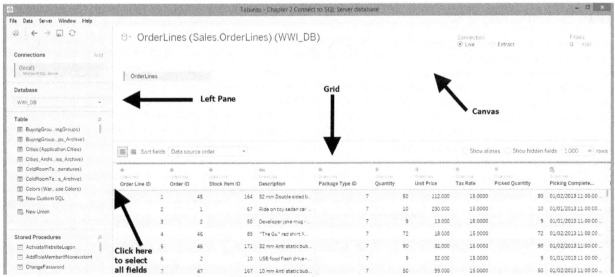

Figure 2-5 Data Source tab options for an SQL Server database

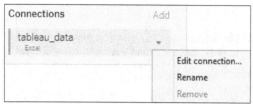

Figure 2-6 Connection shortcut menu

Database Section This section is only available when you connect to a database that is on a server, as shown earlier in Figure 2-5. This includes databases that you have the server software installed for, on your computers hard drive. If you look in the Connections section in Figure 2-5, you will see the word (local), above the server name. That lets you know where the database resides.

The Database drop-down list will display a list of all of the databases in the folder that the database is in, that the workbook is connected to. If you need to join a database in the drop-down list to the current database, you have to create a connection to it.

Files, Sheets Or Table Section The name of this section depends on the data source type. **Files**, as shown in Figure 2-7 are for individual files that are in the same folder. **Sheets** denote the sheets/tabs in an Excel workbook. **Table** denotes the tables in a database.

Clicking the magnifying icon in this section, displays the Search field, shown at the top of Figure 2-7. This field is used to search for files. If this section has a lot of files, a scroll bar is automatically added to the section. It is probably easier to use the scroll bar, then search for a file.

Clicking the button at the end of the Search field, displays the options on the right side of Figure 2-7. The options are used to select how you want to search for the criteria that you entered in the Search field.

When you hold the mouse pointer over a file (or table), you will see the button shown in Figure 2-8. Clicking this button opens the dialog box shown in Figure 2-9 and displays data in the file or table. This dialog box is helpful if you need to view data in a more compact format, or view the data before adding the file or table to the canvas.

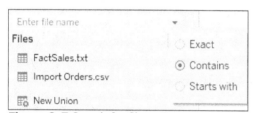

Figure 2-7 Search for file options

Figure 2-8 View Data button

If you see "10,000 rows", in the upper left corner of the dialog box, it means that there are more than 10,000 rows in the table.

Figure 2-9 View Data dialog box

The **NEW UNION OPTION** is only displayed if the data source supports unions. This option is used to append data from another table, in the same connection, to a table that already has a connection. For example, you may have several tables that store sales by month in the same data source. You would create a connection to one of the files, then use the New Union option to select the other files that you want to append.

The **NEW CUSTOM SQL** option opens the dialog box shown in Figure 2-10.

This option is available when you are connected to a SQL database. When this option is dragged to the canvas, it is used to edit existing SQL code, create a parameter or connect to a specific query, instead of connecting to the entire data set.

Figure 2-10 Edit Custom SQL dialog box

Canvas Section

This is the section where you drag a table or file to, from the Left pane, to create a data set.

Clicking the button to the left of the data source, displays a list of all of the data sources in the workbook, as shown in Figure 2-11.

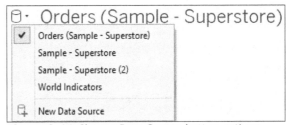

Figure 2-11 Change Data Source button options

Connection Options The options in this section are used to select a **LIVE CONNECTION** (the default) or create or edit an **EXTRACT CONNECTION** for the data source. Extracts have the following benefits:

☑ Creating an extract can improve performance.
☑ The data is compressed and the extract file can be saved to your computers hard drive.
☑ The data can be viewed remotely, meaning your computer does not have to be connected to the data source to have access to the data.

The **FILTERS** option is used to add, edit and delete filters, using the dialog box, shown later in Figure 2-26. Filters can be created for the live and extract connection options. Filters and extracts are covered in more detail in the next chapter.

Grid Section

The options in this section are used to modify the data as needed, to get it ready to create visualizations. The lower portion of this section displays the data in the file or table that is selected. If tables have been joined, data from the joined tables are displayed.

By default, up to the first 1,000 rows of data are displayed, but you can increase or decrease the number of rows displayed. In addition to being able to view data, the following tasks can be completed in this section.

☑ Rename fields
☑ Sort by row or column
☑ Create calculated fields
☑ Create aliases

 Resizing Columns
Columns in the grid can be resized the same way that they are resized in a spreadsheet.

Grid Toolbar

Figure 2-12 shows the grid toolbar. The options on the toolbar are explained below.

Figure 2-12 Grid toolbar

Resizing The Grid
The height of the grid can be resized by placing the mouse pointer on the gray light above the toolbar, as shown above in Figure 2-12. Drag the line up or down to resize the height of the grid.

The **PREVIEW DATA SOURCE BUTTON** displays the data in the grid, as shown earlier in Figure 2-5. This is the default view when the Data Source tab is displayed.

The **MANAGE METADATA BUTTON** displays the information shown in Figure 2-13. Metadata is data about other data. The metadata grid displays the fields as rows. This lets you make changes to the fields using the options on the shortcut menu shown in the figure. This grid is the default grid layout displayed, when the data source is **CUBE DATA** (also known as an **OLAP CUBE** or **DATA CUBE**). This grid displays the fields as rows. This allows you to view the structure of the data. Hiding and renaming fields can be done on this grid.

The options on the shortcut menu are explained below.

Select the **COPY VALUES** option to copy the selected values. This option works the same as using the CTRL + C keys.

CREATE CALCULATED FIELD [See Chapter 6]

CREATE GROUP [See Chapter 5]

CREATE BINS This option is used to group, categorize or put values into buckets (which Tableau calls **BINS**). Bins can be created from dimensions or measures. When created from a measure, a new dimension is created.

DESCRIBE displays information about the field.

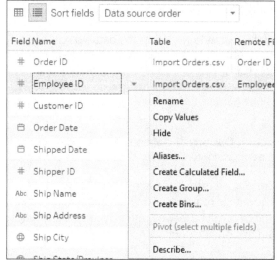
Figure 2-13 Metadata grid and shortcut menu

The options in the **SORT FIELDS DROP-DOWN LIST** are used to select how the data is initially sorted. **DATA SOURCE ORDER** is the default sort option. This means that the data is displayed in Tableau, in the order that it was added to the data source file (the spreadsheet or database, for example).

What Is An Alias?

An alias is a different name for specific values in a **DIMENSION**. It is a way to rename a field, if you will. An alias name is created to make it easier to understand the data in the field. IT people, me included, often abbreviate field names. Some companies have field naming conventions, which must be used. Many of these conventions were established decades ago. Back then, people outside of IT were almost never given access to the actual data and most people did not create their own data source. Yes, I remember life before Excel was first released in the 1980's <smile>.

An alias can be created on the Data Source tab or on the Sheet tab. They cannot be created for date fields, **CONTINUOUS DIMENSIONS** or **MEASURES**. The terms in bold are explained in Chapter 4.

Selecting the **ALIASES** option, shown above in Figure 2-13, opens the dialog box shown in Figure 2-14. An alias is used to modify the values for the member (values) of the field. To create or modify an alias, click in the Value (Alias) column.

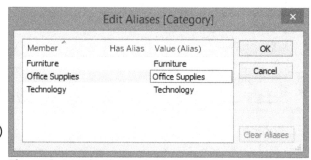
Figure 2-14 Edit Aliases dialog box

Checking the **SHOW ALIAS** option above the grid will display the alias names in the grid.

Checking the **SHOW HIDDEN FIELDS** option will display fields in the grid, that were previously hidden.

The **ROWS** option is used to select how many rows of data are displayed in the grid. The default is 1,000.

Grid Options

Figure 2-15 shows the grid. The options covered in this section are used to modify the data.

# OrderDetails Unit Price	# Orders Order ID	🗓 Orders Order Date	Abc Orders Customer Name	Abc Orders Sales Rep	🗓 Orders Shipped Date	# Orders Order Amount	Abc Products Product Name	Abc Products Size
230	1	01/01/2013	Aakriti Byrraju	Kayla Woodcock	01/02/2013	23,153.23	Ride on toy sedan car (...	1/12 scale
13	2	01/01/2013	Bala Dixit	Anthony Grosse	01/02/2013	55.24	Developer joke mug - ol...	null

Figure 2-15 Grid with fields from more than one table

Changing The Data Type

At the top of the grid, above each column (field name), you will see the **DATA TYPE ICON**. Clicking on this icon displays the shortcut menu shown in Figure 2-16. The options are used to change the data type for the field. The **GEOGRAPHIC ROLE** option is used to change the data type to Geographic. On a field that has the geographic data type, you can see how Tableau has classified the data in the field. In the figure, the data in the field has been classified as being states.

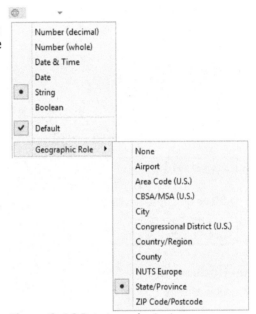

Below the data type icon is the name of the sheet or table the field is stored in. As shown above in Figure 2-15, data from more than one sheet is displayed in the grid.

When you hold the mouse pointer near the data type or field name, to the right of the data type icon, you will see a button that displays the shortcut menu shown in Figure 2-17. The options on the shortcut menu are explained below. The options displayed on the shortcut menu vary, depending on the data type of the field, as shown in Figure 2-18.

To the right of the field name is a button that is used to sort the data in the grid, by the fields that you select. The shortcut menu shown in Figure 2-19 is displayed when two or more columns are selected.

Figure 2-16 Data type shortcut menu

Date & Time Data Type
In the exercise that you just created, the date fields have the Date & Time data type. My guess is that most of the time, you will not have a need to display the time with the date on a chart. When that is the case, change the data type to Date.

The **DATA TYPE** can also be changed on the Sheet tab.

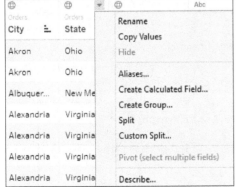

Figure 2-17 Shortcut menu for a text field

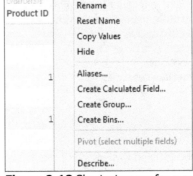

Figure 2-18 Shortcut menu for a numeric field

Figure 2-19 Shortcut menu when two or more columns are selected

SPLIT This option automatically divides the content in the field, based on the common separator that Tableau finds in the field. A field can automatically be separated in up to ten new fields. This option is often used when the first and last names are stored in the same field. The Product ID field, shown in the first column in Figure 2-20, is automatically split into the other three fields shown in the figure.

CUSTOM SPLIT Selecting this option opens the dialog box shown in Figure 2-21. The options are used to select the separator that will be used to split the data in the field and how many columns should be created.

Select the **RESET NAME** option when you want to restore the original field name used in the data source.

PIVOT [See Chapter 3, Pivot Data]

The **MERGE MISMATCHED FIELDS** option is used when the field names that you need to use to create a union, do not match.

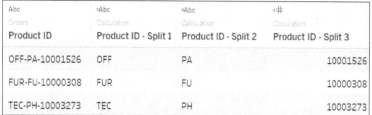

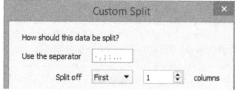

Figure 2-21 Custom Split dialog box

Figure 2-20 Result of Split option applied to the Product ID field

Cube Data Tips
① The Left pane is not displayed for cube (multidimensional) data.
② The grid does not display for cube (multidimensional) data.
③ If the data source is a cube, the canvas displays the queries and cubes or the catalog. This is how you select the data set that you need.

Menu Options

This section explains options on the menu that are specific to Tableau.

File Menu

Figure 2-4 shows the File menu. The options are explained below.

The **PASTE DATA AS CONNECTION** option is enabled when you have copied data to the clipboard to paste into Tableau. Doing this will let you create a new data source or connection.

Select the **IMPORT WORKBOOK** option to add the contents of another workbook, either a **PACKAGED WORKBOOK FILE (.TWBX)** or another Tableau workbook to the current workbook.

The **REPOSITORY LOCATION** option is used to select a new location for the repository. This option is also helpful if you cannot remember what the default location is, where you store files. When you select this option, the current default location is displayed.

Tableau Public has the following save options:
SAVE TO TABLEAU PUBLIC and **SAVE TO TABLEAU PUBLIC AS**.

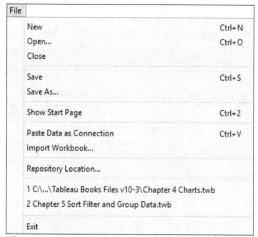

Figure 2-22 File menu

Repository Location

Changing the default repository location is helpful when any of the following is true.

☑ You want a way to keep all files for a project in a folder that you create. For example, you may be working on visualizations for the Finance department now and a few months from now, you start a project for the Sales department. You would create a new folder for the Sales department to save those workbooks in. This way, you will know which project, files are for.

☑ Your company wants you to save the workbooks that you create on a server, instead of on your computers hard drive.

Changing The Default Repository Location
Chapter 1 covered the My Tableau Repository folder structure and location. It is not a requirement to save the workbooks that you create in this location. If you save a workbook to a different folder, like the folder that you created in Exercise 2.1, the repository and folders shown earlier in Chapter 1, Figure 1-6, will automatically be created in the new folder location. If this is what you want to do, it would be a good idea to use the Repository Location option discussed above to change the default location.

How To Create Another Repository Location

As covered above, you may want or have the need to have another repository location. When this is the case, the steps below show you how to set up another repository.

1. In Windows Explorer, create a folder (probably at the root of the C drive, but this is not a requirement) using a name that is meaningful to the workbooks and files that will be stored in it (Sales Dashboards and 2016 Historical Financial Data, are examples).

2. In Tableau, select the Repository Location option shown above in Figure 2-22 ⇒ Navigate to the location where you created the folder.

3. On the right side of the window, click on the folder that you selected. You should see the folder name in the **FOLDER** field at the bottom of the dialog box ⇒ Click the **SELECT FOLDER** button. You will see the message shown in Figure 2-23.

When you re-open Tableau, the default repository location will be changed to the one that you just selected.

All of the folders shown in Chapter 1, Figure 1-6 will be added to the new repository.

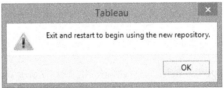

Figure 2-23 Restart to use the new repository message

Data Menu

Figure 2-24 shows the Data menu. The options that have not already been covered are explained below.

The **NEW DATA SOURCE** option displays the Connect panel shown earlier in Figure 2-3.

Use the **REFRESH DATA SOURCE** option to get the most recent version of the data in the selected sheet or table. This is one way to keep data in the workbook current.

The **DUPLICATE DATA SOURCE** option makes a copy of the data source that is displayed.

The **PASTE DATA AS DATA SOURCE** option is enabled when you have copied data to the clipboard. This option will create a new connection and paste the data in the clipboard into the new data source, which you can rename. Once pasted, at the bottom of the Data menu, you will see an entry that starts with the word "Clipboard" and today's date. That is the new data source, as shown at the bottom of the Data menu.

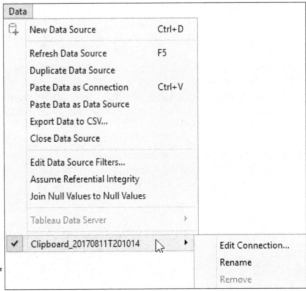

Figure 2-24 Data menu

Select the **EXPORT DATA TO CSV** option when you want to save the data displayed on the Data Source tab to a .csv file.

The **CLOSE DATA SOURCE** option displays the message shown in Figure 2-25, if you have created a visualization based on the data source. More than likely, you do not want to select this option.

The **EDIT DATA SOURCE FILTERS** option is used to modify filters that have been created for the data source. Filters can also be created and deleted on the dialog box shown in Figure 2-26.

Select the **ASSUME REFERENTIAL INTEGRITY** option when the data in one table has matching data in another table and you want to try and improve the performance of the query. Selecting this option only enforces referential integrity in Tableau, not in the data source.

Use the **JOIN NULL VALUES TO NULL VALUES** option when you want to create a join on fields that have null values. This will display the word "Null" in each field that does not have a value. This lets you display fields from the row that does have a value and could be helpful if you need to see rows that are missing data from more than one table.

The last option(s) on the menu, are the data sources in the workbook. Each data source has options to edit the connection, rename or remove the connection, for the selected data source, as shown above in Figure 2-24.

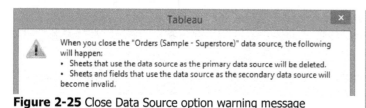

Figure 2-25 Close Data Source option warning message

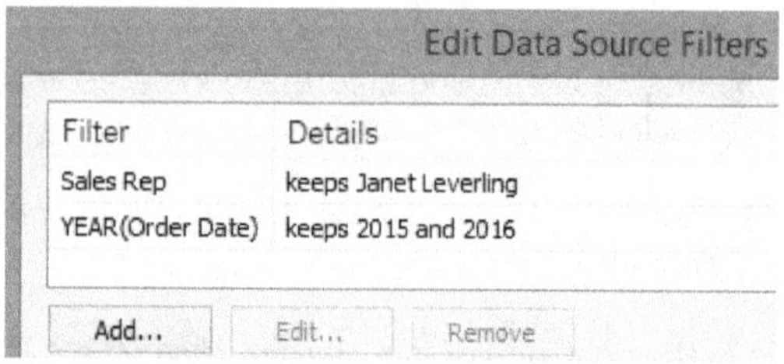

Figure 2-26 Edit Data Source Filters dialog box

Server Menu

Figure 2-27 shows the Server menu. The options are explained below.

The **OPEN WORKBOOK** option is used to open a workbook that is on a server.

The **PUBLISH DATA SOURCE** option is used to put a copy of a data source that you want to share on a Tableau Server or Tableau Online.

The **TABLEAU PUBLIC** option is used to create a Tableau Public account (profile), save workbooks to Tableau Public and open workbooks that have been saved to the Tableau Public Server.

Figure 2-27 Server menu

Window Menu

Figure 2-28 shows the Window menu. The options are explained below.

The **SHOW STATUS BAR** option displays/hides the options shown earlier in the lower right corner of Figure 2-4. These options are really not used from the Data Source tab. They are covered in Chapter 4.

Figure 2-28 Window menu

BOOKMARK [See Chapter 5, Exercise 5.21]

Help Menu

Many of the options shown in Figure 2-29 are standard for most help menus. The options at the top of the menu provide help in different formats.

The **OPEN HELP** option displays the online help file in a web browser.

The **WATCH TRAINING VIDEOS** option displays the videos that are available. What I like is that the video catalog is updated, when new functionality is added to the software.

The **SETTINGS AND PERFORMANCE** options shown in the figure are mostly used to increase and view that performance of a workbook.

If you do not want Tableau to be updated automatically, clear the check box for the **ENABLE AUTOMATIC PRODUCT UPDATES** option.

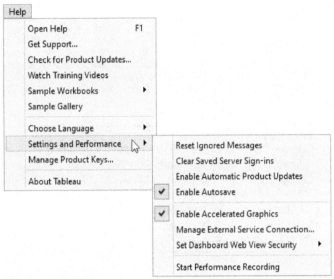

Figure 2-29 Help menu

Data Source Tab Toolbar

Figure 2-30 shows the toolbar that is in the upper left corner of the workspace, below the menu. The options are explained in Table 2-2.

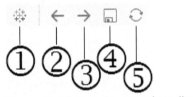

Figure 2-30 Data Source tab toolbar

Button	This Button . . .
①	Displays the Start Page.
②	Removes the last action that was applied.
③	Reapplies the last action.
④	Saves the workbook.
⑤	Refreshes the data.

Table 2-2 Data Source tab toolbar buttons explained

Text Files

Each text file that you connect to, can only contain the equivalent of one table. Below are the two text file types that are most commonly used. Some of the other text file types that can be connected to are **.JSON**, **.TAB** and **.TSV**.

☑ **.TXT** This file type does not contain any formatting. This file type is usually created in NotePad, or something similar. Figure 2-31 shown below, shows part of a text file.

☑ **.CSV** This file type is often created when there is data in a database that the user does not have access to. This file type is often created as an export file from a database, especially when moving data between systems or applications.

Connecting To An XML File
While there is no connector for **XML FILES**, it is possible to connect to one. This is done by creating a calculated field that stores the path to the XML file, then create a **URL ACTION** to open the file.

Text (.txt) files do not have any formatting like bold, italic or font size. To be used in Tableau, this file type has to have rows of data, as shown in Figure 2-31. Each row of data has fields (columns). An advantage of text files is that they can handle millions of rows of data. The fields are usually separated by commas. While the comma is the most used separator for text files, other separators like quotes, can also be used.

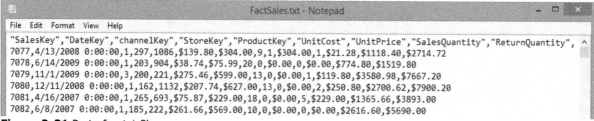

Figure 2-31 Part of a .txt file

 Text File Tips
One way to know that there is a problem with a text file is that all of the fields have been imported into one column, when displayed on the Data Source tab. To use a text file, it must meet certain criteria in addition to having the .txt file extension. On your own, if you are having trouble importing the data in a text file, open the file in Note Pad and confirm the following:
① The file does not have anything other than a header row and the rows of data. If used, the header row has to be the first row in the file.
② The separator between fields is valid.

Exercise 2.3: Create A Connection To A TXT File

In the previous exercise, a connection was created for a CSV file. Even though the Fact Sales.txt file was displayed in the Files section, there was no connection for it. This exercise will show you how to create a connection for this text file.

1. Open a new workbook.

2. On the Sheet 1 tab, click the Connect to Data link ⇒ Click on the Text file link.

3. Double-click on the Fact Sales.txt file. This text file has over 2 million rows of data.

Update Now And Automatically Update Buttons

These buttons are available when a filter, table or join has been added, edited or deleted.

The **UPDATE NOW BUTTON** refreshes the data.

The **AUTOMATICALLY UPDATE BUTTON** refreshes the data, every time a change discussed above is made. Once clicked, I could not find a way to turn the option off from the Data Source tab. Auto update can be stopped from a sheet tab, by clicking the **PAUSE AUTO UPDATES** button on the toolbar.

If you have set up a live and extract connection for the same data source and click the Automatically Update button, it is applied to both connections.

 If you know that the structure of the data source has changed, for example, a new, deleted or renamed field, refresh the data before clicking either update button, shown in Figure 2-32. Otherwise, you will probably see an error message.

Figure 2-32 Update buttons

Changing The Data Type

In this part of the exercise, you will learn how to change the date data type. If you look at the dates in the Date Key column, you will see that they have the Date/Time data type. If you know that you do not need the time portion, changing the data type makes sense.

1. Click the date type icon for the Date Key field ⇒ Date ⇒ Click the Update Now button, shown at the bottom of Figure 2-32. The dates in the field are displayed without the time.

2. Save the workbook as `E2.3 Connect to a txt file`.

   In Tableau Public, you will be prompted to create a data extract. Click the **CREATE DATA EXTRACT** option ⇒ Click the **EXTRACT** button on the Extract Data dialog box ⇒ Save the extract files in the Data sources folder.

Microsoft Excel And Access Driver Requirements

Tableau uses Microsoft Office drivers to connect to Excel files and Access databases, if the bit version of Office and Tableau are the same, (32-bit or 64-bit). For example, if you have the 32-bit version of Office installed and the 64-bit version of Tableau installed or vise versa, you will have to install the Microsoft Access Database engine. If you do not have Office 2007 or higher installed, you will have to install the Microsoft Access Database engine. If your bit versions match, you do not have to install any drivers.

This link has the file to download. Download and install the version (32 or 64 bit) that matches the version of Tableau that you have installed. www.microsoft.com/en-us/download/details.aspx?id=13255

Exercise 2.4: Create A Connection To An Access Database

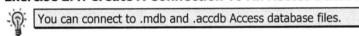 You can connect to .mdb and .accdb Access database files.

1. Open a new workbook.

2. On the Sheet 1 tab, click the Connect to Data link ⇒ Click on the Access link.

3. Click the Browse button ⇒
   Select the importdb.mdb file.
   The path to the database is shown in Figure 2-33.

   This database does not require a password or Workgroup Security.

Figure 2-33 Options to connect to an Access database

4. Click the Open button, shown above in Figure 2-33.

   Once connected, you will see the tables in the database, as shown in Figure 2-34.

   TABLEAU PUBLIC ONLY, add the Orders table to the canvas.

Figure 2-34 Tables in the Access database

5. Save the workbook as `E2.4 Connect to an Access database`.

Change A Data Source Location

There may be times when the location of a data source file changes. If this happens, the current connection that you have will not work. This scenario happens more with non database files, like Excel or text files. When this is the case, the path to the new location of the file can easily be changed. This can be done, even after charts have been created.

Exercise 2.5: Change The Location Of The Data Source

In this exercise, you will learn how to edit the path of the data source. The current location of the file is the Tableau Book Files folder. In this exercise, the new location of the file is the More Data folder in the Tableau Book Files folder.

1. Save the E2.2 workbook as `E2.5 Data source location changed`.

2. Data Source tab ⇒ In the Connections section, display the shortcut menu for the Import Orders file ⇒ Edit Connection.

3. Navigate to the More Data folder and double-click on the Import Orders.csv file.

 The steps that you just completed can also be used if the file name of the data source has changed.

 Change The Data Source Location From A Sheet Tab
The steps below show you how to change the data source location from a sheet tab.
1. Select a Sheet tab that uses data from the data source that has to be changed.
2. Data ⇒ Select the data source at the bottom of the menu ⇒ Edit Data Source.
3. Select the file from the new location.

Using Databases On A Server

Earlier in this chapter, you learned how to connect to an Access database. The process of connecting to it, was basically the same as connecting to an Excel file or text file. In a corporate environment, connecting to a database on a server requires you to log on with your security credentials to gain access to the database. This login process is controlled by the database, not Tableau. I am bringing this to your attention because the next section shows you how to connect to a database on a server, but does not require logging in.

Connecting To SQL Server Databases

 Tableau Desktop Professional, is the only edition the can connect to SQL Server databases.

This is one of the most popular databases currently available. If you need to connect to this type of database, the steps below show you how. To follow these steps, you need access to a SQL Server database. Completing the steps below is optional.

1. Open a new workbook.

2. Connect panel ⇒ In the Server section, select Microsoft SQL Server.

3. If the SQL Server database that you want to connect to is on your hard drive, type (local) in the Server field. If the database is on a server, type in the full path to the database.

4. Select one of the Sign in options. Select the one that you have used on your own, to connect to the database.

   The options shown in Figure 2-35 are for connecting to a SQL database that is on your computers hard drive.

Figure 2-35 SQL Server connection options for a database on your computers hard drive

5. Click the Sign In button.

6. On the Data Source tab, open the Select Database drop-down list and select the database that you want to use, as shown in Figure 2-36. Once selected, you will see the tables and other files that you have rights to, like views and stored procedures, as shown in Figure 2-37.

Figure 2-36 Select Database options

Figure 2-37 Tables in the database

ODBC Connection Option

This option is only available in Tableau Desktop Professional. In Chapter 1, you saw the types of data sources that you can connect to. If the database that you need to connect to is not listed, select the **OTHER DATABASES (ODBC)** option. This will open the dialog box shown in Figure 2-38. The options are used to create a connection to the data source that you need.

The options in the **DSN** drop-down list are connections to data sources that are already set up on your computer. If you have connected to the same data source in another software package that you need to use now in Tableau, either the ODBC connector for it should already be set up, or the driver may already be installed.

Select the DSN or driver option to connect to the database, then click the Connect button. If the driver that you need is not in the drop-down list, see www.tableau.com/support/drivers.

Once connected to the server, fill in the fields in the Connection Attributes section, then click the Sign In button.

Figure 2-38 Other Databases (ODBC) dialog box

Using Data In A PDF File

At one time, a popular way to distribute tables of data was on web page. Now, more and more data is saved in PDF files and distributed. This is great when you only need to view data. If you have tried, you know that getting data out of a PDF file to paste into another document can be a nightmare.

Tableau has a connector that allows you to connect to PDF files, and use any tables that have data in a column format, as a data source. A blog post stated that currently, the PDF connector does not support hierarchical data. Some place else, I read that password protected PDF files are not supported, but otherwise, you should be able to use tables in a PDF file. You may have the need to clean the data from a PDF file.

Exercise 2.6: Create A Connection To A PDF File

In this exercise, you will learn how to connect to a PDF file and scan the file for the table(s) that you want to use.

1. Open a new workbook.

2. On the Connect panel ⇒ PDF File ⇒
    Select the Population Challenges PDF file, in your folder.

    The options shown in Figure 2-39 are used to select the pages to scan for tables that have data.

    You may find it easier to view the PDF file before connecting to it and write down the page number(s), that the PDF Reader uses (not the page numbers that are on the document itself). Doing this will allow you to enter the page number(s) on this dialog box.

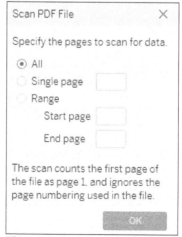

Figure 2-39 Scan PDF File dialog box

3. On the dialog box shown above, select the **RANGE** option ⇒ Type 15, as the Start page number and 18 as the End page number ⇒ Click OK.

You should see the tables shown in Figure 2-40.

Notice that there are two tables on page 16. If you looked on this page in the PDF file, you will only see one table. That is because Tableau considers the "A" section one table and the "B" section (of the same table in the PDF file) another table or sub table. The same is true of the three tables retrieved from page 18.

Figure 2-40 Tables retrieved for the PDF file

4. Drag the table from page 15 to the canvas. You should see the fields shown in Figure 2-41. The fields would need to be renamed.

Abc	Abc		Abc	Abc
Page 15 Table 1	Page 15 Table 1		Page 15 Tab...	Page 15 Tab...
F1	F2	Σ	F3	F4
1	India		16.5	22
2	China		8.4	33
3	Pakistan		3.1	37
4	United States of Ame...		2.8	40

Figure 2-41 Fields from a table in the PDF file

5. Save the workbook as E2.6 Connect to a PDF file.

PDF File Connection Shortcut Menu

Figure 2-42 shows the shortcut menu for a PDF file shortcut connection.

The **RESCAN PDF FILE** option is used to scan the PDF file again, to select other pages in the PDF file that have tables.

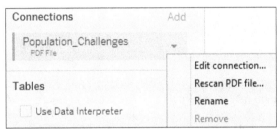

Figure 2-42 PDF file connection shortcut menu

Use Some Of The Data Menu Options

As the heading of this section indicates, you will learn how to use some of the options on the Data menu. Being able to use these options will broaden your skills for working with data sources.

 On your own, if you are replacing a data source with a database on a server, the process is the same as described in Exercise 2.7. The difference is that some of the dialog boxes will be slightly different.

Exercise 2.7: Replace A Relational Data Source

Exercise 2.5 showed you how to select a different location for the same data source. There may be times when you start off using data in one format, like a spreadsheet and the data in the spreadsheet is moved to a SQL Server database. If you know that you data source will change from one file format to another one, it will be helpful to get a copy of the new table layout, so that you will know how to map the fields. This will save you a lot of time, because you will need to know if any of the field names have changed.

In this scenario, all of your work (12 charts for example) will not have to be redone once the data is in a database. You can connect an existing workbook to the new data source. In this exercise, you will replace the Excel file with an Access database.

1. Open a new workbook.

2. Create a connection to the Customer.xlsx file.

3. Save the workbook as `E2.7 Replace a spreadsheet file with a database`. Notice that the third column name is Customer Name.

Select The Replacement File

1. Data menu ⇒ New Data Source.

2. On the New Data Source pane, select the Access option.

3. Click the Browse button to select the importdb.mdb file ⇒ Click Open. Notice that the database has different tables then the Excel workbook has. That is not a problem.

4. Drag the Customer table to the canvas. Notice that the third column is named Company Name.

 The replacement table does not have to have the same name as the one that it is replacing.

Switch To The New Data Source

In this part of the exercise, you will learn how to replace the original data source (the Customer tab in the Excel workbook) with the Customer table in the Access database.

 To enable the **REPLACE DATA SOURCE** option, the Tableau workbook needs at least one sheet to have a field added to the view. On your own, if your workbook has at least one chart, skip step 2 below.

1. On the sheet tab, click on the original data source on the **DATA PANE**, as illustrated in Figure 2-43.

Figure 2-43 Original data source illustrated

2. In the **DIMENSIONS** section of the Data pane, drag the Region field to the Rows shelf, as shown in Figure 2-44.

    In Tableau Public, delete the field that you added to save the workbook.

Figure 2-44 Field added to the Rows shelf

3. Data menu ⇒ Replace Data Source, as shown in Figure 2-45. You should have the options shown in Figure 2-46 ⇒ Click OK. If you do not have the data sources shown in the figure, open the drop-down list and select the data source.

Figure 2-45 Data menu

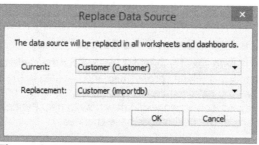

Figure 2-46 Replace Data Source dialog box

How To Change The Field Reference

If a field in the original data source was changed in the new data source and the original field was used, you will see a red exclamation mark next to the field on the Data pane shown in Figure 2-47. The background color of the field on a shelf would also be red and the chart would be disabled.

Every field that has an exclamation mark after a data source has been replaced, has to be changed. When you hold the mouse pointer over the field, you will see a message letting you know what the problem is with the field, as shown in Figure 2-48. The message shown is letting you know that the field is not in the replacement data source. Most of the time, this means that the field has been renamed. Tableau refers to this as a **FIELD REFERENCE**. To resolve this, you would follow the steps below.

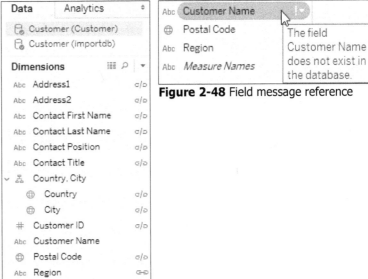

Figure 2-48 Field message reference

Figure 2-47 Field changed after table replacement

1. Open the drop-down list for the field, as shown in Figure 2-49 ⇒ Replace References.

Figure 2-49 Dimension field shortcut menu

2. On the dialog box shown in Figure 2-50, select the field to replace the field with the error. The fields on this dialog box are from the new data source. In this exercise, you would select the Company Name field.

    Once the reference field is selected, the error message will go away and the chart will be enabled.

    On your own, if you are not sure which field to select, you can look at the data from the new data source on the Data Source tab or ask the person that created the new data source.

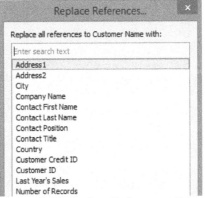

Figure 2-50 Replace References dialog box

> **Using A New Data Source**
> As covered in the previous exercise, the biggest change that you may have to work on when switching to a new data source is changing some field names. The other change that you have to take into consideration, is that the data type of a field could be different in the new data source.

Exercise 2.8: Paste Data As A Data Source

This option is useful when you have data that can be copied to the clipboard, like an HTML table on a web page or part of the data on a spreadsheet or data in a word processing document.

When this data is pasted into a Tableau workbook, a data source is automatically created and a new connection is created in the workbook. The data is automatically saved as a text file in the repository when the workbook is saved.

In this exercise you will learn how to paste some of the data in a text file that has over 2 millions rows of data, into a workbook.

1. Save the E2.4 workbook as `E2.8 Paste data from a text file`.

2. Open the Fact Sales.txt file in Notepad or your favorite text editor (not a word processing package).

3. Starting with the first row, select 25 or more rows of data. The number of rows that you select does not have to be exact ⇒ Press Ctrl+C.

> **Using An Unsaved Workbook**
> If you followed the steps in this exercise, but are using a new unsaved workbook, in step 4, you would use Data ⇒ Paste, on the Sheet tab.

4. If you are using Tableau Public, go to step 5.
   In the Tableau workbook, on the Data Source tab ⇒ Data menu ⇒ **PASTE DATA AS DATA SOURCE**.

   You should see a connection like the one shown in Figure 2-51. The first few numbers of the file name are the date. The numbers after the letter T are the time.

Figure 2-51 Connection created for data pasted into the workbook

5. On the Sheet tab ⇒ Data menu ⇒ Paste.

6. File ⇒ Saves As ⇒ Select the location where you want to save the text file. Selecting File ⇒ Save, or clicking the Save button on the toolbar does not give you the option to select where you want to save the file. You would see the dialog box shown in Figure 2-52.

Figure 2-52 Clipboard Data Saved dialog box

7. On the Sheet tab, right-click on the Clipboard data source ⇒ Rename ⇒ On the dialog box shown in Figure 2-53, type `Pasted from FactSales file`.

Figure 2-53 Rename Data Source dialog box

Exercise 2.9: Export Data To A CSV File

There may be times when you need to use data that is in Tableau, in other software. If that is the case, you can export the data to a csv file. The following are some reasons when you would want to export the data.

☑ To clean and transform the data in other software, in ways that Tableau does not offer.

☑ You have joined data from different data sources into one table.

Not surprising, data can be exported from the Data Source and Sheet tabs. In this exercise, you will learn how to export data to a csv file from both tabs.

Export Data From The Data Source Tab

The data that is exported from this tab is the data from the data source after it has been cleaned or transformed.

1. Save the E2.4 workbook as E2.9 Export to csv.

2. Add the Orders table to the canvas.

3. Data ⇒ Export Data to CSV ⇒ Navigate to your folder ⇒ Type E2.9 Export from data source tab as the file name.

Export Data From The Sheet Tab

The data that is exported from this tab is the data that was used to create the visualization.

1. Sheet tab ⇒ Drag the Order Amount field to the Columns shelf.

2. Drag the Ship Via field to the Rows shelf, after the Customer ID field.

3. **TABLEAU PUBLIC ONLY,** If you have any other field on the Columns or Rows shelf, delete it ⇒ Data menu ⇒ Orders (importdb) ⇒ Export data to CSV ⇒ Go to step 5.

4. Across from the Dimensions section heading, click the **VIEW DATA** button (the first button).

   You will see the dialog box shown in Figure 2-54 ⇒ Click the **EXPORT ALL** button on the dialog box.

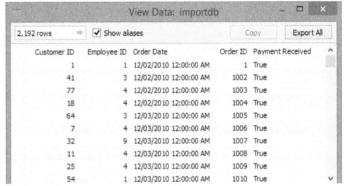

Figure 2-54 View Data dialog box

5. Navigate to your folder ⇒ Type E2.9 Export data from sheet tab, as the file name.

Exercise 2.10: Import A Workbook

 This exercise cannot be completed in Tableau Public, because it does not have the Import Workbook option, that is used in this exercise.

Earlier in this chapter, you learned that the contents of one workbook can be added to another workbook. In this exercise, you will import the E1.2 workbook into a workbook created earlier in this chapter.

1. Save the E2.3 workbook as E2.10 Imported workbook.

2. File ⇒ Import Workbook.

3. Select the E1.2 Basic Charts.twb file, which is in the Workbooks folder, shown in Chapter 1, Figure 1-6.

4. If you click on the Sheet 1 tab, you will see the chart that you created in Exercise 1.2. At the top of the Data pane on the left, you will see two data sources, Fact Sales and Orders Superstore. The Orders data source was imported from the E1.2 workbook because it was used to create the chart.

Saving Workbooks vs Saving Data Sources

This is an important concept and distinction to understand. When a workbook (.twb) is saved, the data source connection, changes and new work that you added is saved. An icon for the workbook is automatically added to the Open section of the Start Page.

When a data source file (.tds) is saved, the connection information is saved. The connection is displayed in the Saved Data Sources section of the Start Page. On your own, once you have the connections created that you will use, you probably will not have a need to change them.

PREPARING DATA FOR ANALYSIS

 After reading this chapter and completing the exercises you will:

- ☑ Know how to filter data on the Data Source tab
- ☑ Be able to create a data extract
- ☑ Know how to join sheets or tables
- ☑ Understand how blends work

CHAPTER 3

Is The Data Ready For Visualizations?

The previous chapter showed you how to connect to a variety of data sources. Once you have connected to a data source, you need to make sure that the data can be used to create the visualizations that you need. By that I mean the following:

☑ Do you need all of the rows of data in the table, to create the visualizations?
☑ Is the data in the format that you need? Some chart types require data to be structured in a specific layout.
☑ Do you need data from more than one table to create the visualizations?
☑ Do you need data that does not exist in the data source?
☑ Are the fields that you need formatted properly? For example, do you need currency fields to be displayed with a dollar sign.
☑ Are the field names appropriate to display on a visualization?

Depending on the data that you will use, there may be other data preparation functionality that needs to be implemented. Based on experience, I have found that it can take longer to prepare the data then it takes to create the visualization. My advice is not to rush through the data preparation portion of your projects, because it can become frustrating, really quickly, when you are creating a chart, but do not have all of the data that you need. When this happens, you have to stop creating charts (the fun part) and get the data that you need.

While Tableau's focus is displaying data visually, many of the principals for gathering and selecting the right data, are the same as creating printed reports. The next few sections have been adapted from books that I have written for software tools that are used to create reports that are printed, both text based and visually, to fit into the functionality that Tableau provides. Keep in mind that charts, visualizations and dashboards are reports.

Report Design Process

I know that you are anxious to create more reports, but there are several items that need to be addressed and worked out before you create a report, whether this is your first report or your 100th report. This is especially true if you are just starting out. While I know that you may be tempted to skip this section, I hope that you don't because it provides information to help you gather the data and figure out what is needed to create charts on your own. This section is an overview of the design process. Report design could be an entire chapter or two all by itself, but I am giving you the abridged version <smile>. The design process is part of what is known as the "Business Requirements" phase of a project. As you gain experience, you will see that if you do not get the business requirements right, the project will be delayed, potentially be over budget and not produce the results that the business owner (requestor) or client is looking for. Many call this a "bad career move".

When you understand the report design process concepts presented in this chapter, it will be easier for you to create visualizations. On your own, you should write down the answers to the questions that will be presented in the design process discussion. The more planning that you do before you create a chart, the less you will have to modify it, after it is created. There are four main steps to the report design process. Each step can have multiple tasks.

You will see how these steps come together through the exercises in this book. When creating reports, especially ones that other people will use, it is imperative that you fully understand the requirements, which often includes you asking a lot of questions. This is not something that you can be bashful about. Not asking questions or worse, asking the wrong questions will more than likely cause you grief down the road.

Based on my experience as a report designer, equally important as understanding the report requirements, especially if you are replacing existing reports, is that the people that will use the reports, have a vision of what the reports (rarely, will you get a request for **one report** from someone <smile>) should look like. Whether you like their vision or not, you need to respect it, for the following reasons:

① It is the right thing to do.
② They are the people using the reports, day in and day out.
③ Directly or indirectly, they are paying your salary.

This does not mean that you do not have input. The best way to have input in my opinion, is to clearly demonstrate how your ideas will make it easier for them to do their job or how your ideas will make the reports better.

Step 1: Define The Purpose Of The Chart

Yes, I know what you are saying: "How hard can it be to figure out the purpose of a chart or visualization?". The answer is it depends on how well the person or group of people are able to explain what they want the chart to provide and how well you understand what they tell you.

The majority of reports that you create will probably be used by someone other than yourself, which means that you should meet with the person or group of people that will use the report. These meetings are part of the report requirement gathering process. Keep in mind that you may have to have more than one meeting to get a good idea of what the report needs to include, because the users may not tell you or be able to clearly articulate their needs in one meeting. Reports are often used as a decision making tool, which means that poor decisions will be made or the decision making process will be ineffective, due to missing or incorrect data that is displayed on the report. The data must be presented in a logical manner, so that it can be an effective decision making tool.

Your role as the report designer is to gather the information needed to create the report. If the information is not presented on the report, in a way that works for the users, trust me, they will let you know and you will be spending a lot of time making modifications.

In my opinion, the more that users have you modify a report, the quicker your credibility goes down hill. That is not something that you want to happen. What I have discovered is that if you create a prototype of the report for the users, they can discuss what they like and do not like about the prototype. Usually, you will gain valuable information that is often hard to get users to discuss in a regular meeting.

The worst thing that you can do in many cases, is give the users the impression that you know more about their needs then they do. I am not saying that in some cases that you won't know more about their data or needs, just don't give them that impression, if you know what I mean <smile>. To define the expected outcome of the report, write a descriptive sentence or two about the purpose of the report or what the report needs to accomplish. Below are some sample purpose statements. Each of these statements would be used to create a different chart. The charts could be displayed on the same dashboard.

① The purpose is to compare last years sales totals to this years sales totals, by region.
② The purpose is to show products that are low on inventory and need to be reordered.
③ The purpose is to show the top 10 best selling products, by sales team.

Step 2: Determine The Chart Type

Now that you have determined the purpose of the charts, you need to determine the fields needed and the best chart type to use. If you are creative, you will like this step. In addition to determining the best chart type, you need to determine the following:

① Create a list of fields that are needed to create the chart. If you know what database and table each field is in, include that on the list. If the data does not currently exist, include that on the list also. You will use this list to complete tasks in future steps, in the design process.
② Which fields on the chart need totals, statistical information or a calculated field. (**Hint**: Calculated fields do not exist in a table.)

Step 3: Find The Data For The Chart

This step is very important because without the data there is no chart. As the person creating the chart, life will be much easier for you, if you are familiar with the data that is needed and how it is organized. If you are not familiar with the data or are not technical, you may have to rely on Information Technology specialists, like database administrators, to help you with the tasks in this step. There are three tasks that you have to work on, to complete this step successfully.

Task 1 The first task that you have to complete is to find out which files, like a spreadsheet or tables in a database have the data for the report. Use the list of fields that you created in step 2 to find the data sources. You may also have to find out what servers the databases are on.

Task 2 This task involves selecting the actual fields in the tables that are needed for the chart. Use the list of fields that you created in step 2. Determine any formatting that may be needed for each field. You also have to determine if the field names in the table are the best choice for the field headings that will be displayed on the chart. One example of when a field name needs to be changed is for fields that have the word "ID" as part of the field name.

This is because most users do not know what "ID" means. The good thing is that most of the time, ID fields are not displayed on a chart.

Task 3 Now that you have found some of the data in the tables, there are probably fields left on the list that you created in step 2, that you have not found. More than likely, many of the fields that are left on the list need to be created. This task involves creating formulas for these fields, which are known as calculated fields.

In order to be able to create calculated fields, you have to become familiar with the data types that were explained earlier in Chapter 2. Some functions are designed to only work with specific types of data. Examples of calculated fields include:

① List price times quantity
② Number of days between the order date and the ship date
③ Calculating a persons age
④ Calculations that conditionally format data or the background color of cells or rows

Step 4: Clean And Transform The Data

This step involves organizing all of the data.

Task 1 This task includes completing as many of the following as necessary to prepare the data to be analyzed, once the connections have been created.

① Create the joins or blends.
② Clean and transform the data.
③ Create the calculated fields.

Task 2 To complete this task you have to organize all of the data, both from the data tables and calculated fields, as well as, any other data source. Organizing the data means at a minimum, answering the following questions.

① Does the data need to be sorted? If so, which field(s) should the data be sorted on?
② Does the data need to be grouped? If so, which field(s) should the data be grouped on?
③ Does the report need to have any data flagged? If so, how should the data be flagged? The primary reason data would be flagged is so that it can easily be identified on a report. Make a list of any data that needs to be flagged. Tableau has several options that can be used to indicate that the data is flagged. A popular option is applying conditional formatting.

Task 3 Another way that you organize the data is by selecting which records will actually appear on the report. This is important because most reports do not require that all records in a table appear on the report. For example, if the report needs to display sales (orders) for a specific sales rep, you would create filters that would only allow orders for the particular sales rep to appear on the report. Another example would be to display all customers that purchased a specific product or category of products.

In addition to record selection, it may be necessary to create parameters which will make the report more flexible in terms of record selection. Parameters allow the person viewing the report to select the criteria that will be used to retrieve the records that will appear on the report. Parameters work like filters. The difference is that the person viewing the chart, selects the filter criteria. An example of this would be an order report. If the chart had filters for the order date, order amount and sales rep fields, all of the following charts and more, could be displayed using one chart.

① Show all orders for a specific date.
② Show all orders for a specific sales rep.
③ Show all orders over or under a specific total order amount.
④ Show all orders in a date range.
⑤ Show all orders in a date range for a specific sales rep.

Task 4 Depending on the company, it may be necessary to have the person or group of people sign a document that states that all of the tasks discussed above will produce the report that they need.

And this concludes the basics of the report design process. Hopefully, you gained some insight of what goes on behind the scenes.

Public Data Sets

Earlier, I discussed that all of the data that you need, may not be in a data source that you have access to. You may have the need to do analysis that needs historical data. Public data sets may be a solution. The following connectors are used to connect to public data sets. The web sites are links to the public data sets.

- ☑ Google Big Query https://cloud.google.com/bigquery/public-data/
- ☑ Microsoft Azure Marketplace https://azuremarketplace.microsoft.com/en-us/marketplace/
- ☑ ODATA (Open Data Protocol)

Another public data set is Data.gov. The web site is www.catalog.data.gov/dataset. If you do a search for "public data sets", you may find the data that you need.

What Experience Has Taught Me About Where Data Is Stored

With all of the sophisticated databases and data stored in the cloud, I have noticed that often, the data people use most is stored in spreadsheets. This data could be exported to a spreadsheet from a database, pasted in from another data source or initially created in a spreadsheet. People like spreadsheets because they are free form, meaning you can place data anyplace you want and in any layout that you want.

An example of this is the data shown later in Figure 3-5. In reality, there is nothing wrong with that layout, as long as the data stays in the spreadsheet. The problem arises, the minute that the data needs to be used in an application that requires structure. Tableau is an example of such an application.

In addition to a less than desirable data structure, there are other issues that need to be addressed with data stored in a spreadsheet. This includes data that is missing, incorrect data being entered (because spreadsheets do not have data validation), and data in a layout that will not allow you to create the charts that you need in Tableau. At the end of the day, using data that was created in a spreadsheet, can cause you to have to spend several hours getting it in shape, to be used in Tableau. Having good, clean data, regardless of the source, is important, because the data needs to be analyzed.

> **Using Named Ranges**
> Tableau supports named ranges and named tables in Excel. If the data that you need to use in Excel is in a named range or a defined table, you can connect to them in Tableau. Figure 3-1 shows the sheets in an Excel workbook. Notice the following:
> ① The first sheet (named Excel Table) is based on an Excel table. Yes, I know that the sheet name is not original <smile>.
> ② The Order Named Ranges sheet, is the sheet that two named ranges were created on.
> ③ The Order Details and Order Header sheets, contain the data for the named ranges that were created on the Order Named Ranges sheet. Notice that these two sheets have a different icon, which represents a named range. When you hold the mouse pointer over either of these sheets, you will see (**NAMED RANGE**), after the sheet name, as shown in the figure.

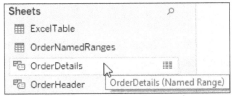

Figure 3-1 Excel table and named ranges

Depending on the data source, you may have the option of making changes to the data before you connect to it in Tableau. This is known as cleansing the data. If that is the case, cleaning the data in the data source is a good option. To be honest, in my opinion, Tableau does not have robust data cleansing functionality. After completing the exercises in this chapter, you should have a pretty good idea of whether or not, there is enough functionality to handle your data cleansing and data transformation needs.

While the Data Source tab provides a lot of options to prepare your data, keep in mind that changes made to the data on this tab, will be applied to every visualization, in the workbook, that is created using the data. If that is not what you want, make the change on the sheet(s) that need it.

Exercise Tips
Below are some tips that will help make completing the exercises easier.
1. When instructed to add a sheet or table on the Data Source tab, drag it from the Connect pane on the left, to the **DRAG SHEETS HERE** section, on the workspace. Double-clicking on the sheet or table will also add it to this section.
2. At the end of each exercise, save the workbook.
3. When you see the Update buttons at the bottom of the grid section, click the Update Now button.

Exercise 3.1: Learn About The Data Interpreter

In this exercise, you will learn about the data interpreter. This workbook will also be used as the starting point for other exercises in this chapter. To view the results of the data interpreter, you need to have Excel installed.

1.   Open a new workbook.

2.   Create a connection for the tableau_data.xlsx file.

3.   **TABLEAU PUBLIC ONLY**, Add the Orders table.

4.   Save the workbook as E3.1 Data interpreter.

Data Interpreter

This tool is available for Excel workbooks, text files and Google Sheets. It runs automatically when a connection is created for any of these file types. The Data Interpreter cleans all of the data that is connected to the data source. **The data is not changed in the data source.** Figure 3-2 shows the Data Interpreter option.

As shown in Figure 3-2, Tableau has detected that some of the data in the data source may need to be cleaned.

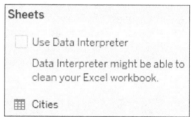

Figure 3-2 Data Interpreter option

The Data Interpreter is enabled when Tableau thinks that it can optimize the data for analysis purposes. This tool has the ability to:

☑ Detect empty rows or columns.
☑ Remove formatting that may cause a problem when creating visualizations.
☑ Remove headers or footers that are not needed.
☑ Detect hierarchical headers.
☑ Detect sub-tables that you may have a need to use. **SUB-TABLES** allow you to use a subset of the data, independent of the other data in the table.

Is The Data Interpreter Always Available?

The answer is Yes and No. Every time that you connect to an Excel file, text file or Google Sheet, the Data Interpreter runs. It is not enabled for any other data source type. As you saw earlier in Chapter 1, Exercise 1.2, when you connected to the Sample Superstore Excel workbook, you did not see a prompt for the Data Interpreter, like you saw above in Figure 3-2. The reason that it was not displayed in Chapter 1, is because Tableau did not find any data that could be improved. Just keep in mind that just because you do not see the Data Interpreter, does not mean that the data is ok. Below are some other reasons that you may not see the Data Interpreter.

☑ Data in Excel that is saved in CSV format is not supported.
☑ There are more than 2,000 columns.
☑ There are more than 150 columns and more than 3,000 rows of data.

Use The Data Interpreter

1. Check the **USE DATA INTERPRETER** option ⇒ When you see the **REVIEW THE RESULTS** link, click on it. This will open a copy of the data source and display the key for the Data Interpreter tab.

2. If prompted that there is a problem with some content . . ., Click Yes.

    The dialog box shown in Figure 3-3 informs you of the repairs that were made ⇒ Click Close.

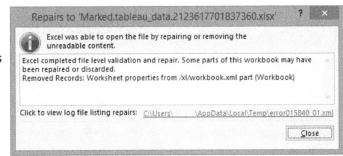

Figure 3-3 Repairs dialog box

Figure 3-4 shows the information on the Data Interpreter tab. It explains how to understand the results.

While the intended goal of the Data Interpreter is to help people clean some types of data problems, it can be annoying, because it does not allow you to select the types of problems that you want to check for. The example that comes to mind is the check for sub tables. Having sub tables is not a problem.

In all my years, I have never heard of or seen such, when it comes to checking for problems. If I only need to use a portion of the data in a table, I can create a query to select the records that I want when I import the data.

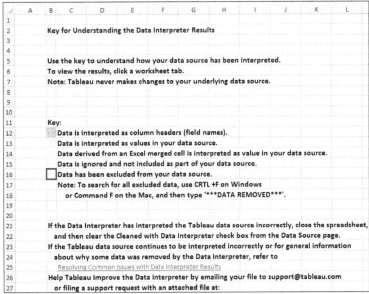

Figure 3-4 Key for the Data Interpreter tab

Or once the data set is in Tableau, I can create a filter or query to select the subset of data that I want to display or analyze. Do I use the Data Interpreter? Nope.

3. Close Excel. For the purposes of this book, there is no need to save the changes.

Cleaning Up The Data Interpreter Files

If you use this tool, temp files will be created on your computers hard drive. You can delete these files when you are finished using this tool. The path to the temp files is C:\Users\YourUserAccount\AppData\Local\Temp\TableauTemp.

Data Cleansing Options

In my opinion, Tableau's strongest features are its ability to create a wide variety of visualizations and a large toolset to customize visualizations and dashboards. This gives you the option of displaying the same data in a number of different ways, to be able to easily determine which graphical representation of the data best depicts the point that you need the data to make. Where it needs to be improved, is in the data cleansing and transformation areas.

Data in Excel, as well as, data in other non database data sources, can be very messy when it needs to be imported into another software package. The reason that I am focusing on Excel is because I know that many companies keep large amounts of data in Excel, either by creating it there or importing data from other sources into Excel or importing data into a Power Pivot database in Excel.

Empty rows or columns are a problem. For example, Figure 3-5 shows part of a balance sheet that was created in Excel. The first few rows would present a problem in Tableau. While the Data Interpreter can handle some issues, it is not as robust as other data cleansing tools that I have used. Two that come to mind (because I wrote a book about each of them - no shame book plug <smile>) are the Power Query tool in Excel or in Power BI Desktop. Power Query and the Query Editor in Power Bi Desktop, have the same functionality. They just have different names. Data can be imported from a lot of sources in Tableau. My guess is that the list is at least 60 different data source options. In addition to data cleansing, combining data from different data sources and types is also available.

	A	B	C	D	E	F	G	H	I	J	K	L	M
1						Balance Sheet							
2						Current Assets, Income & Expenses							
3													
4		January	February	March	April	May	June	July	August	September	October	November	December
5													
6	Current Assets												
7	Cash	17580	12100	74770	44425	74770	17580	44425	12500	343434	17580	74770	17580
8	Inventory	31783	45700	21006	12230	21006	37874	12230	45700	12230	31783	21750	31783
9	Receivables	59560	27500	54321	34567	54321	59560	44567	27500	34567	12345	54321	59560
10													
11	Total Assets	108923	85300	150097	91222	150097	115014	101222	85700	390231	61708	150841	108923
12													
13													
14	Avg Cash	44729			YTD Cash	223645							
15	Avg Inventory	26345			YTD Inventory	325075							
16	Avg Mthly Receivables	46053.8			YTD Receivables	522689							
17													
18	Income												
19	Mail Order	163,000	144,425	227,500	154,321	144,725	53,000	12,540	27,500	44,425	254,321	27,500	63,000
20	Kiosk	37,500	12,230	45,700	22,050	12,230	57,500	21,006	45,700	12,230	21,006	45,700	57,500
21	Store	50,000	12,100	74,770	31,783	12,100	50,000	31,783	74,770	12,100	31,783	74,770	50,500
22	Internet	23,000	7,700	54,730	59,560	7,700	23,000	59,560	54,730	7,500	62,600	43,850	23,000
23													
24	Total Income	273,500	176,455	402,700	267,714	176,755	183,500	124,889	202,700	76,255	369,710	191,820	194,000

Figure 3-5 Balance sheet

I did a little research to see what other options are available to help clean data, in particular, free options <smile> and came across the first three options below. The tools listed below are used to clean and transform data, help provide data discovery and data prep. DISCLAIMER: I have not used the first three options listed below, so I cannot tell you anything more about them.

☑ Tableau add-in for Excel. These links have information about the add-in.
https://community.tableau.com/docs/DOC-9169
https://community.tableau.com/thread/211781
This link has the zip file with the add-in https://community.tableau.com/docs/DOC-10394

☑ Tableau add-in for Power Pivot. https://www.tableau.com/support/drivers#powerpivot This link also has drivers for other software, like SQL Server and My SQL in the Data Source drop-down list. Once you select the driver that you want to install, scroll down the page to get the file (32 or 64 bit) to download.

☑ www.trifacta.com/products/wrangler free (works with these file types, .txt, Excel, .csv, .json)

☑ Power Query in Excel (comes with some editions of Excel)

☑ Power BI Desktop www.powerbi.com

Aggregated Data

This type of data is often created in spreadsheets. Aggregated data is totals, counts and averages, as shown later in Figure 3-22. Aggregate data needs to be removed, either in the spreadsheet, before connecting to the workbook or by using the Data Interpreter to remove it.

Built-In Data Cleansing Options

The data cleansing options covered so far have been external to Tableau. This section covers data cleansing options that come with Tableau.

① **ALIAS NAME** [See Chapter 2, Figure 2-14]

② **NULL VALUES** This type of data can be tricky to correct, especially if you are not familiar with the data. In many instances, it is ok for a field to have null values (no data in the field), as shown in Figure 3-6.

If every row of data has a null value in the field in question, more than likely, the field isn't needed in the data source and could be deleted. The null values could also indicate that Tableau cannot match the data type. Whatever the outcome of a field that is null for every record, using it to create a visual, isn't a good idea.

There are a few options to handle null values, as explained below.

Abc Sheet1 Store	# Sheet1 Year	# Sheet1 Total
Atherton	2010	19.700
null	2011	17.100
null	2012	18.300
null	2013	14.800
null	2014	19.800
null	2015	24.500
Berkeley	2010	14.400
null	2011	18.000

Figure 3-6 Fields with null values

☑ Fix the data in the data source.
☑ Create a filter for rows with null values in the field, to keep them from being used to create a visual.
☑ Create a group for the rows with null values

③ **CREATE GROUPS** [See Chapter 5, Grouping Data]
④ **GEOGRAPHY FIELD PROBLEMS** There are times when the built-in mapping does not recognize a location. When this is the case, a gray **PILL** is displayed in the lower right corner of the map. Clicking on this pill will display the locations that are not recognized.

Built-In Data Transformation Options

Data transformation is used to change the appearance of or manipulate the data.

Options that fall into this category include changing the data type, splitting data in a field and renaming fields.

RENAME A FIELD This is similar to creating an alias name for a field. The difference is that renaming a field changes the field name in the workbook, but not in the data source.

Using CSV Files That Have Rows With Different Numbers Of Columns

 The concept of a csv file that has rows of data with different numbers of columns is known as a **JAGGED CSV FILE**.

Most of the time, the CSV files that you will use, will have the same number of columns of data for each row. As shown in Figure 3-7, some of the cells do not have data. In Excel, this is not a problem.

The **TEXT FILE CONNECTOR** also supports files, where each row does not have data in the same number of columns, as shown in Figure 3-8. By "support", I mean that the data can be connected to, even though there is a problem with the data. Keep in mind that connections do not verify the quality of the data in the data source. Connections only provide access to the data.

Looking at the data in Excel, you can see that the first row of data has a date as the last field. It is easier to see that there is a problem with some of the data in Excel, then in Notepad. When you see something like this, you should look at the source data to figure what the cause is for the jagged file, then correct the problem, so that the data is moved to the correct column.

To use this file in Tableau, it would have to be modified. To fix this file, commas would need to be added to some rows, because some rows do not have data for each field. For example, rows 2, 3 and 4 in Figure 3-8, need a comma after the Employee ID field because these rows do not have a Customer ID value.

As shown in Figure 3-9, the last three columns have **NULL VALUES**. I imported the data without making any modifications, so that you can see how the data would look, if it wasn't modified. Some fields are hidden in this figure.

The null values and empty cells indicate that there is no data in the cell. The columns data type determines whether null values or empty cells are displayed when the field does not have any data.

	A	B	C	D	E	F	G	H	I	J	K	L	M	N	O
1	Order ID	Employee ID	Customer ID	Order Date	Shipped Date	Shipper ID	Ship Name	Ship Address	Ship City	Ship State/Province	Ship ZIP	Ship Country	Shipping Fee	Payment Type	Paid Date
2	9	27		01/15/2006	01/22/2006	2	Karen Toh	789 27th Street	Las Vegas	NV	99999	USA		Check	01/15/2006
3	3	4		01/20/2006	01/22/2006	1	Christina Lee	123 4th Street	New York	NY	99999	USA		Credit Card	
4	4	12		01/22/2006	01/22/2006	2	John Edwards	123 12th Street	Las Vegas	NV	99999	USA			
5	33	6	8	01/30/2006	01/31/2006	3	Elizabeth Andersen	123 8th Street	Portland	OR	99999	USA			
6	34	9	4	02/06/2006	02/07/2006	3	Christina Lee	123 4th Street	New York	NY	99999	USA	4		02/06/2006
7	35	3	29	02/10/2006	02/12/2006	2	Soo Jung Lee	789 29th Street	Denver	CO	99999	USA	7	Check	02/10/2006
8	36	4	3	02/23/2006	02/25/2006	2	Thomas Axen	123 3rd Street	Los Angel	CA	99999	USA	7	Cash	02/23/2006
9	37	8	6	03/06/2006	03/09/2006	2	Francisco P,rez-Olaeta	123 6th Street	Milwaukee	WI	99999	USA	12	Credit Card	03/06/2006
10	38	9	28	03/10/2006	03/11/2006	3	Amritansh Raghav	789 28th Street	Memphis	TN	99999	USA	10	Check	03/10/2006
11	39	3	8	03/22/2006	03/24/2006	3	Elizabeth Andersen	123 8th Street	Portland	OR	99999	USA	5	Check	03/22/2006
12	40	4	10	03/24/2006	03/24/2006	2	Roland Wacker	123 10th Street	Chicago	IL	99999	USA	9	Credit Card	03/24/2006
13	41	1	7	03/24/2006			Ming-Yang Xie	123 7th Street	Boise	ID	99999	USA	0		

Figure 3-7 CSV file in Excel

Figure 3-8 CSV file in Notepad

Figure 3-9 CSV file imported into Tableau

Exercise 3.2: Split Data In A Column

A popular use for this option is to split the first and last names that are in the same field.

1. **TABLEAU PUBLIC ONLY**, Create a connection to the tableau_data.xlsx file ⇒
   Save the file as `E3.2 Split a name field` ⇒ Go to step 4.

2. Save the E3.1 workbook as `E3.2 Split a name field`.

3. Clear the check mark for the Data Interpreter option.

4. Add the Financial Data sheet to the canvas.

5. Scroll to the right until you see the Sales Reps column ⇒ Display the shortcut menu for the field ⇒ Split.

6. On the shortcut menu for the Split 1 column, select **RENAME** ⇒
   Change the field name to `Sales Rep First Name`.

   The three columns should look like the ones shown in Figure 3-10.

Abc	=Abc	=Abc
FinancialData	Calculation	Calculation
Sales Rep	Sales Rep First Name	Sales Rep - Split 2
Michael Suyama	Michael	Suyama
Margaret Peacock	Margaret	Peacock
Nancy Davolio	Nancy	Davolio

Figure 3-10 Sales Rep field split and one field renamed

Filters

Filters have several uses, including the following:

① To select which records can be displayed on a chart.
② To select records that have incorrect data, records that need to be updated or records that need to be deleted.

Tableau was designed to handle large amounts of data. By large, I mean millions of rows of data per table. More than likely, you will not have the need to have millions of rows of data displayed on a visualization, but if you do, Tableau can handle it. It is also very possible that you will not want to view all of the data in any table.

One way to select the records that will be displayed on a visualization is to create filters. In a way, filters work like queries. The benefit is that filters are easier to create. Each data type has its own way of selecting the records that will be included or excluded on the visualization. Filters can be created for charts before, during or after a chart is created. The data displayed is the same, regardless of when in the process, the filters are created.

Filters can be created for Live and Extract connections. Before creating a filter, select the table or sheet that you want the filter applied to, then select the connection type.

The previous chapter covered filters. I stated that creating a filter to create a data extract could improve performance. Creating a filter for a live connection can also improve performance. Filters reduce the number of rows that have to be processed. In Exercise 2.3, a connection was created for a text file that has over 2 million records. More than likely, the visualizations that you would create would not need 2 million rows of data.

 Each field can only have one filter.

Filter Order Of Operations

In addition to being created on the Data Source tab, filters can also be created on a Sheet tab. As you will see, filters can be created in a variety of places. There are no rules that require filters to be created in a specific order. If you create filters on a sheet tab, then create a filter for the same data source, on the Data Source tab, that is fine. Just keep the following in mind. The filters are processed in the order listed below.

① Extract filters (Data Source tab) (1)
② Other filters on the Data Source tab (1)
③ Context filters [See Chapter 5, Context Filters]
④ Filters created for a dimension field (2)
⑤ Filters created for a measures field (2)

(1) Filters created on the Data Source tab are applied to all visualizations in the workbook, that use the sheet or table, that the filter is created for. Filters created on a sheet are only applied to the chart, on the sheet.
(2) This type of filter can be created on the Columns, Rows or Filters shelf on a Sheet tab. At the end of this chapter, you will see where the filter order of operations fits into the order that Tableau processes all ACTIONS (also known as OPERATIONS).

Live vs Extract Connection Options

Figure 3-11 shows the connection and filter options. They are explained below.

Connection			Filters	
○ Live	⊙ Extract	Edit Refresh	4	Edit
Extract includes subset of data. 05/19/2017 4:05:06 AM				

Figure 3-11 Connection and Filter options

Select the LIVE OPTION to update the data in the workbook when the data in the data source file changes.

Select the EXTRACT OPTION when you do not need the data in the workbook to be updated continuously. This means that the data used in the workbook is static. If the data source has a lot of data, it can cause the connection to be slow. If that is the case, you may want to use the Extract option and only refresh the data when necessary.

A filter can be created for the Extract option to reduce the number of records displayed. This reduces the number of records that will be available when visualizations are created. The extract option is how a **DATA EXTRACT (.TDE)** file is created and how data is added to the data extract file.

The **EDIT OPTION** is used to create, edit or delete a filter for an extract connection. (3)

The **REFRESH OPTION** is enabled after the extract file has been created. It is used to refresh the data in the extract file. (3)

The **ADD BUTTON** in the Filters section is used to create, edit or delete a filter for a live connection.

The number below the Filters heading is the number of filters that have been created for the live connection for the data source.

(3) This option is only available when the Extract option is selected.

How Do I Choose Between A Live And Extract Connection?

This topic is important and I want you to understand the pros and cons for each option. Table 3-1 is a summary.

Live Connection	Extract Connection
Requires a connection to the data source to use. If the data source is on your computer, this isn't a consideration.	Does not require a connection to use the data, once the extract is created.
Data is refreshed automatically.	Data is not refreshed automatically. It can be refreshed, when connected to the data source.
Performance can be an issue, especially if the data source has a lot of records, or is used by a lot of people at the same time.	Better performance than a live connection because the data source is not being used.
Files are not compressed.	Extract files are compressed, which makes the file size smaller.

Table 3-1 Live vs Extract connection options

 A data source can have a live and extract connection. When you save extract connection options, you can switch back to the live connection option if necessary and not loose the extract options that you have set.

Not all data sources can use both connection options. For example, data sources saved in the cloud have to use the Extract connection option. OLAP cube files cannot use the Extract connection option.

Exercise 3.3: Create Filters For A Live Connection

In this exercise you will create two filters that will display two years of orders for a sales rep.

Create The Sales Rep Filter

1. Save the E3.2 workbook as E3.3 Filters for a live connection.

2. In the upper right corner of the Data Source tab, click the **ADD BUTTON** ⇒ On the Edit Data Source Filters dialog box, click the **ADD BUTTON** ⇒ On the dialog box shown in Figure 3-12, select the Sales Rep field ⇒ On the dialog box shown in Figure 3-13, select the Sales Rep, Janet Leverling ⇒ Click OK.

Create The Order Year Filter

In this part of the exercise, you will create a filter that will only display orders for two years.

1. On the Edit Data Source Filters dialog box, click the Add button ⇒ On the Add Filter dialog box, select the Order Date field.

2. On the dialog box shown in Figure 3-14, select the **YEARS** option ⇒ Click Next.

    The options shown, depend on the fields data type that the filter is being created for. Figure 3-15 shows the filter options for a numeric field. The values shown in Figure 3-16 are the years found in the table, for the Order Date field.

3. Check the years, 2015 and 2016, as shown above in Figure 3-16.
   Figure 3-17 shows the filter criteria that has been created ⇒ Click OK.

Figure 3-12 Add Filter dialog box

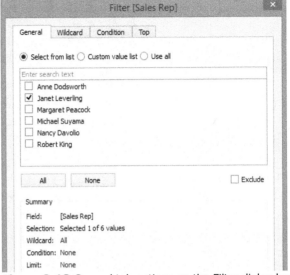

Figure 3-13 General tab options on the Filter dialog box

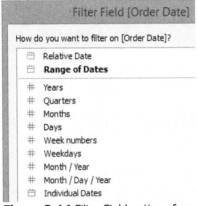

Figure 3-14 Filter Field options for a date field

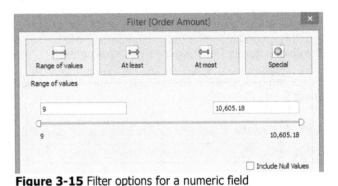

Figure 3-15 Filter options for a numeric field

Figure 3-16 Criteria options selected for the Order Date field

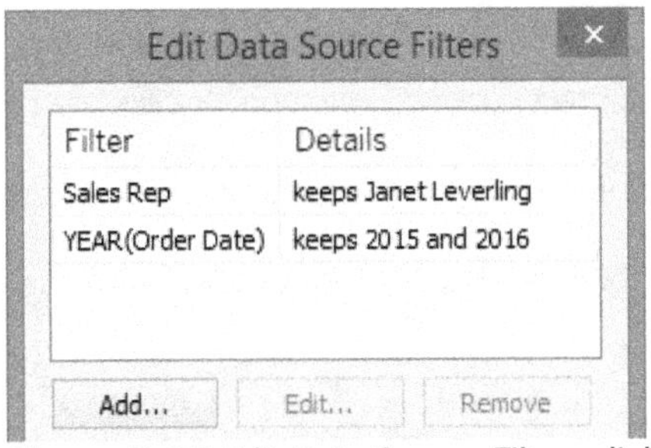

Figure 3-17 Edit Data Source Filters dialog box

In the Filters section on the canvas, you should see that there are two filters. You will see the data shown in Figure 3-18. If you do not see the data, click the Refresh button or the Update Now button. If you scroll down the data in the grid, you will see that all of the records have the same sales rep and the order date is in 2015 or 2016.

Order Date	Order DateTime	Required Date	Ship Date	Ship Via	Customer Name	City	State	Sales Rep
01/02/2015	06/08/2014 8:13:30 AM	01/09/2015	01/03/2015	FedEx	Trail Blazer's Place	Madison	WI	Janet Leverling
01/02/2015	01/27/2014 8:54:14 AM	01/09/2015	01/03/2015	FedEx	Trail Blazer's Place	Madison	WI	Janet Leverling
01/04/2015	02/05/2014 7:51:32 AM	01/10/2015	01/05/2015	UPS	Backpedal Cycle Shop	Philadelphia	PA	Janet Leverling
01/04/2015	06/22/2014 9:34:24 PM	01/04/2015	01/04/2015	Purolator	Cyclist's Trail Co.	Sterling Heights	MI	Janet Leverling

Figure 3-18 Records retrieved from the filter criteria

Data Extracts

If you know that all of the visualizations that will be created in the workbook will only use historical data, select the Extract connection option. An example would be analyzing data for the previous calendar year.

Another reason to use the extract option, is that it saves a copy of the data with the workbook. This means that the workbook does not have to be connected to the data source. This is a good solution if you need to share the workbook with someone that does not have access to the data source.

Data extracts can also be used when you have the need to combine (aka append) data from different tables. For example, Figure 3-19 shows the tabs for three monthly invoice files. The data on these tabs could be combined into one extract file, using the **NEW UNION** option.

March2017	April2017	May2017

Figure 3-19 Files that can be combined

A data extract can be a subset of the data. What may not be obvious is that the Extract connection option is how the **DATA EXTRACT (.TDE)** file is created.

Exercise 3.4: Create A Filter For An Extract Connection

 This functionality is not available in Tableau Public.

This exercise will show you how to create a filter that selects the data that will be saved in the extract file.

1. Save the E3.1 workbook as E3.4 Extract data file.

2. Add the Orders sheet.

3. Select the Extract connection option ⇒ Click the Edit button.

4. On the Extract Data dialog box, click the Add button ⇒ Select the Territory field.

5. Select the following Territories: Far West, Mideast, Southeast. You should have the options shown in Figure 3-20.

Figure 3-20 Extract Data dialog box

6. Click on the Sheet tab ⇒ On the Save Extract As dialog box, type `E3.4 Orders extract data file`.

If you tried to save the workbook without creating the data extract file, you would see the warning shown in Figure 3-21.

It lets you know that the extract file has not been created.

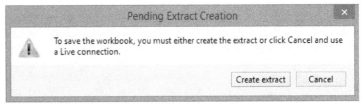

Figure 3-21 Pending Extract Creation warning message

Understanding How Much Work A Workbook Can Need

Earlier in this chapter, the design process was covered. Hopefully, you came away with the understanding that the process described is for each chart that needs to be created. In Tableau, you can think of each sheet as a report. Each sheet can only contain one visual. A dashboard usually stores two or more sheets and a story contains two or more sheets or dashboards.

In a perfect environment, all of the data that you need to create a visualization would already be in one file. In the real world, the data that you need may come from a variety of data sources, including web pages (which is also known as public data), databases, PDF files and spreadsheets. Keep in mind that multiple visualizations, dashboards and stories can be created in one workbook. You may have a dashboard that displays financial data from a database, another dashboard that displays sales for several product lines, sheets for orders by product line, per country and a story that displays new business opportunities, all in one Tableau workbook. More than likely, to create all of these visualizations, the data will be in different data sources. The good thing is that all of the data can be imported into one Tableau workbook.

Exercise 3.5: Add Another Data Source To A Workbook

So far, all of the workbooks that were created, only have a connection to one data source. Workbooks support more than one data source. Even better, the data sources do not have to be the same type. In this exercise, you will add an Access database to a workbook that already has an Excel data source.

1. Save the E3.1 workbook as `E3.5 Workbook with different data source types`.

2. On the Data Source tab, click the Add button in the Connections section ⇒ Select the Access option.

3. The importdb.mdb connection information should be filled in, on the Access dialog box ⇒ Click Open.
    You will see the database listed in the Connections section and the tables in the database below it. If you click on the Excel connection, you will see the sheets from the workbook.

4. Save the workbook.

Pivot Data

Data in Excel is often set up as a **CROSSTAB** or **PIVOT TABLE**, as shown in Figure 3-22. This layout style displays data in a grid format. The data is usually summarized. This is known as a Columnar table layout, meaning the variables (in this figure, the years) are the column headers. Tableau uses a Row table layout, as shown in Figure 3-23. In this layout, the variables are stored in the columns named Year and Year Total.

 | Excel pivot tables are not supported in Tableau. |

(In Millions)

Store	FY 2013	FY 2014	FY 2015	FY 2016	FY 2017	Total
Atherton	$19.70	$17.10	$18.30	$14.80	$19.80	$89.70
Berkeley	$14.40	$18.00	$16.40	$16.70	$19.30	$84.80
Carmel-by-the-Sea	$18.80	$13.50	$18.70	$13.90	$15.70	$80.60
Cupertino	$12.00	$16.20	$17.50	$17.80	$13.80	$77.30
Fresno	$19.20	$15.60	$19.60	$15.90	$14.40	$84.70
Laguna Beach	$18.90	$14.60	$16.70	$12.10	$13.90	$76.20
Mailbu	$18.70	$17.80	$14.00	$18.50	$13.70	$82.70
Pasadena	$17.00	$19.40	$17.10	$17.30	$17.30	$88.10
San Francisco	$14.40	$14.00	$13.90	$15.40	$18.30	$76.00
Total	$153.10	$146.20	$152.20	$142.40	$146.20	$740.10

Figure 3-22 Data in a crosstab or pivot table layout

Store	Year	Year Total
Atherton	2013	$19.70
Atherton	2014	$17.10
Atherton	2015	$18.30
Atherton	2016	$14.80
Atherton	2017	$19.80
Berkeley	2013	$14.40
Berkeley	2014	$18.00
Berkeley	2015	$16.40
Berkeley	2016	$16.70
Berkeley	2017	$19.30
Carmel-by-the-Sea	2013	$18.80
Carmel-by-the-Sea	2014	$13.50

Figure 3-23 Data in a row table layout

The **PIVOT** and **ADD DATA TO PIVOT** options, on the column shortcut menu in the grid, takes the data in a pivot table layout, as shown above in Figure 3-22, or data that is in a non tabular format and changes it to a flat file (unpivoted layout), shown above in Figure 3-23. This process is known as changing the **DATA STRUCTURE**.

If you have a spreadsheet that looks like the one shown above in Figure 3-22, you will appreciate how the Add Data to Pivot option can help you use non table data in Tableau. This option is used to change the layout into one that Tableau supports. By support, I mean that the data will be changed to a layout that can be used to create a visualization.

Exercise 3.6: Working With Pivot Data

This exercise will show you how to pivot the data shown earlier in Figure 3-22, to the columnar format shown in Figure 3-23.

1. **TABLEAU PUBLIC ONLY,** Open a new workbook ⇒ Connect to the tableau_data.xlsx file ⇒ Add the Pivot Data sheet ⇒ Save the workbook ⇒ On the Sheet tab, delete the field that you added to save the workbook ⇒ Go to step 4.

2. Save the E3.1 workbook as `E3.6 Pivot crosstab data`.

3. Add the Pivot Data sheet.

4. Select the FY columns 2013 to 2016 ⇒ Open the shortcut menu for the first selected column (FY2013) ⇒ Select Pivot. You will see two columns that start with "Pivot Field", at the beginning of the grid.

5. Open the shortcut menu for the FY2017 column ⇒ Select **ADD DATA TO PIVOT**. You should see the unpivoted data shown in Figure 3-24.

    This option adds the selected column(s) to the existing pivot columns. I did this to demonstrate how going forward, if the table has more year columns added to it, that needs to be pivoted, it can be done.

Abc	#	Abc
Pivot	Pivot	PivotData
Pivot Field Names	Pivot Field Values	Store
Fy 2013	19.70000	Atherton
Fy 2013	14.40000	Berkeley
Fy 2013	18.80000	Carmel-by-the-Sea
Fy 2013	12.00000	Cupertino

Figure 3-24 Unpivoted data

Pivot Fields

As shown above in Figure 3-24, there are two pivot fields, as explained below.

① The **PIVOT FIELD NAMES** column (also known as the attribute column) contains the data for each pivot column heading in the data source.

② The **PIVOT FIELD VALUES** column (also known as the value column) contains the data for each cell in the data source. The columns in the data source become rows, once the pivot option is applied.

> **Pivot Data Tips**
> Keep the following in mind when using pivot data.
> ① All fields used to create the pivot have to be from the same connection.
> ② Pivot fields cannot be used in calculated field formulas.
> ③ Pivot fields can be used as the join field.

Renaming Pivot Fields

These fields (columns) can be renamed, like fields in the data source.

1. Rename the Pivot Field Names field to `FY Year`.

2. Rename the Pivot Field Values field to `Year Total`.

> **How To Remove/Undo Pivot Columns**
> In the grid, open the shortcut menu for one of the pivot fields ⇒ Select **REMOVE PIVOT**. All of the pivot fields will be removed and the original fields from the data source will be restored.

What Is A Relationship?

In order to be able to use data from multiple tables to create a chart, there has to be a connection between the tables. The connection is called a **JOIN** or **LINK**. The result of a link between tables is called a **RELATIONSHIP**. The ability to create relationships between tables and use the data from multiple tables to create one chart, is one reason that makes Tableau popular.

Relationships are created between a column of data that two tables have in common. Relationships between tables also allow for a higher level of analysis. For example, data in one table can be filtered by data in another table, which provides even more flexibility and control over the data that is displayed on a chart.

Relational Databases

The reason that tables can have relationships created between them is because there is at least one column of data in each table that has the same data, thus the term "Relational Databases". Yes, this is a complicated topic and there are a lot of books on the concepts associated with relational databases and how to create them, so I won't bore you with all of the details, but please hear me out and don't skip this section. Creating relationships in Tableau and creating relationships in a database have things in common.

While databases are not the primary focus of this chapter, it is important that you understand a little more than the fundamentals. My goal is to explain, as painless as possible, how all of the components fit together <smile>. The reason that you need to understand this database concept is because it is one of the building blocks for the reports that you will create and modify. If you have never created a database, or have very little experience creating them, the next few sections in this chapter will be your crash course in databases and relationships. Figures 3-25 and 3-26 illustrate the layout of two tables. These tables will be referred to several times in the next few sections.

Orders			
Order ID	Order Date	Order Amount	Cust ID
1000	1/2/2015	$263.99	48
1001	1/2/2015	$322.45	57
1002	1/3/2015	$196.00	3
1003	1/4/2015	$124.99	48

Table Name
Field Names
Records

Figure 3-25 Orders table

Orders Detail		
Order ID	Product ID	Quantity
1000	43	4
1000	76	2
1001	76	3
1001	10	2
1003	10	1
1004	25	3

Table Name
Field Names
Records

Figure 3-26 Orders Detail table

Primary Key Fields

Primary key fields and ID fields are terms that are used interchangeably. I prefer to use the term ID field because primary key fields in databases often have "ID" as part of the field name. I have also seen the word "Key" at the end of a field name to signify that the field is a primary key field.

 ID is short for identification. It is jargon that the computer programming community uses to reference a field that can be used to link one table to another table.

The majority of the tables in the database that is used in this book have at least one ID field. Hopefully, you will find that this is also true out in the real world. The reason ID fields are used is because by design they provide a way for each record in the table to have a unique way to be identified. A **FOREIGN KEY** points back to a primary key in a related table.

I have taught several database classes and almost without fail, this topic caused a lot of confusion. For some reason, people want to create links on string (text) fields. Please don't do that. It can cause you problems and should be avoided. It is a bad table design choice. However, creating relationships using text fields is acceptable, in particular, for data that is imported into a database from a text file.

If you needed to create a report that displays all of the orders and what items were on each order, you would need a way to link the Orders and Orders Detail tables shown above. Think of creating relationships as providing the ability to combine two or more tables "virtually" and being able to display the result of this "virtual linking" on a report. The result of this virtual linking will remind you of a view, that some databases support.

In Figures 3-25 and 3-26 above, the common ID field is the Order ID field. If you look at the data in the Orders Detail table, you will see that some records have the same Order ID number. That's okay. This means that some orders have more than one item. Each record in the Orders Detail table represents one item that was ordered. If you were to virtually join the data in the tables shown above, the virtual table would look like the one shown in Figure 3-27.

This "virtual" join is what happens when tables are **LINKED** (have a relationship). If all of this data was stored in one table instead of two, at the very minimum, all of the fields in the Orders table would be repeated for every record that is in the Orders Detail table, which is exactly what the virtual table, in Figure 3-27, shows.

Orders				Orders Detail		
Order ID	Order Date	Order Amount	Cust ID	Order ID	Product ID	Quantity
1000	1/2/2015	$263.99	48	1000	43	4
1000	1/2/2015	$263.99	48	1000	76	2
1001	1/2/2015	$322.45	57	1001	76	3
1001	1/2/2015	$322.45	57	1001	10	2
1002	1/3/2015	$196.00	3			
1003	1/4/2015	$124.99	48	1003	10	1
				1004	25	3

Figure 3-27 Virtually joined tables

Repetition of data is why data is stored in two or more tables in a database, instead of one. In this example, an additional row would be added to the Orders table for each row in the Orders Detail table. It is poor table design to have the same information (other than fields that are used to join tables) stored in more than one table.

 Usually if you see a record in the Orders Detail table, like Order ID 1004 shown above in Figure 3-27, or any **CHILD TABLE** that is in a **PARENT-CHILD RELATIONSHIP**, there is a problem with the data in at least one of the tables because all of the records in the child table should have a matching record in the parent table. Parent tables are used to get data (also known as **LOOKUP DATA**) from a **CHILD TABLE**. In this scenario, the record for Order ID 1004, in the Orders Detail table, would not be retrieved or shown on a report.

An ID field in the Orders table is how you find the matching record (known as a **ONE-TO-ONE RELATIONSHIP**) or matching records (known as a **ONE-TO-MANY RELATIONSHIP**, which is the most popular type of relationship) in another table. These are the two most common types of relationships. The **MANY-TO-MANY RELATIONSHIP** is a third type of relationship. It is not used as much as the other two relationship types.

Each row in a parent table needs a primary key field. In my opinion, child or lookup tables do not necessarily need a primary key field, as long as it has a foreign key field that the parent table can use to create a relationship with. Some, will disagree with me on this. Having said that, I do understand why all tables have a primary key field, even though the primary key field may not be used.

For the most part, a primary key consists of using the data in one field. There are times (not often though), where data from more than one field is needed to make the "primary key" value unique. When this is the case, the key is known as a composite key. **COMPOSITE KEYS** are a unique value that is created by combining the values in two or more fields. To create this type of key, you have to combine the values in the fields before creating the relationship. One way to accomplish this is by creating a formula that combines the values in the fields needed to create a unique value for each row of data.

How Relationships Work

More than likely, many of the reports that you create will require data from more than one table. Reports that display the equivalent of a Product List report will probably only use one table, so there is no linking involved. The best way to understand the basic concept of creating relationships between tables, especially if you are not familiar with the data, is to take the time to view at least some of the data in the tables that need to have a relationship created.

Depending on the table structure, tables can have more than one field that they can be linked on. An example of this would be the Orders Detail table. This table has an ID field that would be used to link it to the Orders table. There is a Product ID field in the Orders Detail table that would be used to retrieve the Product Name from another table (the Product table) to display on the report, instead of displaying the Product ID number. Displaying the product name is more meaningful then displaying the Product ID field, which is usually a number. If you are asking why the Product Name is not stored in the Orders Detail table, there are a few reasons, as explained below.

① The ID field takes up less space then the Product Name field, thereby keeping the size of the Orders Detail table (and any other table that would potentially store the Product Name field, instead of the Product ID field) smaller.
② If the product name was changed in the Orders Detail table, and a report used the Product Name field in the Product table (which is what should happen), the report would not display the revised product name.
③ Without a Product table, there would be no place to add new products or update the inventory.
④ If a Product Name has to be changed for any reason, it only has to be changed, on one record, in the Product table. Every report that the Product Name field is displayed on, would automatically be updated with the revised product name, the next time the data is refreshed and the report is run. If the product name was stored in the Orders Detail table, every record in the Orders Detail table that had that product name would have to be changed, as well as, any other table that stored the product name. That would be a lot of extra work (for someone) and increase the chance for inaccurate data.

What Is Cardinality?

Lookup tables usually have values in the primary key field that are repeated. This type of table is the "Many" side of a relationship. The primary table usually has values that are not repeated in the primary key field. This type of table is the "One" side of a relationship. This concept of primary and lookup tables is also known as the **CARDINALITY** of a relationship.

Cardinality is the term used to classify the type of relationship (one-to-one or one-to-many) that two tables have. Cardinality refers to the uniqueness of data. Cardinality is helpful for tables that have a lot of records because it can be used to help select how data should be combined. If the related columns have unique values, use joins to combine the tables. If the related columns have a lot of the same data values, use data blending to combine the tables.

Understanding Joins

The purpose of creating a join is to be able to use data from more than one table to create visualizations. As you have seen, Excel workbooks usually have more than one sheet of data and databases have more than one table. Especially in databases, there is usually one main table and several look up tables.

The beginning of this chapter started with the design process. If you followed along, hopefully you came away understanding that more than likely, you would be creating more than one visualization in a workbook. To be able to use the data in more than one table, a join between the tables is needed. Joins can be created anytime during the process of creating visualizations. If you are new to creating joins, you will probably find yourself coming back to the Data Source tab, once or twice to create more joins.

Join Types

Hopefully, you are still with me. Don't worry, the relational database "lecturette" is almost over. There are several types of links that can be created. These different types of links are called **JOIN TYPES**. There are several join types that you can select from. Each join type will display different results from the same tables, which you will see in

Figures 3-28 to 3-31. Joining tables is not permanent. Joins are recreated each time the query is run. There are two main types of joins, as explained below.

   ① **INNER JOINS** The record set (records that are retrieved) only contains records that have a match in both tables.

   ② **OUTER JOINS** The record set contains all records from one table (usually the primary table) and the matching records from the other table (usually the child table).

The four join types that are explained in Table 3-2 are the join types that are the most common. There are other join types that have to be created manually, by creating a **JOIN CALCULATION**. [See bottom of Figure 3-37] Table 3-2 references left and right tables. In the Orders and Orders Detail tables scenario, the Orders table is the **LEFT** table and the Orders Detail table is the **RIGHT** table.

 | The "matching" explained in Table 3-2 is usually done on primary key fields. |

Join Type	How Records Are Selected . . .
Inner	Selects records that have matching records in both tables, as shown in Figure 3-28. This is the default join type.
Left	Selects all records from the table on the left and matching records from the table on the right, as shown in Figure 3-29. If there are no records in the table on the right that match, the values in the columns for the table on the right will be displayed with nulls. You may know this as a **LEFT OUTER** join.
Right	Selects all records from the table on the right and matching records from the table on the left, as shown in Figure 3-30. This join type works the opposite of the Left join type. If there are no records in the table on the left that match, the values in the columns for the table on the left will be displayed with nulls. You may know this as a **RIGHT OUTER** join.
Full Outer	Selects all records from both tables whether or not there are matching records in the other table, as shown in Figure 3-31. Full Outer joins are also known as a **UNION JOIN TYPE**.

Table 3-2 Join types explained

Join Type Examples

When walking through these examples, compare the data in each example to the data shown earlier in Figure 3-27. The examples in this section **only** show the data that would be retrieved, based on the join type that is selected. This is why it is important to understand linking and join types. The arrows between the tables represent the flow of the data. While the examples only show joins between two tables in the data set, joins can and often are created between two or more tables. By that I mean one table in a data set can have joins to two or more other tables in the data set.

In Figure 3-28, the record for Order ID 1002 in the Orders table would not be retrieved in an Inner join because there is no related record in the Orders Detail table.

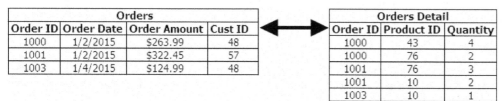

Orders					Orders Detail		
Order ID	Order Date	Order Amount	Cust ID		Order ID	Product ID	Quantity
1000	1/2/2015	$263.99	48		1000	43	4
1001	1/2/2015	$322.45	57		1000	76	2
1003	1/4/2015	$124.99	48		1001	76	3
					1001	10	2
					1003	10	1

Figure 3-28 Inner join record set

In Figure 3-29, the record for Order ID 1004 would not be retrieved from the Orders Detail table in a Left join because there is no related record in the Orders table.

Orders					Orders Detail		
Order ID	Order Date	Order Amount	Cust ID		Order ID	Product ID	Quantity
1000	1/2/2015	$263.99	48		1000	43	4
1001	1/2/2015	$322.45	57		1000	76	2
1002	1/3/2015	$196.00	3		1001	76	3
1003	1/4/2015	$124.99	48		1001	10	2
					1003	10	1

Figure 3-29 Left join record set

In Figure 3-30, the record for Order ID 1002 in the Orders table would not be retrieved in a Right join because there is no related record in the Orders Detail table.

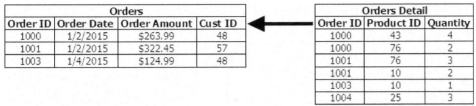

Orders					Orders Detail		
Order ID	Order Date	Order Amount	Cust ID		Order ID	Product ID	Quantity
1000	1/2/2015	$263.99	48		1000	43	4
1001	1/2/2015	$322.45	57		1000	76	2
1003	1/4/2015	$124.99	48		1001	76	3
					1001	10	2
					1003	10	1
					1004	25	3

Figure 3-30 Right join record set

In Figure 3-31, all records would be retrieved from both tables in a Full Outer join, whether there is a related record in the other table or not.

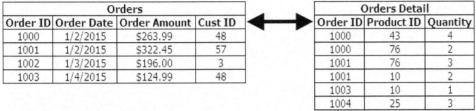

Orders					Orders Detail		
Order ID	Order Date	Order Amount	Cust ID		Order ID	Product ID	Quantity
1000	1/2/2015	$263.99	48		1000	43	4
1001	1/2/2015	$322.45	57		1000	76	2
1002	1/3/2015	$196.00	3		1001	76	3
1003	1/4/2015	$124.99	48		1001	10	2
					1003	10	1
					1004	25	3

Figure 3-31 Full Outer join record set

The Join Dialog Box

To display this dialog box, two tables have to be added to the canvas. Once the tables are added, you will see the link (also called a **UNION**), between the tables, as illustrated in Figure 3-32. Click on the link to display the dialog box shown in Figure 3-33. This dialog box is used to join tables.

Figure 3-32 Link between tables illustrated

Figure 3-33 Join dialog box

The shortcut menu shown above in Figure 3-32, is available for all tables. The options are explained below.

The **FIELD NAMES** option is selected when the tables have field names.

The **GENERATE FIELD NAMES AUTOMATICALLY** option is used when a union is created and there are no matching field names (in the tables) or the table does not have field names.

The **CONVERT TO UNION** option converts the join into a union.

The **DUPLICATE** option adds a copy of the table to the canvas. This is often done to create a **RECURSIVE JOIN**.

Select the **REMOVE** option to remove the table from the canvas.

The symbol displayed above each join type in Figure 3-33, indicates the type of join that has been created. If you hold the mouse pointer over each icon, you will see a tooltip that explains the type of join that will be created. As shown, the inner join is the default join type. If a join type is not enabled (dimmed out), you cannot create that type of join.

New Union Option

Creating a union is not a join. A union is a way to combine (append) data from two or more tables. The data from one table is appended to the data in another table. This option appears below the files in the data source, on the left pane, if the data source type supports the Union functionality.

An example would be the three tabs of data, shown earlier in Figure 3-19. When the New Union option is selected, the dialog box shown in Figure 3-34, is displayed. To create a union, the following must be true.

① The tables that you want to combine have to come from the same connection.
② The tables have to have the same structure, meaning that the fields must have the same data type, tables must have the same number of fields and the same field names.

Figure 3-34 Union dialog box

What Is The Star Schema?

Hopefully, now that you have a better understanding of data models, it is time to clearly define what the data model will be used for. Data models are used for storing, analyzing and reporting on data. The three **SCHEMA TYPES** for data models are:

① **STAR** Has one level of **CHILD TABLES**.
② **SNOWFLAKE** Can have multiple levels of child tables. Some people say that this schema can cause performance issues because of the increased number of relationships. My advice is to try it and see for yourself.
③ **CONSTELLATION** Is used when there is more than one fact table.

The Star schema has what is called a **FACT TABLE** (the **PARENT** or **PRIMARY TABLE** in the data model). My personal preference is the Star schema, because it handles large data sets. That, and it is easy to understand.

The primary table is surrounded by the other tables in the data model, forming, you guessed it, a star, as shown in Figure 3-35. The Orders table is the fact table in this figure. This is also known as **DIMENSIONAL MODELING** because it describes the logical way that data should be structured to obtain the best performance. More than likely, the table that has the most relationships, with other tables, is the fact table.

Fact tables contain data for a business process (for example, the quantitative information, metrics or measurements). This table is at the center of a star schema or snow flake schema and is surrounded by dimension tables. This data is used for analysis purposes. An example of data in a fact table is sales information. The fields in a fact table that can be analyzed are known as **MEASURE COLUMNS**. These fields can be aggregated.

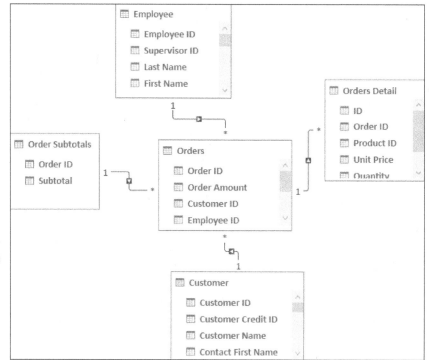

Figure 3-35 Star schema

The fact table usually has some or all of the following characteristics:

① It has measurable data, meaning that it will answer a question. For example, the Orders table has an order amount. This field could be used to answer which five states have the most sales.
② Other tables are linked to it.
③ It has one or more date fields, which confirm when something happened, like when the order was placed or the date of each basketball game.
④ Fact tables usually have more of rows of data, then any other table in the data model. (Date tables are not included when determining the fact table, because they do not contain data that will be analyzed).

A **DIMENSION TABLE** (also known as a **CHILD TABLE**) contains data about how the data in a fact table can be analyzed. These tables contain supporting data, if you will, that provide additional information about a field in the fact table. For example, in Figure 3-35 above, the Customer table contains information on who placed each order. The Order Details table contains the items for each order. Notice that each dimension table is linked to the fact table and none of the dimension tables are linked to each other.

Dimension tables can be linked to each other. An example would be adding a Products table to the schema in the figure. It would be linked to the Orders Detail table, using the Product ID field. That would allow the product name to be displayed on the chart. If the schema rules were strictly followed, adding the Product table would make the star schema shown above in the figure, a Snowflake schema, because the Product table does not have a direct relationship with the fact table (the Orders table).

The concepts in this section are important to understand because dimensions and measures are how Tableau classifies data that is used to create charts.

 | Text and date values are dimensions most of the time. Numeric values are measures. |

Exercise 3.7: Create The Data Sets For The Charts That Will Be Created In This Book

In this exercise, you will create two data sets that will be used as the starting point for the charts that will be created in the rest of this book.

Create A Data Set That Has Joins

In this part of the exercise, you will learn how to create joins. The following tables will be joined:

☑ Orders and Order Details
☑ Order Details and Products
☑ Orders and Sales Reps

1. **TABLEAU PUBLIC ONLY,** Open a new workbook ⇒ Connect to the tableau_data.xlsx workbook ⇒ Go to step 3.

2. Save the E3.1 workbook as `E3.7 Chart data`.

3. Add the Orders table to the canvas ⇒ Add the Order Details table to the canvas.

4. Click on the link ⇒ Select the Left join type ⇒ Close the Join dialog box. If you hold the mouse pointer over the link between the tables, you will see a popup that shows how the tables are linked and the field in each table that was used to create the link, as shown in Figure 3-36.

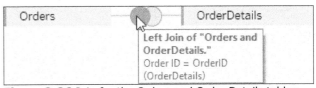
Figure 3-36 Join for the Orders and Order Details tables

5. Add the Products table. The reason that it was automatically linked to the Order Details table is because there is a field in both tables with the same name.

6. Add the Sales Reps table.

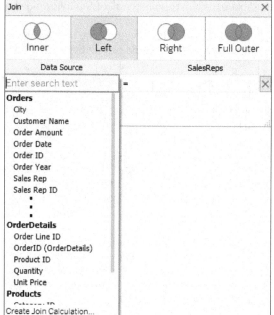

The Join dialog box, shown in Figure 3-37, automatically appears with a list of fields in the tables already on the canvas, because no match on any field name in the Sales Reps table was found in any of the tables on the canvas.

If the fields selected are not the ones that you need, open the drop-down list and select the field that you need, as shown in the figure.

To delete the join fields, click the X to the right of the drop-down list on the right, as shown in the figure.

Figure 3-37 Join dialog box options when the Sales Reps table is added

7. Select the Left join type ⇒ In the drop-down list, select the Sales Rep ID field in the Orders table.

8. In the drop-down list for the Sales Reps table, select the Rep ID field, as shown in Figure 3-38.

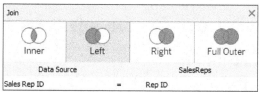

Your joins should look like the ones shown in Figure 3-39. I created the join in step 8 to demonstrate how to create a join when there are no matching fields.

Figure 3-38 Orders and Sales Reps tables join criteria

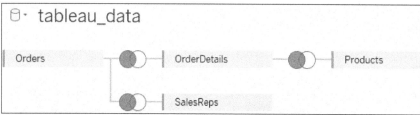

Figure 3-39 Joins for the workbook

 Columns that display the table name in parenthesis in the grid, means that there is another column with the same name in a different table.

Hiding Columns

Several of the columns displayed in the grid will not be used to create a chart. Hiding a field on the Data Source tab, also hides it on the Sheet tabs. The fields are not actually hidden, the color is changed to gray and the fields are still visible. Hidden fields cannot be used to create a chart. In this part of the exercise, you will hide a few columns.

1. From left to right, hide the following columns: Order Line ID, Order ID (Order Details), Product ID (Products) and Category ID.

Renaming A Data Set

Figure 3-39 above, shows the current data set. As shown, the name of the data set defaults to the data source name. It would be helpful if the name represents the data that it contains. Having a better name is especially helpful if the Tableau workbook has more than one data set.

1. Click on the words "tableau_data" ⇒ Type Orders Dataset ⇒ Press Enter. While I used the word "dataset" as part of the name, that is not a requirement.

Add Another Data Source To The Workbook

As you know, a Tableau workbook can support data from more than one data source. In the first section of this exercise, a data set if you will, was created that used several tables from the same data source. Tableau workbooks support multiple data sets. By this I mean that you can add data from other data sources to this workbook and have them in their own data set. This means that when you are creating a chart, you have the option of selecting which data set to use. For example, you can have data from a spreadsheet, Access database and an SQL Server database, all in the same Tableau workbook.

Figure 3-40 Sheets in the tableau_data.xlsx file

Figure 3-40 shows all of the sheets in the tableau_data Excel workbook. Currently, the only sheets that can be used to create a chart are the ones shown above in Figure 3-39.

What if you need to create a chart that needs data from the other sheets? Sheets that have a relationship to a table in the Orders Dataset that was created in this exercise can be joined to that data set. Sheets that do not have a relationship to the Orders Dataset, need their own data set.

The steps below show you how to add another data set in the same workbook.

1. **TABLEAU PUBLIC ONLY**, Save the workbook as E3.7 Chart data.

2. Data menu ⇒ New Data Source.

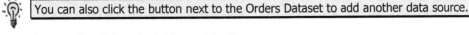
You can also click the button next to the Orders Dataset to add another data source.

3. Select Excel ⇒ Select the tableau_data file.

4. Drag the Financial Data sheet to the canvas.

5. Click the Update Now button.

6. Remove (tableau_data) from the data set name. If you click the button to the left of the data set, you will see both data sets that are in the workbook, as shown in Figure 3-41.

Figure 3-41 Data sets in the workbook

7. A hierarchy was automatically created, that is not needed. To remove it, display the Sheet tab ⇒ Display the shortcut menu for the State, City hierarchy ⇒ Select **REMOVE HIERARCHY**.

8. Save the workbook ⇒ Pin it to the Start page.

On your own, if you needed data from a different data source, including a different filet type (like a database or another Tableau file), select the file type in step 3 above, then select the file.

Creating Other File Types

Tableau Public does not support the file types created in Exercises 3.8 and 3.9.

The majority of exercises so far in this book have created workbook (.twb) files. As covered in Chapter 1, Tableau has the ability to create a lot of file types. The next few exercises will show you how to create some of the other file types.

Exercise 3.8: Create A Data Source File

1. In the E3.7 workbook, click on the Sheet 1 tab.

2. On the Data pane, right-click on the Orders Dataset and select **ADD TO SAVED DATA SOURCES** ⇒ Navigate to your folder ⇒ Type `E3.8 Orders dataset data source file`, as shown in Figure 3-42. The Save as type option should be set to Tableau Data Source (*.tds).

On your own, you may want to save this file in the Data Sources folder, so that it will be displayed in the Saved Data Sources section of the Start Page. [See Chapter 1, Figure 1-2]

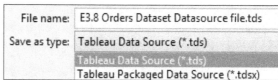

Figure 3-42 Save options for a .tds file

Notice in the figure that a **PACKAGED DATA SOURCE (.TDSX)** file can also be created using the Add To Save Data Sources option.

Exercise 3.9: Create A Packaged Workbook File

1. In the E3.7 workbook, File ⇒ Save As.

2. Type `E3.9 Packaged workbook file`, as the file name.

3. Change the Save as type option to Tableau Packaged Workbook.

Blending Data

In the previous exercise you learned how to join tables so that data from different tables in a data source could be used to create a chart. There will be times when data from different data sources is needed to create a chart. When that is the case, using the join feature will not work. For example, some data is in a database and other data is on a web page. If the tables in the different data sources have a field in common, the tables can be combined, just like joined tables using **DATA BLENDING**.

Data blending allows you to create a left join connection between the data sources. Just like joins, if there is a matching field name, a link will automatically be created. If no match is found, you will have to create the blend using the Edit Relationships dialog box, unless you can rename a field in one of the data sources. In addition to the field names having to be the same, the values in the field have to be the same also. For example, if the tables will be matched on the state field, both tables must use AZ or Arizona. If one table uses AZ and the other table uses Arizona, a match will not be made and the data from the second table will not be included on the chart. If this happens, you will see a message in the lower right corner on the Sheet tab.

The good thing is that you can fix this on a row by row basis. Right-click on the value in the second table, that needs to be changed and select Edit Alias.

> Data blends can only be created on a Sheet tab and are only available for the sheet that it is created on. However, you can duplicate a sheet that has blended data.

Automatic Data Blending

To use automatic data blending, the field name that will be used as the matching field must be the same in both tables. If they aren't, you have to rename the field in the data source or in Tableau.

Automatic blending starts by adding a field in the primary data source to the Columns or Rows shelf on the Sheet tab. The first data source used on the Sheet tab becomes the primary data source. When a field from the other data source is added to a shelf, the data blend is created.

Using The Edit Relationship Dialog Box For Data Blending

The previous section covered how automatic data blending works. There may be instances when renaming fields is not appropriate or you have a scenario that requires two or more dimensions to create the chart. If either is the case, automatic data blending will not handle your needs.

. . . .

Order Of Operations In Tableau

Earlier in this chapter, you learned about the order of operations for filters. They are part of the Order of operations in Tableau. Tableau performs actions in a specific order. You may get unexpected results when filters are applied. That is often because the order that Tableau processes filters in, is different then the order that you think filters are processed in. In addition to filters, different types of calculations are also processed in a specific order, as listed below.

- ☑ Extract filters
- ☑ Data source filters
- ☑ Context filters
- ☑ Sets, Top N filters, Conditional filters, Fixed Level of detail (LOD) (4)
- ☑ Dimension filters
- ☑ Data Blending
- ☑ Include and Exclude Level of detail (LOD) (4)
- ☑ Measure filters
- ☑ Totals (4)
- ☑ Forecasts and Table calculations (4)
- ☑ Trend and Reference lines (4)

(4) This is a calculated field.

CREATING CHARTS

After reading this chapter and completing the exercises you will:

- ☑ Have an understanding of the options on the Sheet tab
- ☑ Learn about the chart types in Tableau
- ☑ Be able to create the following types of charts, line, bar and pie
- ☑ Know how to use some of the menu options that are not directly related to creating a chart

> In Tableau Public, as you create more and more charts in a workbook, you will see that it can take longer and longer to save the workbook. That is because each time that you click the Save button, all charts in the workbook are resaved to the server, whether or not you made changes to them, since the last time that workbook was saved.

CHAPTER 4

Overview

Up to now, this book has primarily focused on the Data Source tab. This chapter covers the Sheet tab workspace. This is where charts are created. Dashboards and stories also have their own workspace.

There isn't anything wrong with creating basic charts, but sometimes adding one or two small touches can make a world of difference. In addition to showing you how to create charts, this chapter also covers features that can be used to enhance charts.

Sheet Tab Workspace

Figure 4-1 shows the workspace where charts are created. The Sheet tab has a lot more options and features then the Data Source tab has. I call it the Sheet tab workspace because the default name of the tab at the bottom of the workspace is named "Sheet". As you will see, many of the options are available from more than one place.

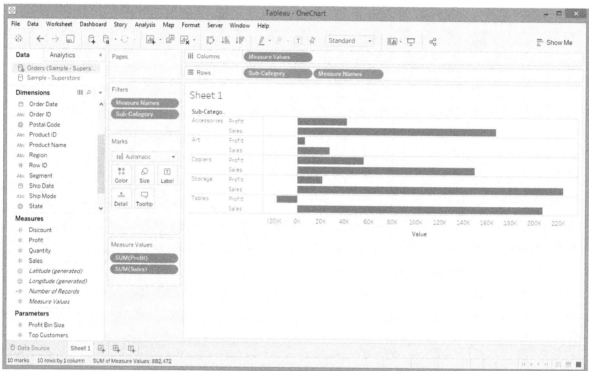

Figure 4-1 Sheet tab workspace

 Tableau refers to charts, dashboards and stories as a **VIEW**.

Menus

The menus have a lot of options. This section will focus on the menu options that you may not be familiar with. The Help menu options were covered in Chapter 2. The dashboard and story menus are covered in Chapter 8. Some menu options have an icon. For the most part, the options with icons are also on the Sheet tab toolbar. These options are explained in the Sheet tab toolbar section, later in this chapter.

 The Analysis and Map menus are not available when a **STORY SHEET** is displayed.

File Menu

Figure 4-2 shows the options on the File menu. The options are explained below.

The **REVERT TO SAVED** option restores the sheet back to the way it was the last time the workbook was saved. While you can click the Undo button several times, to undo the changes, this option may save you time.

Use the **EXPORT PACKAGED WORKBOOK** option when you want to share the workbook with someone that does not have access to the data. A **PACKAGED WORKBOOK (.TWBX)** file will be created, which is the file that you would share.

The **SHARE** option is used to connect to a Tableau server or your Tableau online account. You can also create a table online, using this option.

The **PRINT TO PDF** option is used to export a sheet, including dashboards to a PDF file.

Figure 4-2 File menu

Data Menu

Figure 4-3 shows the options on the Data menu. The options are explained below.

NEW DATA SOURCE [See Sheet Tab Toolbar, later in this chapter]

The **PASTE** option is used to add data from a data source to the workbook. An example is selecting rows of data in a csv file and pasting them into the current workbook. This option can also be used to paste tabular data (data in columns) from a web site into Tableau.

The **REFRESH ALL EXTRACTS** option is enabled if the workbook has at least one extract connection. When enabled, this option will refresh that data in all extract connections at one time.

The **EDIT RELATIONSHIPS** option is enabled when the workbook has connections to two or more data sources. This option is used to create, edit and delete relationships between the data sources in the workbook. The options shown in Figure 4-4 are used to complete these data blending tasks.

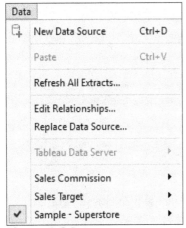

Figure 4-3 Data menu

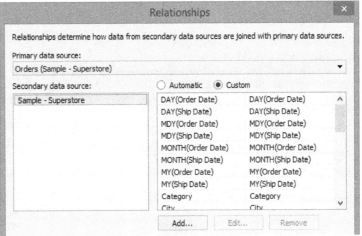

Figure 4-4 Relationships dialog box

The **REPLACE DATA SOURCE** option is used when the data source file name or location has changed, and you need to point to the new location or file name. While this option can be used for databases, it is less likely, because databases tend to not have the named changed or be moved, like spreadsheets or csv files do.

The **TABLEAU DATA SERVER** option is enabled when a data source is stored on a Tableau server. This option is used to refresh data or append data to a workbook, that is stored on a server.

The options at the bottom of the menu are the data sources in the workbook.

Worksheet Menu

The options shown in Figure 4-5 are used for charts. The options are explained below.

NEW WORKSHEET [See Sheet Tab Toolbar, later in this chapter]

Use the **COPY** option when you want to copy an image, data or crosstab of the data, to a file or to the Clipboard, so that it can be pasted into another file.

The **EXPORT** option can export the chart and/or data in one of the following ways:

① Export the chart as an image, using the options shown in Figure 4-6. The image will be saved in the graphic file format that you select.
② The **DATA** option exports the data (used to create the chart) to a database.
③ The **CROSSTAB TO EXCEL** option exports the data to an Excel file, if you have Excel installed. After the data is exported, Excel will open and display the data in a crosstab layout. Figure 4-7 shows the data for the chart shown earlier in Figure 4-1.

Figure 4-5 Worksheet menu

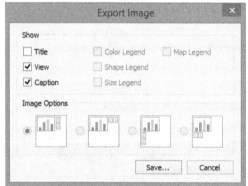

Figure 4-6 Export Image dialog box

	A	B	C
1	Sub-Category	Profit	Sales
2	Accessories	41,937	167,380
3	Art	6,528	27,119
4	Copiers	55,618	149,528
5	Storage	21,279	223,844
6	Tables	-17,725	206,966

Figure 4-7 Chart data exported to Excel

The **CLEAR** option works like the Undo button. The difference is that it only removes changes made to the chart. The enabled options on the sub menu for this option, represent the types of changes that have been made to the chart.

The **ACTIONS** option is used to add the following types of interactive functionality to a chart: filters, highlight parts of the chart, create links to a web page or to another sheet in the workbook. The options shown in Figure 4-8 are used to create actions. [See Chapter 8, What Are Actions?]

Use the **TOOLTIP** option to modify the content in the tooltip that is displayed when the mouse pointer is hovered over the chart.

The following menu options are used to display/hide a section of the workspace: **SHOW TITLE**, **SHOW CAPTION**, **SHOW SUMMARY**, **SHOW CARDS** and **SHOW VIEW TOOLBAR**.

The **DESCRIBE SHEET** option displays the options (the metadata) that were used to create the chart, as shown in Figure 4-9. This documentation is automatically created when the chart is created. The information can be copied into another file.

The **DUPLICATE AS CROSSTAB** option creates a new sheet in the workbook, which displays the data from the chart in a crosstab (text table layout), as shown in Figure 4-10.

The **AUTO UPDATES** and **RUN UPDATE** options are used to select when the data is updated, like the Update buttons on the Data Source tab do. These options are helpful if you need to make a lot of changes to the chart, and the connection to the database is slow or when the data source has a lot of records.

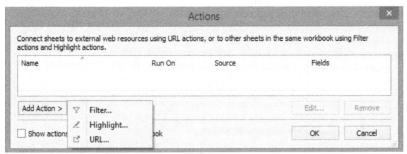

Figure 4-8 Actions dialog box

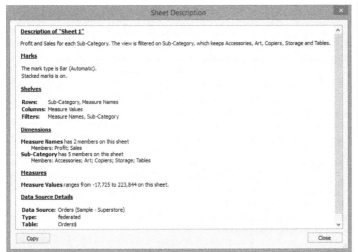

Figure 4-9 Sheet Description dialog box

Figure 4-10 Chart data displayed in a crosstab layout

Analysis Menu

The options shown in Figure 4-11 are used to add forecast features, trend lines and create chart types that are not available on the Show Me button. This menu is not available from a story sheet.

The **SHOW MARK LABELS** option will display/hide the labels on the chart. As illustrated in Figure 4-12, the labels are the actual data values. The labels can be modified to display other types of information, by using the options on the labels shortcut menu on the chart.

The **AGGREGATE MEASURES** option is enabled by default. When enabled, it will display aggregate values like SUM or COUNT on the chart, instead of the values from the data source. The chart shown in Figure 4-12 displays the aggregate values. Figure 4-13 shows the same chart with the aggregate measures option turned off. Not as easy to understand, is it? <smile> (1)

STACK MARKS This option is useful on area or bar charts when the Rows and Columns shelves each have a measure. This causes the marks to be stacked on top of each other. Changing the default option, changes the marks to overlapping, which means that all of the marks will start from the same place on the axis.
Figure 4-14 shows a stacked bar chart with the Stack Marks option enabled.
Figure 4-15 shows a stacked bar chart with the Stack Marks option set to off. (1) (2)

The **VIEW DATA** option displays the data used to create the chart, in summary format or displays all of the rows that are used to create the chart. This option is only available from a sheet tab.

The **REVEAL HIDDEN DATA** option is enabled when some of the data displayed on the chart has been hidden. Selecting this option displays the data on the chart that was hidden. For example, if you right-clicked on the Art sub category, shown in Figure 4-12 and selected Hide, that section of the chart would not be displayed. The Reveal option would redisplay the Art section of the chart.

The **PERCENTAGE OF** option is used to display the data as a percent of the total. The options shown in Figure 4-16 are used to select how you want the percent applied.

The **TOTALS** options are used to add grand totals and sub totals to a chart.

The **FORECAST** option is used to add future estimated values (a projection) to the chart.

TREND LINES are added to a chart to show the relationship of two numerical values.

The **SPECIAL VALUES** option is used to select whether or not null values or unrecognized geographic values (values that cannot be plotted) should be displayed on the chart. (2)

Figure 4-11 Analysis menu

The **TABLE LAYOUT** option is used to display/hide empty rows, columns and field values. The advanced options can be used to set the default number format, number of row and column labels (the default is 6) and label orientation.

The **LEGENDS** option is used to display/hide the legend.

The **FILTERS** option is used to display/hide filters and disable auto update, when a filter is applied.

The **HIGHLIGHTERS** option is used to change the color of a specific mark (data element) or group of marks.

The **PARAMETERS** option is only available when this menu is accessed from a dashboard sheet. It is used to display/hide parameters, if the chart has them.

Use the **CREATE CALCULATED FIELD** option to create a new field whose data will be generated by a formula that you create. This is done when the data that you need is not in the data source.

The **EDIT CALCULATED FIELDS** option is used to modify a calculated field. By default, all sheets have the **NUMBER OF RECORDS** calculated field.

The **CYCLE FIELDS** option switches the order of the fields in the Columns or Rows shelf. Fields can also be moved to other locations on the workspace. The goal of this option is to let you view the same data with a different arrangement of the data. Figure 4-17 shows this option applied to the chart shown earlier in Figure 4-1. In this example, the order of the fields on the Rows shelf were switched.

The **SWAP ROWS AND COLUMNS** option moves the fields on the Rows shelf to the Columns shelf and moves the fields on the Columns shelf to the Rows shelf. Like the Cycle Fields option, you can see the same data from a different perspective.

(1)   These options are often used to create chart types, that are not on the Show Me button.
(2)   By default, this option is enabled.

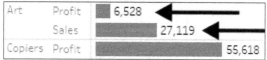
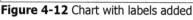

Figure 4-12 Chart with labels added

Figure 4-13 Chart with aggregate measures turned off

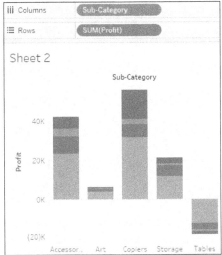

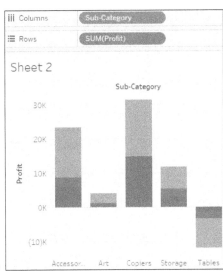

Figure 4-14 Chart with the Stack Marks option enabled

Figure 4-15 Chart with the Stack Marks option disabled

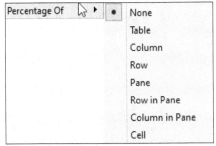

Figure 4-16 Percentage Of options

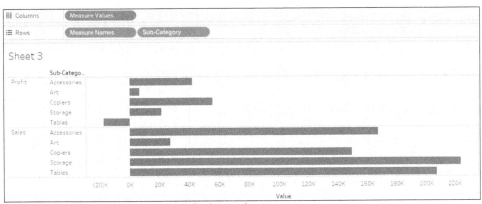

Figure 4-17 Cycle Fields option applied to a chart

Map Menu

The options shown in Figure 4-18 are used to customize a map.

The **BACKGROUND MAPS** option is used to change the map currently being used. The choices are explained below.

☑ Select **NONE** to remove the map image from the background.

☑ The **OFFLINE** option is used when the computer is not connected to the internet and you need to view the map. Keep in mind that offline maps have less detail, then online maps have.

☑ **TABLEAU** is the default background map option. It is the online map.

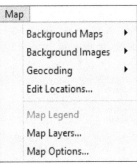

Figure 4-18 Map menu

Format Menu

The options shown in Figure 4-19 are used to customize a chart, dashboard or story. Some of the options are the same as options on shortcut menus, which you may find easier to use.

To save time formatting, format the fields, select the colors, fonts etc., before you create any charts in the workbook. Doing this will apply the same formatting every time you use the field in the workbook.

Selecting the **DASHBOARD**, **STORY** or **WORKBOOK** option, displays the corresponding Formatting pane, which is placed on top of the Data and Analytics pane, as shown on the left side of Figure 4-20. To close the Format pane, click on the X in the upper right corner.

The **CELL SIZE** option is used to customize the size of cells on a text table.

Figure 4-19 Format menu

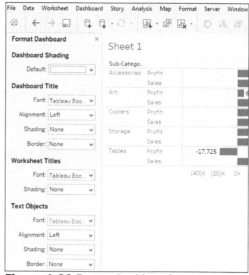

Figure 4-20 Format Dashboard pane

Server Menu

The options shown in Figure 4-21 are primarily used to publish files to Tableau server and to share workbooks.

The **CREATE USER FILTER** option is used to select what data on a chart, a user can see and what charts users can see.

The **TABLEAU PUBLIC** option is used to manage your Tableau public profile, connect to the public server, open workbooks on the server and save workbooks to the public server.

Figure 4-21 Server menu

Window Menu

Figure 4-22 shows the options on the menu.

The **PRESENTATION MODE** option displays the sheets, dashboards and stories in full screen mode. None of the workspace interface is displayed in this mode.

The **SHOW** options display/hide parts of the workspace.

BOOKMARK [See Chapter 5, Exercise 5.21, Create A Bookmark File]

Figure 4-22 Window menu

Sheet Tab Toolbar

Figure 4-23 shows the toolbar. The majority of these options are also on a menu. Some are also available on the tabs, near the bottom of the workspace. Some of the options are only available in Tableau Desktop. The numbered buttons are explained below.

Figure 4-23 Sheet tab toolbar

① This button is used to **ADD A NEW DATA SOURCE** by displaying the Connect window.

② The **PAUSE AUTO UPDATES** button is used to stop the Auto Updates feature from constantly updating the data while you are creating a chart. By default, this option is enabled. The options on the drop-down list let you select to stop the auto update for the worksheet or for filters.

③ The **RUN UPDATE** button is used to update the data when auto update is paused.

④ The **NEW WORKSHEET** button and drop-down list are used to add a new worksheet, dashboard or story sheet to the workbook.

⑤ The **DUPLICATE** button creates a new sheet and places a copy of the selected sheet, dashboard or story on it.

⑥ The **CLEAR SHEET** button deletes everything from the selected sheet, dashboard or story.

⑦ **SWAP ROWS AND COLUMNS** (3)

⑧ The **SORT MEASURE NAMES ASCENDING** button sorts a dimension by the ascending values in a measure.

⑨ The **SORT MEASURE NAMES DESCENDING** button sorts a dimension by the descending values in a measure.

⑩ The **HIGHLIGHT** button enables/disables highlighting. The options on the drop-down list are used to select how you want the values highlighted.

⑪ The **GROUP MEMBERS** button is enabled when two or more dimension headers are selected on the chart or on the Marks card. Doing this combines the values into the same group. Groups are covered in Chapter 5.

⑫ **SHOW MARK LABELS** (3)

⑬ The **FIX AXES** button is used to switch between a locked (fixed) axis, which will only display a specific range on the axis or dynamic (the default), which bases the axis values on the minimum and maximum values on the chart. When this button is clicked, a push pin is displayed next to the axis name, as shown in the lower right corner of Figure 4-24, next to the order date axis label.

⑭ The options on the **FIT** button drop-down list are used to select the size of the window that the chart is displayed in. Think zoom level.

⑮ The options on the **SHOW/HIDE CARDS** button drop-down list are used to select the parts of the workspace (the shelves) and chart, to display or hide. Selecting the **SUMMARY** option displays the window shown in Figure 4-25 to the right of the chart. It provides information about the marks displayed on the chart.

⑯ **PRESENTATION MODE** button [See Window Menu, earlier in this chapter]

⑰ The **SHARE WORKBOOK WITH OTHERS** button is used to publish the workbook to a Tableau server or to Tableau Online.

(3) [See Analysis Menu, earlier in this chapter]

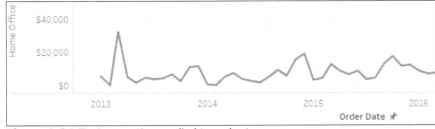

Figure 4-24 Fix Axes option applied to a chart   **Figure 4-25** Summary window

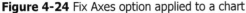

Sheet Tabs

Just like the data source workspace, the sheet workspace has the same tabs at the bottom of the workspace. After the Sheet 1 tab are three buttons. From left to right, they are used to add a worksheet (sheet tab), add a dashboard sheet and add a story sheet.

What Is A Shelf?

A shelf is a section of the workspace that fields are added to, to create or customize charts. The Sheet tab has the following shelves: Pages, Filters, Columns and Rows. The Pages and Filters shelves are covered in Chapter 5. The Columns and Rows shelves are used to create a chart. They are explained below. The Columns and Rows shelf shortcut menus are explained later in this chapter.

Columns Shelf

Fields added to this shelf create columns for the chart. The way that the columns are created depends on whether a continuous measure or discrete dimension is added to the shelf. (The terms, dimensions, measures, discrete and continuous are explained in the new few sections.)

Figure 4-26 shows the Territory discrete dimension field added to the shelf.

Notice that column headings have been created for each member (value) in the Territory field.

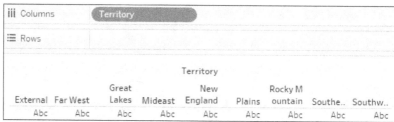

Figure 4-26 Discrete dimension added to the Columns shelf

Figure 4-27 shows the result of adding a measure to the Columns shelf.

A bar is created that has a continuous range of values.

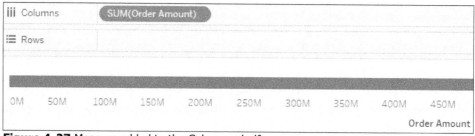

Figure 4-27 Measure added to the Columns shelf

Rows Shelf

Fields added to this shelf create rows for the chart. This shelf works like the Columns shelf. The difference is the direction of the bars. Figure 4-28 shows the Territory dimension added to the Rows shelf. Figure 4-29 shows the Order Amount measure added to the Rows shelf.

Figure 4-28 Dimension added to the Rows shelf

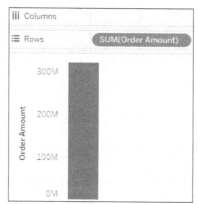

Figure 4-29 Measure added to the Rows shelf

Columns And Rows Shelf Shortcut Menus

Fields added to a shelf have a shortcut menu. The fields data type determines the options that are on the shortcut menu.

Figure 4-30 shows the shortcut menu for a string field.

Figure 4-31 shows the shortcut menu for a numeric field.

Figure 4-32 shows the shortcut menu for a date field. The options are explained below.

The filter options on the shortcut menus are covered in Chapter 5. The calculation options are covered in Chapter 6.

Figure 4-30 String field shortcut menu

Figure 4-31 Numeric field shortcut menu

FILTER [See Chapter 5, Filters Shelf Shortcut Menu]

SHOW FILTER [See Chapter 5, Show Filter Option]

SHOW HIGHLIGHTER displays a filter like the one shown in Figure 4-33. When your mouse hovers over an option in the drop-down list, the corresponding part of the chart is highlighted, as shown on the chart in the figure.

SORT [See Chapter 5, Using The Sort Dialog Box]

FORMAT displays/hides the column or row header on the chart.

INCLUDE IN TOOLTIP displays/hides the field on the tooltip displayed on the chart.

EDIT ALIASES [See Field Shortcut Menu, later in this chapter]

DIMENSION changes the measure to a dimension.

ATTRIBUTE [See Chapter 6, Attribute Option]

MEASURE is used to select a different aggregate function.

EDIT IN SHELF is used to edit the fields calculation on the shelf, opposed to opening a dialog box to edit the calculation.

REMOVE deletes the field from the chart.

DISCRETE changes the field to a discrete value from a continuous value.

CONTINUOUS changes the field to a continuous value from a discrete value.

ADD TABLE CALCULATION [See Chapter 6, Table Calculations]

QUICK TABLE CALCULATION [See Chapter 6, Quick Table Calculations]

Select the **SHOW MISSING VALUES** option when you want to indicate on a chart, that some categories displayed on the chart do not have data. By default, missing values in numeric bins and date ranges are not shown.

EXACT DATE displays the date in the data source.

The numbered sets of date fields on the figure, are explained below.

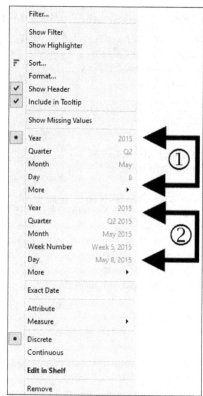

① Selecting an option in this section configures the date fields as a **DISCRETE DATE**. This creates what is known as a **DATE PART**. The options in this section define the granularity of the data as discrete values. If you select Quarter, the chart will combine the data for each quarter, across all years in the data source. This means that if the data source has four years of data (for example, 2014, 2015, 2016 and 2017), the value displayed on the chart for the second quarter, includes data for all of the years that have data for the second quarter.

② Selecting an option in this section configures the date fields as a **CONTINUOUS DATE**. This creates what is known as a **TRUNCATED DATE**. The options in this section define the granularity of the data as continuous values. Using the specs in the previous section, instead of each quarter only being displayed once on the chart, quarters will be displayed individually, one for each year (for example, 2014-Q1, 2014-Q2 . . 2017-Q4). If each year has data for each quarter, the chart would display 16 values (marks).

Figure 4-32 Date field shortcut menu

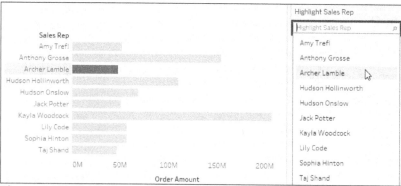

Figure 4-33 Highlighter option

Dimensions And Measures

It is important to understand these terms and their significance in Tableau. I suspect by now that you have seen these words on the Data pane and noticed that each section had fields from the data source. Tableau automatically categorizes each field as a dimension or measure.

As you will see, dimensions and measures work together. Fields are designated as a dimension or measure when you connect to the data source. If you recall, earlier in this book, I urged you, that on your own, you need to check that the fields that you are going to use to create charts, have the correct data type. This is the reason why.

Dimensions

Fields that contain category data are placed in the dimensions section of the Data pane. These are usually date, geographic, boolean and text fields. The numeric fields that are placed in this section do not have quantitative data. Some people will say that numeric dimension fields are those that you do not use aggregate functions with. I don't agree with that 100% because if you need a count of the number of customers per state, there is no measure field that can be used to get the count. The Customer ID field, which is a dimension field, would be used to get the count.

In Tableau, fields that start off as a dimension can become a measure and fields that start off as a measure can become a dimension. Yes, it is a little confusing. Dimensions provide information about measures to categorize the data in the measure. Examples of dimension fields, in the data source used in this book, are category, order date and sales rep.

Date fields are probably the most popular dimension field. I say that because dates can be displayed in several layouts, if you will. The year, quarter, month, week and day can be extracted from a date field and be used to categorize measure values. This means that you have the option to display data by any of these date options.

If you have heard the phrase "slicing and dicing", in reference to data, dimension fields provide this functionality. In Chapter 3, I listed sample purpose statements. The first one was "compare last years sales totals to this years sales totals, by region". In this statement, the region field is the dimension field. What you will notice is that most of the time, the fields after the word "by" are the dimensions. The values in the region field create the categories that the sales totals for last year and this year will be displayed in.

Another way to explain dimension fields is that they are fields that can be used to group other data (measure fields). When a field in the dimensions section of the Data pane, is added to the Rows or Columns shelf, a column header or row header is created on the chart.

 Dimensions cannot be aggregated.

Measures

Measures are numeric fields that can be aggregated. They are the values that are evaluated. In the dimension example above, the measures are the last years and this years sales totals. Calculated fields, that you will learn how to create later, are measures.

A measure references columns. Measures are also known as **CALCULATED FIELDS**. Measures are usually numbers. Keep in mind that non numeric data in a dimension can be used to create a measure (only a count measure). If you need to use more than one aggregation (like distinct count and sum), for the same field, you have to create multiple measures for the same field. It is a good idea to name measures something that indicates what the formula creates.

Unlike dimension formulas which are calculated for every row in a table, measures are formulas that are used to aggregate (for example Sum) the values in a column. One way to determine whether you need to create a measure or dimension is whether or not the value needs to be calculated for each row of data (create a dimension) or calculated for a group of rows (create a measure).

The background color of a measure is green. After a measure is added to a shelf, it can be changed to a discrete value, the same way that a dimension can be changed to a measure, as discussed earlier.

Continuous And Discrete

This section will explain these terms and how they relate to dimensions and measures.

Continuous

This term means without interruption. Fields in the Measures section of the Data pane are continuous by default. That is because they can be aggregated. When a measure is added to the Rows or Columns shelf, a continuous axis is created, as shown earlier in Figure 4-27.

Discrete

This term means distinct or individually separate. Fields in the Dimensions section of the Data pane are discrete, by default. Fields in the Dimensions section that are added to the Columns or Rows shelf are initially DISCRETE and have a blue background.

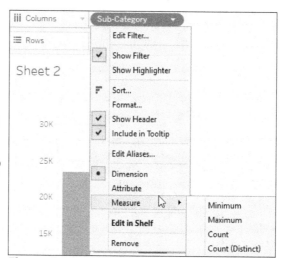

By that I mean that after the dimension is added to the chart, the field can be changed to a measure by opening the drop-down list, selecting Measure, then selecting an aggregate function, as shown in Figure 4-34. When this happens, the background color of the field will change to green and a continuous axis will be displayed, instead of the column or row headers.

Figure 4-34 Options to change a dimension to a measure

 Only date field and numeric dimensions can be continuous without converting the field to a measure.

 Tableau refers to fields that have been added to a shelf, as a PILL. I suspect that is because the background color of a field on a shelf, is shaped like a medicine pill.

 Understanding What The Blue And Green Background Pill Colors Indicate
A fields background color indicates if it is discrete (blue) or continuous (green). Continuous values have an infinite number of values. Discrete values have a finite number of values. The background color does not indicate whether a field is a dimension or measure. What determines whether a field is a dimension or measure is whether or not it can be aggregated. Keep in mind that numeric and date field dimensions can be discrete or continuous and that all measures can be discrete or continuous.

Options For Starting A Chart

Believe it or not, there is more than one way to start creating a chart. The options are explained below.

① Double-click on fields on the Data pane.
② Drag fields in the Data pane onto a shelf or card.
③ Drag a field to the words DROP FIELD HERE, in the section (of the canvas) that you want to add the field to, as shown in Figure 4-35. The chart will start as a text table, but you can change the chart type.
④ Select at least one field on the Data pane, then select an enabled chart type on the SHOW ME button.

Figure 4-35 Tableau chart canvas

Navigation Bar

Figure 4-36 shows the navigation bar that stores each chart, dashboard and story saved in the workbook, in addition to the Data Source tab.

Figure 4-36 Navigation bar

The last three buttons on the right of the bar are used to add another sheet to the workbook. From left to right, the buttons are used to add a new worksheet, a new dashboard sheet and new story sheet.

Sheet Tab Shortcut Menu

Figure 4-37 shows the shortcut menu for a sheet tab. The same shortcut menu is also available for the dashboard and story tabs. The options are explained below.

COPY/PASTE makes a copy of the content on the tab and pastes the copied content on another tab that you select.

RENAME SHEET is used to give the sheet (tab) a different name.

DUPLICATE creates a new sheet that has a copy of the content on the tab that this option was selected from.

DUPLICATE AS CROSSTAB [See Worksheet Menu, earlier in this chapter]

EXPORT creates a workbook file (.twb) or packaged workbook file (.twbx), which has a copy of the selected sheet.

COPY/PASTE FORMATTING copies the formatting (font, color, etc) used on the sheet and applies it to another sheet that you select.

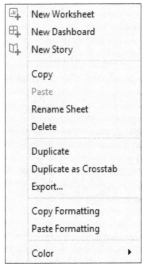

Figure 4-37 Sheet tab shortcut menu

COLOR applies a color line to the bottom of the tab, on the navigator bar shown earlier in Figure 4-36.

 Exercise Tips
Below are some tips to help make completing the exercises easier.

① All charts in a chapter will be saved in the same workbook. Rename each sheet using the exercise number. For example, when working on Exercise 4.2, right-click on the tab for that chart ⇒ Select **RENAME SHEET** (as shown above in Figure 4-37) ⇒ Type E4.2. If you want to include the chart type (area, bar, scatter, etc) as part of the sheet name, that is fine, but not required.
② Most of the exercises will not use the chart title. If you want to hide the title, use one of the options below.
    ☑ Open the drop-down list at the right of the title on the chart and select **HIDE TITLE**.
    ☑ Right-click on a blank space on the canvas ⇒ Select the Title option shown in Figure 4-38. If you need the title later, open this shortcut menu and select the Title option.
③ Starting with Exercise 4.2, if the first step does not duplicate an existing sheet, add a new sheet to the workbook.
④ All of the exercises in this chapter use the Orders Dataset. As shown later, at the top of Figure 4-41, you can select the data set that you need.
⑤ When instructed to drag a field, it means to drag the field from the Data pane, unless stated otherwise.

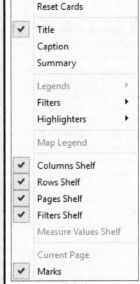

Figure 4-38 Canvas shortcut menu

Exercise 4.1: Create A Bar Chart

As you learned in Chapter 3, the purpose of creating a chart is to provide an answer to a question. In this exercise you will learn how to create a chart that displays each sales reps total sales.

1. Save the E3.7 workbook as Chapter 4 Charts.

2. Rename Sheet 1 as E4.1 Bar chart.

3. **TABLEAU PUBLIC ONLY**, Delete the field that you added to the sheet to save the workbook.

4. Drag the Order Amount field to the Columns shelf.

5. Drag the Sales Rep field to the Rows shelf.

6. On the **SHOW ME BUTTON**, select the Horizontal bars chart.

    The chart should look like the one shown in Figure 4-39. Each bar represents the total sales amount for a sales rep, for all of the orders in the data source. Later, you will learn how to create a filter that will let you select a specific year to show data for.

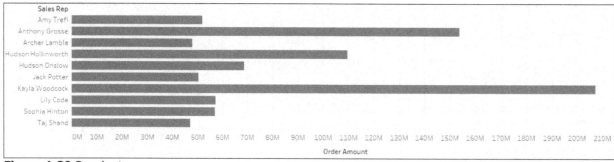

Figure 4-39 Bar chart

How To Create A Vertical Bar Chart

The previous exercise showed you how to create a horizontal bar chart. While there is no vertical bar chart option on the Show Me button, a vertical bar chart can be created. If you want to try this, duplicate the E4.1 sheet to follow along.

1. On the toolbar, click the **SWAP ROWS AND COLUMNS BUTTON**. [See Figure 4-23, button 7]

    The chart shown above in Figure 4-39, now looks like the chart shown in Figure 4-40.

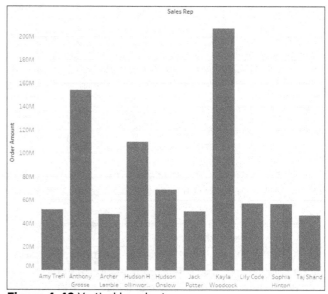

Figure 4-40 Vertical bar chart

Data Pane

This pane (tab) is on the left side of the workspace. As shown in Figure 4-41, it contains the fields from the data set(s) and has two default sections, Dimensions and Measures.

Notice that to the left of each field is the data type icon. They are the same icons that are on the Data Source tab. The data type has some control over the actions that the field can perform.

You can click on this icon to change the data type or **GEOGRAPHIC ROLE**. In addition to features and options for fields, there are also options to organize the Data pane.

As shown in the figure, the two data sets that were created in the previous chapter are displayed at the top of the pane. Either data set can be used to create a chart. When a data set is selected, the corresponding tables and fields are displayed on the Data pane.

You can rename a field, by clicking on the field name. The field will have a gray background, as shown in Figure 4-42. Type in the new field name and press Enter.

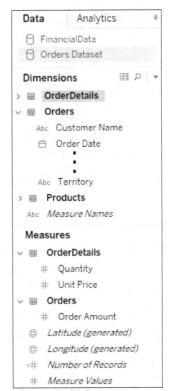

Figure 4-42 Field selected to be renamed

Figure 4-41 Data pane

Shortcut Menus

The Data pane has three shortcut menus, data source, dimensions and field, as explained below.

Data Source Shortcut Menu

Figure 4-43 shows the shortcut menu for a data source (at the top of the Data pane, as shown above in Figure 4-41).

The options that have not already been explained, are explained below.

EDIT DATA SOURCE FILTERS is used to create, edit or delete filters for the data source.

DATE PROPERTIES is used to select the default day, that the week starts on, the month the fiscal year starts with and the default format to display dates in.

PROPERTIES displays the connection properties for the data source.

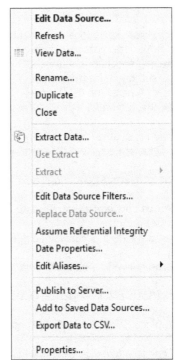

Figure 4-43 Data Source shortcut menu

Dimensions Section Shortcut Menu

Clicking the down arrow button across from the Dimensions section heading, displays the shortcut menu shown in Figure 4-44.

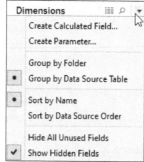

Figure 4-44 Dimensions section shortcut menu

Field Shortcut Menu

Each field, in the Data pane, has a shortcut menu, like the ones shown in Figure 4-45 and Figure 4-46.

Measures have the **CONVERT TO DIMENSION** option in place of the Convert to Measure option, shown in Figure 4-45.

The options that you may not be familiar with are explained below.

ADD TO SHEET adds the field to the canvas if no chart is displayed. If a chart has already been created, the field is added to the chart.

SHOW FILTER adds the field to the Filters shelf, so that it can be used to create a filter for the chart. [See Chapter 5, Show Filter Option]

DUPLICATE creates a copy of the field.

CREATE has options to create additional information, for the selected field. All data types can create calculated fields, groups, sets and parameters, using options on the sub menu for this option. Depending on the data type of the field, there are other options on the sub menu.

Figure 4-45 Data pane field shortcut menu for a numeric field

Figure 4-46 Data pane field shortcut menu for a string field

TRANSFORM This option is enabled for string and geographic field data types. The data in a field can be split or pivoted. When two or more fields are selected, different options are available for this option.

CONVERT TO DISCRETE converts a continuous field to a discrete field.

CONVERT TO CONTINUOUS converts a discrete date field to a continuous date field.

CONVERT TO MEASURE converts a dimension field to a measure.

CONVERT TO DIMENSION converts a measure field to a dimension.

DEFAULT PROPERTIES [See Default Properties Options]

GROUP BY is used to place fields into folders. These options are only available for relational data sources.

FOLDERS is used to create a folder to place fields in, to create a group.

HIERARCHY [See Chapter 5, Creating A Hierarchy]

. . . .

REPLACE REFERENCE is used to create a name to use instead of the field name, as a way to refer to the field.

DESCRIBE displays information about the field.

Generated Fields
At the bottom of the Dimensions and Measures sections on the Data pane, you will see fields with an italic font. These fields are automatically created for each data source. They are explained below.

Dimensions Generated Fields
MEASURE NAMES This field contains the name of each measure. (4)

Measures Generated Fields
LATITUDE (GENERATED) This field uses latitude coordinates. (5)

LONGITUDE (GENERATED) This field uses longitude coordinates. (5)

NUMBER OF RECORDS This field provides a count of the number of rows in the data source.

MEASURE VALUES This field contains the values of each measure. (4)

(4) These fields are used together to blend measures. If these fields are added to a chart, each field can have its own legend or the legends can be combined. These fields are like containers because they store more than one measure. They can be added to a chart when you try and add more than one measure to the same axis.
(5) This field is only generated if the data source has geographic fields. The field can be used when you create a map. Behind the scenes, Tableau geocodes the data to create these fields.

Other Sections On The Data Pane
In addition to the dimensions and measures sections, the Data pane will also display the sections discussed below, as needed.

① PARAMETERS This section stores parameters that you create. They are place holders in formulas (calculated fields) that you create.
② SETS This section stores custom fields that are created using dimensions.

Default Properties Options
This DEFAULT PROPERTIES option, shown earlier in Figure 4-45 is used to select default formatting for a field. The options that you select will be applied to every chart in the workbook that uses the field. The options are explained below.

☑ The COMMENT option displays the dialog box shown in Figure 4-47. This dialog box is used to enter content that you want displayed on the tooltip, in the Data pane, for the field, when the mouse pointer is hovered over the field. The content will also be displayed on the Calculated Fields dialog box. This is helpful if you need to store or display information about the field.
☑ The COLOR option is used to change the default color for the fields values, when displayed on a chart.
☑ The SHAPE option opens the Edit Shape dialog box. The options are used to change the default shape for each data item (value in the field). This option is only available for non numeric fields.
☑ SORT option [See Chapter 5, Changing The Default Sort Order For A Field]
☑ The NUMBER FORMAT option displays the dialog box shown in Figure 4-48. The options are used to set default formatting for the field. An example is that you do not want the value to display decimal places on the chart. If the field has large values, you may want to select one of the options in the Units field drop-down list. (6)
☑ The AGGREGATION option is used to change the default SUM aggregate function to something else. [See Aggregate Functions] (6)
☑ The TOTAL USING option is used to calculate sub totals.

(6) This option is only available for numeric fields.

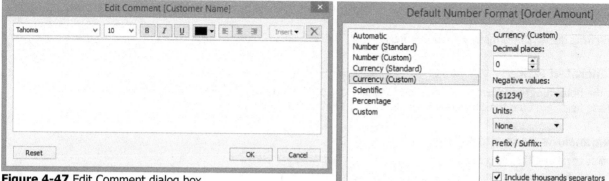

Figure 4-47 Edit Comment dialog box

Figure 4-48 Default Number Format dialog box

 A word to the wise. If you need to use the same data source, with the same formatting, in more than one workbook, it may be a good idea to create a workbook with the data sources that have fields that need formatting and set the formatting up. This would be the equivalent of creating a template. Then save the workbook with the formatting with another name and use that workbook to create the charts in.

Aggregations

Aggregations are used to group or summarize data. The way that data is displayed in a table, by default, makes it difficult to see trends in the data or answer "What-If" analysis type questions. For example, if you looked at the data in the table shown in Figure 4-49, can you tell which sales rep had the most sales or what the top five selling products were? Probably not. When added to a visualization, aggregations will group or summarize the data to answer these questions and much more. If you have written calculation formulas in SQL, many of the functions available in Tableau will be familiar. Most functions in Tableau are calculated at the database level.

SalesOrderID	OrderDate	DueDate	ShipDate	CustomerID	SalesPersonID	SubTotal
71842	6/1/2004	6/13/2004	6/8/2004	460	285	$11.687
71841	6/1/2004	6/13/2004	6/8/2004	10	285	$102,044.1...
71840	6/1/2004	6/13/2004	6/8/2004	571	286	$1,117.094
71839	6/1/2004	6/13/2004	6/8/2004	611	279	$68,030.1615
71838	6/1/2004	6/13/2004	6/8/2004	319	286	$13,724.1893
71837	6/1/2004	6/13/2004	6/8/2004	579	275	$36,189.4664
71836	6/1/2004	6/13/2004	6/8/2004	254	280	$81,644.2102
71835	6/1/2004	6/13/2004	6/8/2004	621	280	$64,801.7394

Figure 4-49 Table of data

Aggregate Functions

Figure 4-50 shows the aggregate functions that you can use. They are explained in Table 4-1.

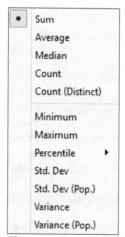

Figure 4-50 Aggregate functions

Aggregate Function	Description
Average	Calculates the average of the values.
Count	Returns a count of the number of rows that have a value in the selected field.
Count(Distinct)	Returns a count of the number of rows that have a unique value in the selected field.
Maximum	Returns the largest value in the field.
Median	Finds the middle value of all of the values in the field.
Minimum	Returns the smallest value in the field.
Percentile	Is used to select a percent between zero and 100, that will calculate the percentile of the values in the field. This will display the average percentile for all of the values in the column or row.
Std. Dev	The standard deviation function calculates how far from the mean (the average) each value in the selected field deviates.
Std. Dev (Pop.)	Calculates standard deviation, based on the entire population specified in the arguments in the formula.
Sum	Adds the values in the field to get a total.
Variance	Calculates the variance of the values in the scope.
Variance (Pop.)	Calculates the population variance of the values in the scope.

Table 4-1 Aggregate functions explained

Show Me Button

Tableau uses the word VIEW, instead of chart. Figure 4-51 shows the charts on this button. As you have figured out by now, this button displays the chart types that can be created. Currently, there are 24 chart types, on this button. The bottom of the window displays how many dimensions and measures are needed to create the selected chart type.

The fields that you select, initially determine the chart type that you can use. What was not obvious to me for a while, was that you can select the fields (dimensions and measures) on the Data pane to enable chart options on the

Show Me button, instead of adding the fields to the Columns and Rows shelves to determine what chart types you can select from. As you select more fields, more chart options will be enabled.

Tableau goes a step further, to help you select a chart type. One of the chart types that you can use based on the fields that you have selected, will have a red border around it, on the Show Me button. This is the chart type that Tableau thinks will best display the data in the fields that you have selected. You can use the chart with the red border or any chart that is enabled.

The **CHART TYPES** are explained below, in the order that they appear on the Show Me button.

Figure 4-51 Show Me button

TEXT TABLES will remind you of a grid, spreadsheet or pivot table. Data is displayed in a non graphical layout.

HEAT MAP uses color and size to display data in different categories. The higher the value, the larger the square is.

HIGHLIGHT TABLE is a version of the text table. The difference is that the cells have a background color that represents the value in the cell. It is also similar to a heat map because categories are displayed with different colors.

SYMBOL MAP displays values on a geographical map using symbols or pie charts. When a pie chart is used to display values on the map, the pie chart can display three values (categories). Doing this provides a break down of the total value for each category. If some marks are difficult to see, changing the color (using the Color button on the Marks card) will help. The size of the circle corresponds to the size of the value that it represents.

FILLED MAP displays the values of one measure on the map, using shades of the same color.

PIE CHART only displays one series of data. Each slice of the pie represents a value. This chart type displays values as a percent of the total (which is always 100%). A pie chart is best suited when the values are greatly different, because data is often not represented accurately (by the size of the slice) in this chart type.

HORIZONTAL BARS shows differences between items and relationships between multiple groups of data. The length of the bar represents the value. If a measure is added to the Color button on the Marks card, the bars on the chart will be displayed in different colors. This is probably the most used chart type.

STACKED BARS displays more than one series of data on each bar on the chart. This chart type is similar to a pie chart in that it shows how each element makes up part of the total. To keep the chart reasonable, it is best not to use too many dimensions.

SIDE-BY-SIDE BARS is a good alternative to a stacked bar chart, when you need to display a lot of categories (dimensions). The bars are color coded to visually show which measure they represent. When this chart type is selected, the **MEASURE VALUES** and **MEASURE NAMES** generated fields are automatically added to help create the chart.

TREE MAPS display data by using space. Select this chart type when you need to show how each value relates to the total. It requires one or more measures and only one dimension. This chart type does not display data on a map, like the Filled Map chart does. The values are displayed using rectangles. The rectangle in the upper left corner of each section, displays the largest value, in the category. The rectangle in the lower right corner of each section, displays the smallest value.

This is different from how tree maps work in other software. The difference is that in other software the data does not have to be segmented, like it is in Tableau. This means that the largest value displayed in the upper left corner is for all of the values displayed on the chart.

This chart type can be used instead of a pie chart. Like a pie chart, a Tree Map displays how each part contributes to the whole. Labels are displayed to indicate the category. This chart type is also similar to a Scatter chart because it can be used to analyze two measures. (7)

CIRCLE VIEWS will remind you of a bubble chart. The values are displayed using circles by default, but the circles can be changed to a different shape. Select this chart type when you want to display the distribution of data. Adding dimensions to the Marks card will break up the views. There may be times when you do not need to display the data aggregated. When that is the case, open the Analysis menu ⇒ Clear the Aggregate option. (7)

SIDE-BY-SIDE CIRCLES works the same as a side-by-side bar chart. The values for each dimension are displayed in their own section of the chart. The data is displayed with colored circles. (7)

LINES (CONTINUOUS) is used to display a time series of data consecutively, without any breaks. (8)

LINES (DISCRETE) is used to display a time series of data with breaks in the time. This means that the lines are not connected, like they are in a continuous line chart. Examples of time breaks are year and month. This chart type is effective, if you need to see data by quarter or season (spring, fall, etc.). (8)

DUAL LINES displays data using different axis range values. The values are displayed on the lines over time. (9)

AREA CHARTS (CONTINUOUS) is similar to the line (continuous) chart in that data is displayed over time. One difference is that each member (of the dimension) is stacked on top of each other to indicate the totals. Each dimension is divided by color. (8)

AREA CHARTS (DISCRETE) is similar to the line (discrete) chart. (8)

DUAL COMBINATION is similar to a dual line chart. This chart type provides the ability to display different information on the same chart. This is accomplished by displaying one measure with bars and another measure with a line. Each measure has its own axis and range of values. (9)

SCATTER charts are used when you need to display relationships, if any, between numeric values. This chart shows how two or more values (measures) are related (like month of year and order amount) and how a change in one value affects the other value. This chart type is used to show if there is a trend or correlation between the values. The X and Y axis must display numeric data. If data like dates or months can be converted to numeric data, it can be used with this chart type. Scatter charts can also display ratio data by displaying plot points. If you hold the mouse pointer over this chart type on the Show Me button, you will see that two measures (minimum) are needed. What may not be clear is that the Columns and Rows shelves, each need at least one measure. If you want the plot points to be displayed by size, based on their values, use a third measure and add it to the Size button on the Marks card. As needed, a dimension can be added to the Marks card to divide the data. This chart type is also known as an **XY SCATTER CHART**.

HISTOGRAM charts display the frequency of a data element in a data set. This chart type places the data into buckets (which are range intervals on the x axis) and displays a count of the records in each bucket. Usually, you will not see more than eight bars on a histogram chart, regardless of how many ranges (buckets) there really are. This chart type is used to show the distribution of values in intervals (known as **BINS** in Tableau). A parameter can be created, that will allow the range of values for the buckets to be changed. This chart type is also known as a **FREQUENCY TABLE**.

BOX AND WHISKER charts summarize the distribution of one or more groups of data based on their rank. The boxes on the chart have a line at the top and bottom of the box, which represent the lowest and highest value. This chart type is best used to display discrete data. Tick marks are used to indicate a value in the range. The colors represent the quartile ranges. The boxes display the middle 50 percent of the data and the whiskers indicate the complete range of data.

GANTT charts are often used to display project management data (on a horizontal bar chart) like the start and end dates of tasks on a project plan. Gantt charts need a date field. For example, the vertical axis would display the project tasks and the horizontal axis would display the time frame. The marks on the chart represent the duration of the task. The length of the color on the bar represents the length of time for the task.

BULLET charts are often used in a dashboard because they can display a lot of data in a small space. This chart is a variation of a bar chart. It displays data on a bar chart and is often used to compare one measure to one or more other measures. The black vertical lines are reference lines, which are used as a comparison to the data displayed on the bars. The examples that come to mind for using this chart type are a comparison of sales for this year and last year or actual sales versus projected sales. (7)

PACKED BUBBLES display data using color and size. Dimensions are used to create the bubble and a measure is used to create the size of the bubbles. The bubbles are not very precise, especially if the values being displayed are close in range.

(7) This chart type is a good option when you need to display data in a small space.
(8) A difference between area and line charts is that in an area chart, the area (the space) between the lines is filled in with color.
(9) Each measure can have its own axis and use different units (scales) of measurement. For example, one axis can display data in currency and the other axis can display data in percents.

> **An Easy Way To Create A Chart**
> If you select fields on the Data pane and then click on a chart type on the Show Me button, the fields will be added to the Columns or Rows shelf.

You may find the tip above helpful if you are still trying to figure out which shelf a field should be added to. Using the tip will shield you from that, because the fields are added to a shelf. After the initial chart is created, there are a lot of options that are available to customize a chart.

Selecting The Best Visual To Display Data

As you just learned, Tableau has several chart types. The goal of the chart and the amount of data that needs to be displayed, will influence the type of chart that will best display the data, so that the expected outcome is achieved. The charts in Figures 4-52, 4-53 and 4-54, all use the same fields and display the same data.

Figure 4-52 displays the data as pie charts. Depending on the fields selected, the data may be displayed on one pie chart or multiple pie charts. The pie charts shown in the figure display each category in its own chart. Pie charts show each part as a comparison. While a common chart type, pie charts are not effective when you need to display exact comparisons. It is hard to tell what each value, on each chart, represents.

Figure 4-53 displays the data in a table. While the data is easier to understand then it is on the pie charts, tables make it difficult to tell the low and high values.

Figure 4-54 displays the data in a bar chart. The bars on the chart make it easy to see the low and high values for each category.

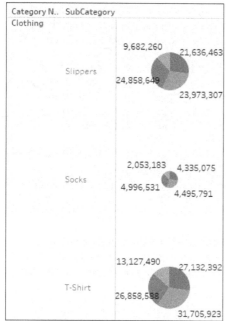

Figure 4-53 Data displayed in a table

Figure 4-52 Data displayed on pie charts

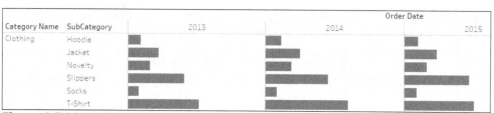

Figure 4-54 Data displayed on a bar chart

Exercise 4.2: Create A Text Table

In this exercise you will learn how to create a table that displays category and sub category totals by order year.

1. Select the Order Date, Category Name, Sub Category and Order Amount fields.

2. Select the Text table chart option. The chart should look like the one shown earlier in Figure 4-53.

3. Rename the sheet to E4.2 Text table.

Combined Field Option

The **COMBINED FIELD** option requires at least two fields to be selected. It is used to combine values from different fields (dimensions) into one field. This option creates a new field with data from the selected fields. The name of the new field is a combination of the original field names. A combined field can be used to create a chart, like fields from a data source. [See Figure 4-46, Create ⇒ Combined Field]

 To display the selected fields in a specific order, right-click on the field that you want displayed first, before selecting the Create option on the fields shortcut menu.

Creating And Using A Combined Field

This section demonstrates how a combined field works. If you want to follow along, duplicate the E4.2 chart, then follow the steps below.

1. Select the Sales Rep and Sales Rep ID fields.

2. Right-click on the selected field that you want displayed first. In this example, right-click on the Sales Rep ID field ⇒ Create ⇒ Combined Field. On the Data pane, below the Products table, you should see the Sales Rep ID and Sales Rep fields.

3. Drag the combined field to the end of the Columns shelf. The table should look like the one shown in Figure 4-55. Compare this table to the one shown earlier in Figure 4-53.

		Order Date / Sales Rep ID & Sales Rep (Combined)					
		2013					
Category Name	SubCategory	2, Kayla Woodc..	3, Hudson Onsl..	6, Sophia Hint..	7, Amy Trefl	8, Anthony Gro..	13, Hudson Hol..
Clothing	Hoodie	1,479,727	570,312	341,145	269,994	82,416	1,065,156
	Jacket	2,854,462	1,096,634	1,303,297	690,800	173,930	2,786,551
	Slippers	5,297,246	2,597,518	1,939,827	1,391,697	337,156	4,802,711
	Socks	1,473,369	191,408	246,216	280,069	80,162	1,062,234
	T-Shirt	7,023,215	3,195,412	2,254,111	2,037,267	443,429	4,920,884
Clothing Novelty	Novelty	2,004,238	843,629	663,175	439,026	162,595	1,561,812

Figure 4-55 Table created with a combined field

The Marks Card

A **MARK** is a value from a field that is displayed on a chart. Figure 4-56 shows the Marks card. The options on this card are used to control how the data values are displayed on the chart. This includes changing the appearance of the marks and the level of detail displayed on the chart.

The options on the drop-down list are used to select the type of chart (mark) that you want displayed. **AUTOMATIC** is the default option. With this option selected, Tableau will select what it thinks is the best mark type for the chart.

The following buttons are below the drop-down list: Color, Size, Label, Detail and Tooltip. When a field is added to the Color, Size or Shape button, a legend is displayed to show how the values in the field are related to the data displayed on the chart.

These buttons are always available. Depending on the option selected in the drop-down list, other buttons will be displayed. For example, when the Pie mark is selected, the Angle button is available. When a discrete line chart is created, the Path button is available. When you click on some of these buttons, the customization options are displayed. Figure 4-57 shows the customization options for the Color and Label buttons.

Figure 4-56 Marks card

Dragging a field to a button, creates a filter, as shown at the bottom of Figure 4-56, and displays the field on the tooltip. As shown at the bottom of Figure 4-56, to the left of each field, an icon is displayed that represents the button that the field was added to. The icons correspond to the ones on the buttons. You can move the field to a different button by clicking on the icon and selecting a different button in the drop-down list, as shown at the bottom of the figure.

The options selected in Figure 4-56, change the chart shown earlier in Figure 4-39, to the one shown in Figure 4-58.

The Marks card controls how marks are displayed on the chart. For example, in Exercise 4.1, the Order Date field was added to the Columns shelf and the Order Amount was added to the Rows shelf. If the fields were added to the opposite shelf, the chart would look different.

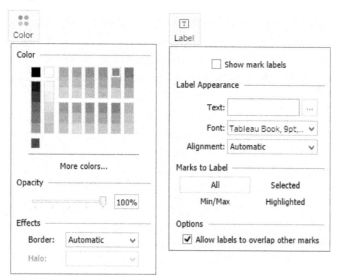

Figure 4-57 Color and Label button customization options

Figure 4-58 E4.1 Bar chart modified by using the Marks card options

 It is important to note that the shelf that fields are added to, to create a chart, makes a difference.

Marks Card Buttons

A field can be dragged to these buttons. These buttons are used to break up the values displayed on the chart, by doing things like displaying each category of data in a different color or removing the aggregation from a field. All chart types do not have all of the buttons that are explained below.

COLOR The options shown above in Figure 4-57 are used to display or change the color on some or all of the chart. (10)

SIZE The field dragged to this button is used to select the size of the objects (lines, bars, slices, etc.) on the chart. Because this option orders values from small to large, it is best to use it when the data is ordered by year or month. (10)

TEXT This button is only available for text tables. The options are used to customize the numeric value.

LABEL This button is not available for text tables, but provides the same functionality, as the Text button. The options shown above in Figure 4-57 are used to customize how the labels are displayed on the chart.

DETAIL Fields dragged to this button remove the aggregated function from the field. This is usually done so that the field can be added to the tooltip for the chart.

TOOLTIP This button is used to customize the content displayed on the charts tooltip.

PATH This button is available for line and polygon charts. When a dimension is added to this button, the marks are connected, based on the members in the dimension. For example, if the dimension is a date field, the order is based on the date order.

SHAPE This button is used to give each member a different shape. (10)

(10)   This button supports continuous and discrete fields.

· ·

Exercise 4.3: Use The Marks Card Color Button

1. Add a sheet ⇒ Rename it to E4.3 Marks card.

2. Drag the Order Amount field to the Rows shelf.

3. Drag the Category Name field to the Columns shelf.

   The chart should look like the one shown in Figure 4-59.

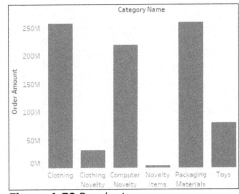

Figure 4-59 Bar chart

4. Drag the Order Amount field in the Measures section, to the **COLOR** button on the Marks card.

   Notice that the bars on the chart are now different colors.
   The colors represent each categories profit.

   You will see the legend shown below the Marks card, in Figure 4-60, to the right of the chart.

   I moved the legend below the Marks card, to make it easier to see in the figure.

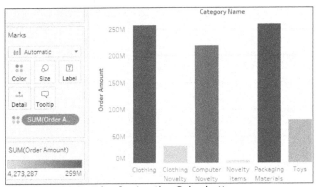

Figure 4-60 Result of using the Color button

Exercise 4.4: Create A Highlight Table

This exercise will show you how to create a table that displays a background color (using a gradient color scheme), which represents the value in the cell. The default is that lighter colors represent smaller values.

1. Duplicate the E4.2 chart ⇒ Rename it to E4.4 Highlight table.

2. On the Show Me button, select the Highlight tables chart. The chart should have different shades of a blue background.

Change The Highlight Background Color

1. On the Marks card, click the **COLOR** button ⇒ Click the **EDIT COLORS** button ⇒ Open the Palette drop-down list and select Orange.

2. If the Marks card drop-down list is not set to **SQUARE**, select this option now.

The chart should look like the one shown in Figure 4-61. Notice that the Novelty Items category only has data for 2016. The color legend shown in Figure 4-62, displays the lowest and highest values displayed on the table. The color helps you see where values are in the range of values.

Category Name	SubCategory	Order Date			
		2013	2014	2015	2016
Clothing	Hoodie	4,952,430	6,164,464	5,484,850	2,144,163
	Jacket	11,838,591	13,371,035	12,501,359	5,505,267
	Slippers	21,636,463	23,973,307	24,858,649	9,682,260
	Socks	4,335,075	4,495,791	4,996,531	2,053,183
	T-Shirt	27,132,392	31,705,923	26,858,588	13,127,490
Clothing Novelty	Novelty	8,493,622	10,204,366	8,793,880	3,631,925
Computer Novelty	Mug	42,789,622	49,776,616	50,287,724	20,695,715
	Office Misc	1,034,469	906,032	852,707	454,593
	USB Drive	13,351,569	15,291,372	16,411,297	6,905,534
Novelty Items	Chocolate Candy				4,273,287
Packaging Materials	Air Cushion	3,127,473	3,411,575	3,333,600	1,525,279
	Bag	4,001,479	4,630,355	4,091,852	1,657,199
	Bubble Wrap	21,174,354	23,765,985	25,925,243	9,882,621

Figure 4-61 Highlight table

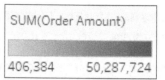

SUM(Order Amount)

406,384   50,287,724

Figure 4-62 Highlight table legend

Exercise 4.5: Create A Pie Chart

This exercise will show you how to create a pie chart that displays the order amount for each category. You will also learn how to resize a pie chart and customize the labels on the chart.

1. Select the Category Name and Order Amount fields ⇒ Select the Pie chart.

2. To make the chart larger, press and hold the CTRL and Shift keys, then press the B key, five times.

3. On the Marks card, click the SIZE button ⇒ Drag the slider right, to the next tick mark.

4. On the Marks card, click the LABEL button ⇒ Check the Show mark labels option.

5. On the Marks card, open the drop-down list for the Sum(Order Amount) field that has the ANGLE ICON ⇒ Select Format.

6. As shown below in Figure 4-63, on the Format PANE tab on the left, open the Default Numbers drop-down list ⇒ Select CURRENCY (CUSTOM).

7. Change the Decimal places option to zero, as shown in Figure 4-63 ⇒ At the top of the pane, across from the Word "Format", click the X, to close the Format pane.

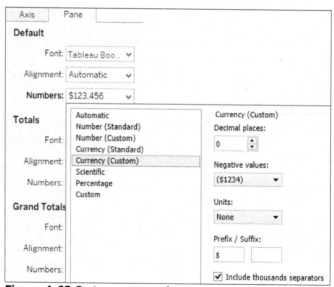

Figure 4-63 Custom currency formatting options

8. From the Data tab, drag the Category Name and Order Amount fields to the Label button on the Marks card. Doing this will display both values as labels on the chart.

9. Rename the sheet to `E4.5 Pie chart`.

   To the right of the chart, you should see the legend.

   The chart should look like the one shown in Figure 4-64.

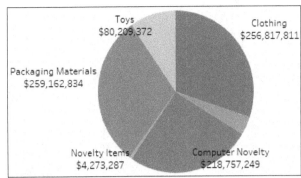

Figure 4-64 Pie chart

Status Bar

The status bar is at the bottom of the workspace. Figure 4-65 shows the status bar. The options are explained below.

| 282 marks | 3 rows by 1 column | SUM(Sales): $2,297,201 | | ◄ ◄ ► ►◄ | ⠿ ▨ ■ |

Figure 4-65 Status bar

The left side of the status bar displays the following information about the chart: The number of marks on the chart, the number of rows and columns and the total value of the marks.

On the right, you will see four VCR buttons. They are automatically enabled when there are more tabs then can be displayed on the status bar.

On the far right are three buttons. They are explained below.

① The **SHOW SHEET SORTER BUTTON** displays the window shown later in Figure 4-78. It is primarily used to rearrange the order of the tabs displayed at the bottom of the workspace. Drag a sheet to where you want it moved to.

② The **SHOW FILM STRIP BUTTON** displays a thumbnail of the chart, dashboard or story, in addition to the sheet names, the section above the status bar, as shown later in Figure 4-80. The layout shown in the figure, works like the Sheet Sorter window, in that you can use drop and drag to rearrange the sheets in the workbook.

③ The **SHOW TABS BUTTON** is the default view, which displays the view that you have used up to this point.

Exercise 4.6: Create A Side-By-Side Bar Chart

The chart that you will learn how to create in this exercise will display sales (order amount) by category name and order year. This will let you see which years a category of products did well in and not so well.

1. Select the Order Date, Category Name and Order Amount fields.

2. Select the Side-by-side bar chart.

3. Place the mouse pointer to the right of the Novelty Items column heading on the chart, and drag the vertical line to the right, a little. The chart should look like the one shown in Figure 4-66.

4. Rename the sheet to `E4.6 Side by side bar chart`.

As you can see, the Toys category of products is not doing well. The Novelty Items category only has data for one year. Overall, sales in 2016 are down significantly in all categories.

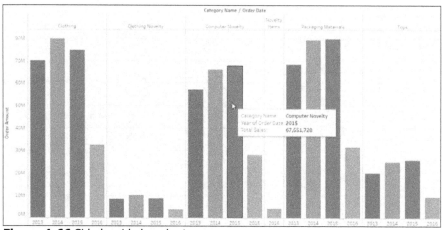

Figure 4-66 Side-by-side bar chart

Exercise 4.7: Create A Stacked Bar Chart

In this exercise, you will modify the E4.1 chart so that it is a stacked bar chart that uses the Shipped Via field to show how the orders were shipped.

1. Duplicate the E4.1 sheet ⇒ Rename it to E4.7 Stacked bar chart.

2. Drag the Shipped Via field to the Color button.

3. Select the Stacked bars chart.

   The chart should look like the one shown in Figure 4-67.

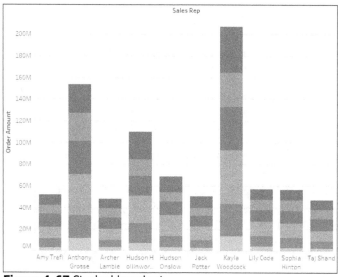

Figure 4-67 Stacked bar chart

Exercise 4.8: Create A Continuous Line Chart

This exercise will display the data in Exercise 4.6, on a continuous line chart.

1. Duplicate the E4.6 sheet ⇒ Rename it to E4.8 Continuous line chart.

2. Select the Line (continuous) chart option.

As shown in Figure 4-68, this layout is not easy to see the trends in the data, like the side-by-side bars chart created in Exercise 4.6.

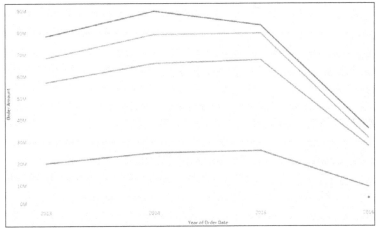

Figure 4-68 Continuous line chart

Exercise 4.9: Create A Discrete Line Chart

This exercise will display the data in Exercise 4.6, on a discrete line chart.

1. Duplicate the E4.6 sheet ⇒ Rename it to E4.9 Discrete line chart.

2. Select the Line (discrete) chart option.

3. On the Columns shelf, click the plus sign on the Year (Order Date) field.

   The data is now displayed by year and quarter, as shown in Figure 4-69.

   As you can see, the data for each year is separate.

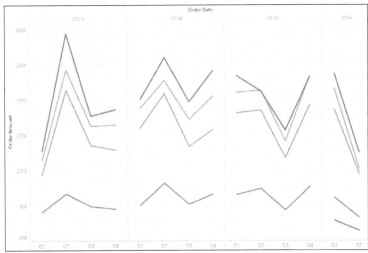

Figure 4-69 Discrete line chart

 Other Ways To Display Parts Of A Date Field
In Exercise 4.9, you clicked on the plus sign for the Order Date field to display data by quarter. This is a way to drill-down to see underlying data. Once a chart with a date field is created, you can click on the plus sign of the date field on the chart, as illustrated in Figure 4-70, to display the quarters on the chart.

You can also display the months in a quarter, by clicking the plus sign on the first quarter. Figure 4-71 shows the data by month for the first two quarters in 2015. You can also drill-down and see the data by day.

As you scroll to the right, the category columns on the left stay visible.

Figure 4-70 Plus sign on a chart illustrated

| Category N.. | SubCategory | Q1 | | | Q2 | | 2015 |
		January	February	March	April	May	June
Clothing	Hoodie	619,368	356,707	528,916	853,227	214,998	383,812
	Jacket	1,515,396	840,349	1,055,728	1,243,334	796,603	951,611
	Slippers	3,084,166	1,434,324	2,324,878	2,835,821	1,398,152	2,357,111
	Socks	712,911	296,886	423,548	667,120	163,688	526,974

Figure 4-71 Data by year, month and quarter

Exercise 4.10: Use The Measure Generated Fields

Earlier in this chapter, the **MEASURE NAMES** and **MEASURE VALUES** fields were explained. This exercise will show you one way to incorporate them into a chart.

1. On a new sheet, add the Category Name and Sub Category fields to the Rows shelf.

2. Drag the Order Date field to the Columns shelf.

3. Rename the sheet to E4.10 Measure generated fields.

4. Drag the Measure Names field to the Columns shelf after the Order Date field.

5. Drag the Measure Values field to the Color button.

6. In the Measure Values section of the Marks card, remove the SUM(Quantity) and SUM(Unit Price) fields.

7. In the Measure Values section, change the SUM(Number of Records) field to the Count aggregate function.

8. Click the Label button ⇒ Check the Show mark labels option.

   The Filters and Marks sections should look like the ones shown in Figure 4-72.

Figure 4-72 Filters and Marks sections

How To Rename A Column Heading

1. On the chart, right-click on the Count of Number of Records heading ⇒ Edit Alias ⇒ Type # of Orders, as shown in Figure 4-73.

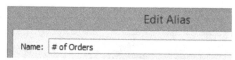

Figure 4-73 New column heading name

2. Change the Order Amount alias name to Total Sales. The table should look like the one shown in Figure 4-74.

Category Name	SubCategory	Order Date							
		2013		2014		2015		2016	
		# of Orders	Total Sales	# of Orders	Total Sales	# of Orders	Total Sales	# of Orders	Total Sales
Clothing	Hoodie	1,421	4,952,430	1,523	6,164,464	1,632	5,484,850	650	2,144,163
	Jacket	3,183	11,838,591	3,208	13,371,035	3,691	12,501,359	1,400	5,505,267
	Slippers	5,625	21,636,463	6,117	23,973,307	6,811	24,858,649	2,612	9,682,260
	Socks	1,136	4,335,075	1,199	4,495,791	1,346	4,996,531	531	2,053,183
	T-Shirt	7,294	27,132,392	7,992	31,705,923	8,447	26,858,588	3,434	13,127,490

Figure 4-74 Table using the Measure Names and Measure Values fields

Exercise 4.11: Separate The Legend

As discussed earlier, when the Measure Values and Measure Names fields are used to create a chart and the Measure Values field is added to the Color button on the Marks card, a single color legend is created by default. If you need to display some measures with different colors, you can create separate color legends. This is what you will learn how to do in this exercise.

1. Duplicate the E4.10 sheet ⇒ Rename it to `E4.11 Separate legends`.

2. On the Marks card, display the shortcut menu for the Measure Values field ⇒
    Select the **USE SEPARATE LEGENDS** option, shown in Figure 4-75.

    To the right of the chart, you will see two legends.

Figure 4-75 Measure Values field shortcut menu options (Marks card)

3. To the right of the Number of Records legend name, display the shortcut menu, shown in Figure 4-76 ⇒ **EDIT COLORS**.

Figure 4-76 Legend shortcut menu

4. On the Edit Colors dialog box, you can select a color scheme from the Palette drop-down list, or click the solid color square after the scale, to select a color scheme. Once selected, the legend and chart will display the color scheme that you select.

Organizing Worksheets

This section focuses on organizing the sheets in the workbook. The next section covers organizing the Data pane. As you have seen, creating more than two or three charts in a workbook almost makes it a requirement to rename them to something more meaningful then Sheet 1 and Sheet 2. If you viewed the Superstore sample workbook, you saw several dashboards, most of which have three or more charts. The reason that you do not see all of the chart tabs, in that workbook, is because they are hidden.

Using The Sheet Sorter Window

This window was discussed earlier in this chapter. It is used to change the order of the sheets, dashboards and stories. If you look at the tabs on your navigation bar, you will see that they are not in exercise order, even though that is the order that the tabs were created in, similar to what is shown in Figure 4-77.

◫ Data Source	Sheet 3	Sheet 4	E4.1	E4.2	E4.4	E4.3 matrix card	E4.5	E4.6	E4.8	E4.7

Figure 4-77 Order of charts on my navigation bar

Changing the order of the sheets is optional for completing the exercises in this book. To rearrange the sheets, follow the steps below.

1. Click the **SHOW SHEET SORTER BUTTON**, in the lower right corner of the workspace. You will see the window shown in Figure 4-78.

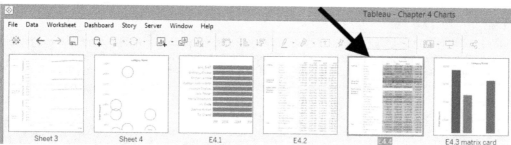

Figure 4-78 Sheet sorter view

2. Click on a sheet that you want to move. You will see a blue border around it, as illustrated above in Figure 4-78.

3. Drag the sheet right or left, up or down, to the location where you want it.

4. Repeat steps 2 and 3 until you have the sheets in the order that you want.

Moving More Than One Sheet At The Same Time
More than one sheet (known as a **THUMBNAIL**, on this view) can be moved at the same time, by clicking on the first one that you want to move, then hold down the CTRL key and click on the other sheets that you want to move. Once you have all of the sheets selected, that you want to move, use the mouse to drag them where you want the sheets moved to.

Sheets can also be rearranged on the tabs at the bottom of the workspace, shown earlier in Figure 4-77, by dragging them.

Thumbnail Shortcut Menu

Each thumbnail on the Sheet Sorter window has the shortcut menu shown in Figure 4-79.

The **REFRESH THUMBNAIL** options at the bottom of the menu, load some or all of the thumbnails into memory.

This is helpful if the workbook will be used as part of a live demonstration and you do not want the demonstration to run slow, in terms of the transition from one sheet to another. Consider trying this option if the workbook has a lot of sheets.

Figure 4-79 Sheet Sorter Thumbnail shortcut menu

Film Strip View

This view displays a thumbnail of each sheet, dashboard and story, at the bottom of the workspace, as shown in Figure 4-80. Right-clicking on a thumbnail in this view, displays a shortcut menu that has the options shown above in Figure 4-79, plus a few other options that have already been covered in this chapter. Sheets can be rearranged from this view.

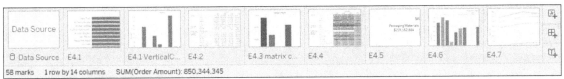

Figure 4-80 Film Strip view

 While the Sheet Sorter and Film Strip views can be used to organize the sheets, they do not display sheets that have been hidden.

Renaming Worksheets

While you can name the sheets whatever you want, it is a good idea to give them a descriptive name. If the charts will be used to create more than one dashboard in the workbook, the sheet names become more important, because it is helpful to know which sheets are for which dashboard.

When I figure out what the dashboard sheets will be named, I often add the dashboard name, or at least part of it to the beginning of the name for the chart sheets that will be used to create the dashboard.

Organizing The Data Pane

Currently, there are two ways to organize the fields on the Data pane.

① **SORTING** The sorting options (shown earlier in Figure 4-44) are only available for relational data sources. You can sort the fields in alphabetical order (the default) or the order that they are in, in the data source.

② **USING FOLDERS** This option can be helpful for tables that have a lot of fields, or if there are a lot of tables displayed on the Data pane.

How To Create Folders

Should you have the need on your own, the steps below show you how to create folders and add fields to a folder.

1. Select some or all of the fields that you want to add to a folder.

2. Right-click on one of the selected fields ⇒ Folders ⇒ Create Folder, as shown in Figure 4-81.

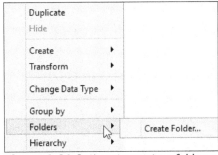

Figure 4-81 Options to create a folder

3. On the Create Folder dialog box, type in a name for the folder. The folder will be displayed at the top of the Dimensions section, as shown in Figure 4-82.

   Notice the folder icon to the left of the folder name. Just like folders in Windows File Explorer, the folders on the Data pane can be closed.

   To add a field to an existing folder, right-click on the field that you want to add to a folder ⇒ Folders ⇒ Add to Folder ⇒ Select the folder that you want to add the selected field to.

Figure 4-82 Folder created

Analytics Pane

The options shown in Figure 4-83 are used to create reference lines, trend lines and forecasts.

The majority of options on this pane are also on the Analysis menu, that was covered earlier in this chapter.

Other options like reference lines are available by editing an axis. The Analytics pane makes it easier to add forecasts, reference or trend lines to a chart.

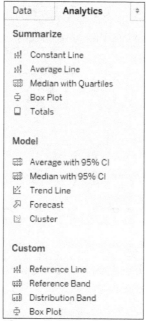

Figure 4-83 Analytics pane

SORT, FILTER AND GROUP DATA

 Overview

After reading this chapter and completing the exercises, you will know how to:

- ☑ Sort data several ways
- ☑ Create a variety of filters, including Top N filters
- ☑ Use the Pages shelf
- ☑ Create a bookmark file
- ☑ View data that was used to create a chart
- ☑ Create groups and sets

CHAPTER 5

Overview

The previous chapter covered the chart types that can be created and showed you how to create several types of charts. As the title of this chapter indicates, you will learn how to sort, filter and group data that is displayed on the chart.

The topics in this chapter will show you ways to change how the data is displayed on a chart. Keep in mind that the topics covered may not be available for all chart types and even more important, they may not enhance the data on all chart types. For example, sorting data displayed on a pie chart, probably will not enhance the appearance of the data displayed. If the pie chart displays a lot of categories, having a filter would be helpful to reduce the number of categories displayed on a pie chart.

Sorting Data

This option is used to change the order that the data is displayed in, on a chart. As you will see, there are several places where you can sort data from. Data is sorted, based on the dimension member values. Data does not have to be sorted using fields displayed on the chart. Any field in the data source can be used to sort the data displayed on a chart. Tableau supports two types of sorting: Manual and computed.

Manual Sorting

This type of sorting is used to rearrange the dimension members to create the exact order that you need. There are two options for manually sorting the data on a chart: Drop and drag the dimension members and use the Sort buttons on the toolbar. This type of sorting is probably the one that you are most familiar with because the sorting is done in ascending or descending order. The toolbar has buttons to sort in ascending/descending order.

Using these options to sort data, does not override the default sort order. It is applied to the way the records are currently sorted. Manual sorting is not permanent, unless you save the workbook with the data sorted.

Computed Sorting

This type of sorting uses rules that define the sort. The shelf that the dimension is placed on, determines the part of the chart that is sorted. If the dimension that will be used to sort on is on the Rows shelf, the rows on the chart will be sorted. Discrete fields can be sorted after they have been placed on any shelf, except the Filters shelf. The dimensions on the Columns or Rows shelf have a sort option on the shortcut menu.

Exercise 5.1: Sort Data In Descending Order

In this exercise, you will sort the data in the E4.1 chart in descending order, so that the largest values will be displayed at the top of the chart. Currently, the E4.1 bar chart is sorted by the sales reps name.

1. Save the Chapter 4 Charts workbook, as `Chapter 5 Sort Filter and Group Data`.

2. Delete all of the sheets except E4.1, E4.2 and E4.6.

3. Duplicate the E4.1 sheet ⇒ Rename it to `E5.1 Sort by order amount`.

4. Hold the mouse pointer over the Order Amount label, at the bottom of the chart. To the right of the label you should see the Sort icon, shown in Figure 5-1 ⇒
Click on the Sort icon. The chart should look like the one shown in Figure 5-2.

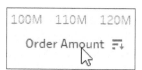

Figure 5-1 Sort icon next to a label

In addition to using the Order Amount label, shown above in Figure 5-1 to sort the data, if you hold the mouse pointer above the chart, you will see the sort icon, as illustrated in Figure 5-2.

The sorting that you just created is known as sorting on an axis. The sort buttons on the axis are intuitive. They automatically create a sort that is based on the chart type. This is a **COMPUTED SORT**.

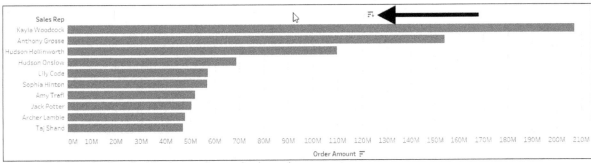

Figure 5-2 Bar chart sorted in descending order by order amount

Exercise 5.2: Sorting Data On A Text Table

Often, an effective use of sorting data in a text table is to display the numeric values in ascending or descending order.

1. Duplicate the E4.2 sheet ⇒ Rename it to `E5.2 Sort text table data`.

2. Hold the mouse pointer to the right of the 2013 column heading. You will see the sort button.

3. Click the Sort button twice.

    The values will be displayed in ascending order, as shown in Figure 5-3.

Sub Category	2013	2014	2015	2016
		Order Date		
Socks	4,335,075	4,495,791	4,996,531	2,053,183
Hoodie	4,952,430	6,164,464	5,484,850	2,144,163
Jacket	11,838,591	13,371,035	12,501,359	5,505,267
Slippers	21,636,463	23,973,307	24,858,649	9,682,260
T-Shirt	27,132,392	31,705,923	26,858,588	13,127,490

Figure 5-3 Text table data sorted in ascending order

Sort By Using Drop And Drag

This sort method can be helpful if the chart has a lot of categories (dimension members) and you want to see them in an order that is not ascending, descending or data source order.

Exercise 5.3: Create A Custom Sort Order

In this exercise, you will create a sort that will display specific sales reps at the top of the chart.

1. Duplicate the E4.1 sheet ⇒ Rename it to `E5.3 Custom sort`.

2. Drag the sales rep (member) Lily Code up and place it below the first sales rep.

    When dragging the dimension member, you should see a black line, as shown in Figure 5-4.

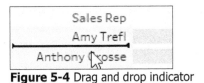

Figure 5-4 Drag and drop indicator

3. Drag the sales rep Sophia Hinton up and place it below the third sales rep ⇒ Click on a blank space on the canvas.

    The dimensions should look like the ones shown in Figure 5-5.

    Compare the order of these dimensions to the order displayed on the E4.1 chart.

Figure 5-5 Custom sort order

Exercise 5.4: Sort Data Using The Legend

Using the legend is another way to use drop and drag to sort the data displayed on a chart. In this exercise, you will create a custom sort on a date field, using the options on the legend. This will make it easier to see how the two years of sales, compare to each other.

1. Duplicate the E4.6 sheet ⇒ Rename it to `E5.4 Legend custom sort`.

2. In the legend, drag the 2013 marker down, below the 2015 marker. The chart and legend should look like the ones shown in Figure 5-6.

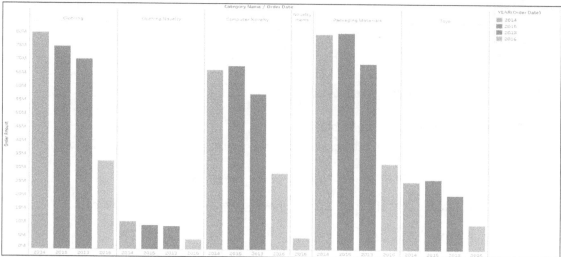

Figure 5-6 Custom sort created by using the legend

Changing The Default Sort Order For A Field

Chapter 4 covered the default properties that can be set for fields. One of the default properties that can be set from the Data pane, is the sort order. The benefit of setting a default sort order, from the Data pane, for some fields is that it will save you time. The Sort dialog box, shown in Figure 5-7 is used to set the default sort order.

Using The Sort Dialog Box

The **SORT** option on a fields shortcut menu, is used to select a sort order for the field on the chart or a default sort order for how the values in the field will be displayed, using the options shown in Figure 5-7. The difference is where you select the sort option from. Sorting from the Data pane creates a default sort order. This means that every chart that uses the field, will have the sort order automatically applied. If you select the sort option any place else on the workspace, the sort will only be applied to the current chart. Figure 5-8 shows the Sort dialog box that is available from the Pages, Columns and Rows shelves.

Using the Sort dialog box is also helpful when you want the values displayed in an order that is not ascending or descending. An example is the territory field values shown in Figure 5-7. You may want all territories in a specific region to be displayed next to each other on the charts that use the field.

Figure 5-7 Sort dialog box

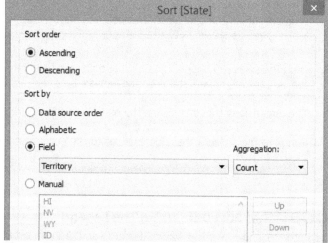

Figure 5-8 Sort dialog box for the Pages, Columns and Rows shelves

Exercise 5.5: Sort On A Field Not Displayed On The Chart

In this exercise you will create a chart that is initially sorted in data source order. Then you will create a sort for a field that is not displayed on the chart.

1. On a new sheet, add the State and Category Name fields to the Rows shelf.

2. Add the Order Amount field to the Columns shelf. As you can see, the data is displayed in state order.

3. Rename the sheet to E5.5 Sort on field not on chart.

4. Display the shortcut menu for the State field on the Rows shelf ⇒ Sort.

5. Select the Field option ⇒ Open the drop-down list and select Territory. This is the field that the states will be sorted by ⇒ Click OK.

   The chart should look like the one shown in Figure 5-9. In reality, you would probably display the Territory field on the chart. Doing that in this exercise would defeat the purpose <smile>.

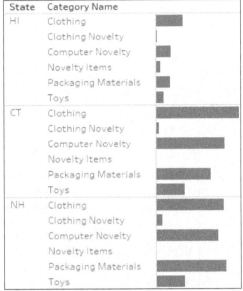

Figure 5-9 Sorted by a field not on the chart

Creating A Hierarchy

A hierarchy is a collection of fields, usually arranged from the highest level to the lowest level. Think of the levels as a way to drill down on the data, which is another way to sort the data. A hierarchy provides the ability to view data at a high level, like a summary report, then drill down as needed to view detail records. Figure 5-10 shows part of a modified version of the E5.5 chart with a hierarchy at the high level. The hierarchy was created using the Territory and State fields. Figure 5-11 shows part of the chart, drilled down to the state level.

The top level field is the one that all other levels are a part of. The next level down is a subset of the level above. All of the fields in the hierarchy can be added to the chart at the same time. Hierarchies are usually used to add drill down functionality to charts. You can create as many levels as you need.

Hierarchy fields display a plus/minus icon in front of the field name. Clicking this icon displays a level of detail records. To close a level, click on the icon again.

 More than one hierarchy can be created in the same workbook.

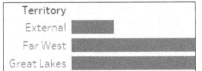

Figure 5-10 High level view of the data

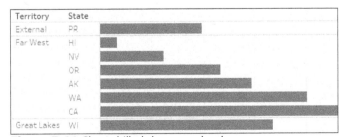

Figure 5-11 Chart drilled down one level

A popular hierarchy to create is Country ⇒ State ⇒ City. On your own, if you have the need, the steps below will show you how to create a hierarchy for the Country, State and City fields.

1. Select one or all of the fields that you need to create the hierarchy for.

2. Right-click on one of the selected fields ⇒ Hierarchy ⇒ Create Hierarchy.

3. On the Create Hierarchy dialog box, type in a name for the hierarchy or accept the default name.

If you need to add another field to a hierarchy, right-click on the field that you want to add ⇒ Hierarchy ⇒ Add to Hierarchy ⇒ Select the hierarchy that you want to add the field to, as shown in Figure 5-12.

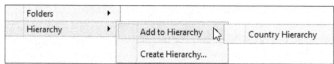

Figure 5-12 Options to add a field to a hierarchy

Filters

In Chapter 3, creating filters on the Data Source tab was covered. The filters created on the Data Source tab are automatically applied to every chart that you create. This section covers creating filters on a Sheet tab. The difference is that the filters created on a sheet tab are only applied to the chart on the tab that the filter is created on. For example, using the same data source, one sheet can filter the data by the first quarter of the year 2016. Another sheet can filter the data by the State field. Filters are used to select which rows of data are used to create the chart.

Filters Shelf

This shelf provides an easy way to create filters for the data that will be displayed on the chart. When you add fields to this shelf, you will see a dialog box, which is used to create the filter criteria. Filters that you create, will appear to the right of the chart, where the legend is displayed.

In addition to dragging a field from the Data pane to the Filters shelf, fields in the Columns and Rows shelves can be dragged to the Filters shelf.

Filters Shelf Shortcut Menu

The majority of options on the shortcut menu for the fields added to this shelf, are the same as the ones for fields added to the Columns and Rows shelves, which were covered in Chapter 4. Figures 5-13, 5-14 and 5-15 show the Filter shelves shortcut menus for different data types. The options not explained in Chapter 4, are explained below.

EDIT FILTER opens the Filter dialog box shown later in Figure 5-17 or 5-23, depending on the fields data type. This allows you to change the filter criteria as needed.

ADD TO CONTEXT [See Context Filters]

APPLY TO WORKSHEETS is used to apply the filter to other worksheets in the workbook.

CREATE SET [See Sets]

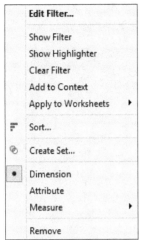

Figure 5-13 String field filter shortcut menu

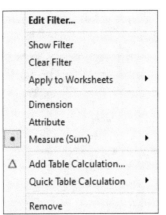

Figure 5-14 Numeric field filter shortcut menu

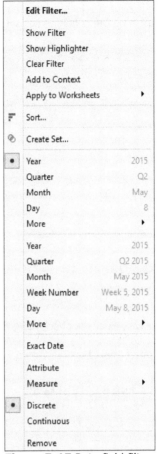

Figure 5-15 Date field filter shortcut menu

Exercise 5.6: Create A Filter For A Date Field

In this exercise, you will learn how to create a filter to select specific years to display on the chart.

1. Duplicate the E4.6 chart ⇒ Rename it to E5.6 Year filter.

2. Drag the Order Date field from the Data pane to the Filters shelf ⇒
    On the dialog box shown in Figure 5-16, click on the Years option ⇒
    Click Next.

    The option that you select on this dialog box determines which options are available on the next screen.

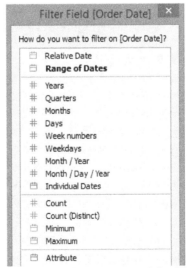

Figure 5-16 First screen of the Filter Field dialog box for a date field

The Filter dialog box, for a date field, has three tabs that can be used to create the criteria. Figure 5-17 displays the values in the field that the filter is being created for. The **SUMMARY** section displays the options selected or created on the dialog box.

The options shown in Figure 5-18 are used to create criteria to select data to display on the chart. Use the options on this tab to either enhance the condition set on the General tab or create additional filter criteria (conditions).

Figure 5-17 General tab options on the Filter dialog box

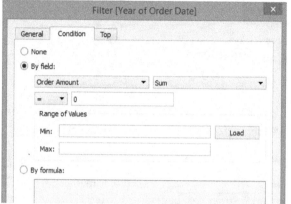

Figure 5-18 Condition tab options on the Filter dialog box

3. On the General tab, clear the check mark for the years, 2014 and 2016, as shown above in Figure 5-17.

4. Click OK. The chart should only display data for 2013 and 2015.

Filter Dialog Box For A String Field

In addition to the tabs shown above in Figure 5-18, the Filter dialog box for a string field also has the tab shown in Figure 5-19.

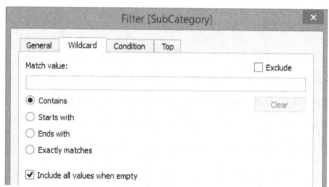

Figure 5-19 Wildcard filter options

Exercise 5.7: Create A Filter For A Category Field

In this exercise, you will learn how to create a filter for a text table, to reduce the number of sub categories displayed on the chart.

1. Duplicate the E5.2 sheet ⇒ Rename it to `E5.7 Sub category filter`.

2. Drag the Sub Category field to the Filters shelf.

3. On the General tab, click the None button to remove all of the check marks ⇒ Check the following members: Action Figure, Air Cushion, Express Box, Mug, Novelty, Packing Knife, Packing Knife - Blades and Slippers.

4. Click the Exclude button.

    The categories that you selected in the previous step will not be displayed on the chart.

    The Summary section should look like the one shown in Figure 5-20 ⇒ Click OK. The table will have fewer rows of data, then the table in Exercise 5.2.

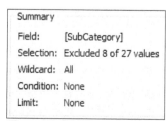

Figure 5-20 Filter criteria

Date Field Hierarchy

Earlier in this chapter, creating a hierarchy manually was covered. Date fields have a built-in hierarchy, which is indicated by the plus sign before the field name when it is added to a shelf, as shown in the left side of Figure 5-21. The date field hierarchy allows you to drill down into the data. When this is done, the chart becomes a nested table.

When you click on the plus sign, a quarter field is automatically created, as shown on the right side of Figure 5-21 and displayed on the chart.

When you click on the plus sign of a quarter field on the chart, the month field is automatically created and displayed on the chart, as shown in Figure 5-22.

Figure 5-21 Year and quarter order date pills

Category N..	SubCategory	January	February	March	April	May	June	July
						Order Date 2013		
		Q1			Q2			
Clothing	Socks	226,408	447,466	342,031	250,932	255,123	453,414	614,229
	Hoodie	205,754	291,146	274,627	447,767	781,160	513,430	653,908
	Jacket	484,067	816,065	786,723	1,478,209	1,482,599	1,302,296	1,522,358
	T-Shirt	1,113,550	1,558,042	1,239,462	3,450,148	3,623,712	3,682,078	3,452,543

Figure 5-22 Chart with year, quarter and month hierarchy fields

Exercise 5.8: Filter Data By The Order Amount

In this exercise, you will learn how to create a filter that only displays data if the sub category has a total order amount for the quarter that is greater than or equal to 3 million dollars. This would be a way to see the sub categories that produce the most revenue.

1. Duplicate the E5.2 sheet ⇒ Rename it to E5.8 Quarters with 3 million.

2. Add the Order Amount field to the Filters shelf.

3. On the Filter Field dialog box, select the Sum option ⇒ Click Next. The options on the next screen provide several ways to create a numeric filter.

4. Click the **AT LEAST BUTTON** ⇒
    In the field, type 3,000,000, as shown in Figure 5-23.

    Typing the commas is optional.

    You can also use the slider to select a value. Maybe it's me, but I find it tricky to use the slider to get a specific value <smile>.

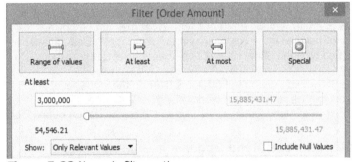

Figure 5-23 Numeric filter options

5. Click OK ⇒ Display the Quarters for each year.

    Figure 5-24 shows the quarters in 2013, that have total order amounts of at least 3 million dollars.

    The empty cells indicate that the sub category did not meet the filter criteria. Someplace on the sheet, it would be helpful to the reader to indicate what the filter criteria is.

Category N..	Sub Category	Q1	Q2	Q3	Q4
		2013			
Clothing	Jacket		4,263,104		
	Slippers	3,856,936	8,026,977	4,663,575	5,088,974
	T-Shirt	3,911,054	10,755,937	5,813,450	6,651,952
Clothing No..	Novelty		3,630,257		
Computer	USB Drive		4,953,561	3,262,862	3,110,319
Novelty	Mug	7,166,151	15,885,431	10,138,281	9,599,758

Figure 5-24 Result of the numeric filter criteria

Exercise 5.9: Create Top 10 Filter Criteria

In this exercise, you will learn how to create filter criteria to display the 10 sub categories with the largest total order amounts in 2015. This will require two filters.

1. Duplicate the E5.2 sheet ⇒ Rename it to `E5.9 Top 10 categories`.

2. Change the chart type to Horizontal bars.

3. Add the Order Date field to the Filters shelf ⇒ Select the Years option ⇒ Click Next ⇒ Clear the check marks for all years, except 2015 ⇒ Click OK.

4. Add the Sub Category field to the Filters shelf ⇒
   Display the **TOP TAB** ⇒ Select the **BY FIELD OPTION**.

   You should have the options shown in Figure 5-25. This filter criteria will select the 10 sub categories that have the largest order totals ⇒ Click OK.

   The chart should look like the one shown in Figure 5-26.

Figure 5-25 Top 10 filter criteria

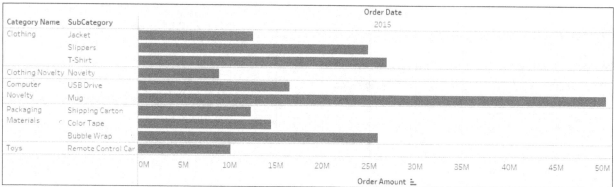

Figure 5-26 Top 10 bar chart

Show Filter Option

In earlier versions of Tableau, the Show Filter option was known as **QUICK FILTER**. The previous exercises showed you how to create several types of filters. What may not be obvious is that the filters that you have created in this chapter cannot be used if the charts are viewed using the Tableau Reader or if the charts are on a Tableau server. Filters created with the Show Filter option, do not have this limitation.

The Show Filter option will place the filter on the workspace, in the same section where the legend is placed. Filters can be added to the workspace by selecting the Show Filter option on any field that has been placed on a shelf. Like many features, the layout and customization options for the filter control, depend on the data type.

Filter Shortcut Menu Options

The options that are selected in Figures 5-27 and 5-28, are the default options for the filter control. Figure 5-27 shows the layout and shortcut menu options for a text field filter. The options on the shortcut menu for a date field are similar. The options on the shortcut menu are for discrete values (filters). Figure 5-28 shows the layout and shortcut menu options for a numeric field filter. The options on the shortcut menu are for continuous values (filters).

The options on the shortcut menus are explained below.

The **EDIT FILTER** option opens the Filter dialog box that you used earlier in this chapter, to create filters.

Select the **REMOVE FILTER** option to remove the filter from the workspace. If the filter was initially on the Filters shelf, it is removed for there also. [See Hide Card, below]

Select the **CUSTOMIZE** option to display/hide parts of the filter control.

The **EDIT TITLE** option is used to change the title (by default, the field name) of the filter control.

The **SINGLE VALUE** and **MULTIPLE VALUES** options are used to change the appearance of the filter control. The icons to the right of each option, indicate how the control will be displayed.

If selected, the **ONLY RELEVANT VALUES** option uses the results of other filters as part of the criteria to select the values displayed. If you do not want other filters to be used to filter the values on the selected filters, select the **ALL VALUES IN DATABASE** option, which displays all values, regardless of the other filters used on the chart.

If selected, the **INCLUDE VALUES** option uses the selected values to filter the data on the chart.

If selected, the **EXCLUDE VALUES** option does not include the selected values in the filter criteria.

The **HIDE CARD** option hides the filter control, but keeps the filter criteria on the Filters shelf.

The **RANGE OF VALUES** option is used to select the lowest and highest values that can be used to select rows of data to display on the chart.

AT LEAST option [See Figure 5-23]

The **AT MOST OPTION** is used to select the highest value that can be used to select rows of data to display on the chart.

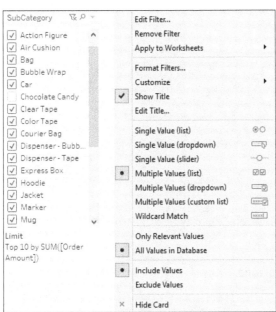

Figure 5-27 Text data type layout and shortcut menu

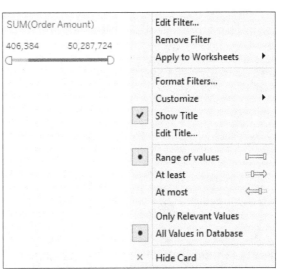

Figure 5-28 Numeric data type layout and shortcut menu

Exercise 5.10: Use The Show Filter Option

By default, the filters that are enabled using the Show Filters option are displayed on a dashboard. This will let people that view the dashboard be able to filter the data on their own. This filter can be customized, like the filters on the Filters shelf can.

1. Duplicate the E5.8 sheet ⇒ Rename it to `E5.10 Show filter option`.

2. Display the shortcut menu shown in Figure 5-29, for the Category Name field on the Rows shelf ⇒ Select the Show Filter option.

   You will see the filter to the right of the chart.

Figure 5-29 Shelf field shortcut menu

3. Create a filter for the Year(Order Date) field on the Columns shelf.

   You should have the filters shown in Figure 5-30.

   You can use the filter options shown earlier in Figure 5-27 to customize the filters that you just created.

Figure 5-30 Filters created from the Show Filter option

Exercise 5.11: Customize Filters On The Chart

In this exercise, you will learn how to customize how the filter is displayed.

1. Duplicate the E5.9 sheet ⇒ Rename it to E5.11 Customize filters.

2. Edit the Order Date filter to display all records.

3. Remove the Top 10 filter criteria from the Sub Category field, by selecting the None option, on the Top tab.

4. Change the chart to a text table.

Create And Customize The Order Date Filter

1. On the Filters shelf, right-click on the Order Date field and select Show Filter.

2. Display the shortcut menu for the Order Date filter control ⇒ Select **EDIT TITLE** ⇒ On the Edit Filter Title dialog box, replace the current title with Select The Years.

Create And Customize The Sub Category Filter

1. On the Filters shelf, right-click on the Sub Category field and select Show Filter.

2. Display the shortcut menu for the Sub Category filter control ⇒ Select the **MULTIPLE VALUES (DROP DOWN)** option.

    The filters should look like the ones shown in Figure 5-31.

Figure 5-31 Customized filters

Slicing Filters

So far, all of the filters that you have created have used fields that were displayed on the chart. A slicing filter is created using a field that is not displayed on the chart. This type of filter is also known as a **CALCULATION FILTER**.

Exercise 5.12: Create A Territory Slicing Filter

In this exercise you will learn how to create a filter that slices a chart that displays order totals by state and category.

1. Duplicate the E5.5 sheet ⇒ Rename it to E5.12 Slice by territory.

2. Add the Territory field to the Filters shelf ⇒ Select all of the Territories, except External.

3. Show the filter on the chart.

4. Change the title to Which Territories?
    As you select and unselect territories on the filter, states will be displayed or hidden on the chart.

Exercise 5.13: Create Year And Quarter Slicing Filters

Popular slicing filters to create are ones that will display data for a specific quarter or quarters for a year.

1. On a new sheet, select the Territory, State and Order Amount fields.

2. Select the Horizontal bars chart type.

3. Rename it to E5.13 Date slicing filters.

4. Add the Order Date field to the Filters shelf ⇒ Select the Years option ⇒ Click Next ⇒ Click the All button ⇒ Click OK.

5. Add the Order Date field to the Filters shelf again ⇒ Select the Quarters option ⇒ Click Next ⇒ Click the All button ⇒ Click OK.

6. Display the Order Year and Quarter filters on the chart.

7. Display the shortcut menu for the Year filter ⇒ Select the Single Value (list) option. Doing this will only allow data for one year to be displayed on the chart at a time.

    The filters should look like the ones shown in Figure 5-32. If your filters are not in the order shown in the figure, click on the title bar of one of the filters and drag it up or down to change the order.

    If the combination of filter options that you select, does not have any corresponding data, no chart will be displayed. For example, selecting the year 2016 and the third quarter, will not display a chart.

Figure 5-32 Slicing filters

Context Filters

Filters are processed individually by default, meaning each context filter processes all records in the data source, without taking into account any other filters for the chart. An existing category filter (like the ones created so far, in this chapter for the category name and sub category fields) can be used as a context filter. Once a context filter has been set up, any other filters for the chart are processed after the context filter. Context filters create a subset of data, that the other filters use, instead of each filter using the entire data source.

Context filters are used to reduce the rows of data. When Tableau queries the data in the data source, to load into Tableau, a temporary table is created. Rows of data that do not meet context and data source filter criteria are not added to the temporary table. Context filters are used to keep the number of rows in the temporary table to a minimum.

Context filters are often used when the chart needs to display Top N data or to improve performance. Behind the scenes, each filter has a query that has to be processed. Having five or six independent filters can make the queries run slow, as they process (read and check) every record in the data source. Having some or all filters use the result data set of a context filter, reduces the number of records each of the other filters has to process.

Creating A Context Filter

Context filters are created like the filters that you have learned how to create in this chapter, up to this point. Then the **ADD TO CONTEXT** option, shown earlier in Figure 5-13, is selected for the filter(s) that you want to use as a context filter. When this option is selected for a filter, on the Filters shelf, the background color of the field is changed to gray on the shelf.

Context filters are moved to the top of the Filters shelf and cannot be rearranged on the shelf, unless the **REMOVE FROM CONTEXT** option is selected on the shortcut menu. Context filters can be edited like other filters. They can also be displayed with the chart.

Exercise 5.14: Create A Context Filter For The Year

As covered earlier, a context filter is processed before the other filters for the chart are processed. Once processed, the other filters for the chart are processed using the data set created by the context filter. A popular context filter to create is for a year, as many charts only need to display one year of data at a time.

1. Duplicate the E5.12 sheet ⇒ Rename it to E5.14 Year context filter.

2. Add the Order Date field to the Filters shelf ⇒ Select the Years option ⇒ Click Next ⇒ Select all of the years ⇒ Click OK.

3. Right-click on the Year field filter ⇒ Select **ADD TO CONTEXT**.

4. Right-click on the Year field filter ⇒ Select Show Filter.

5. Change the Year filter control to the Single Value (list) option.

Pages Shelf

This shelf is used to analyze the data displayed on a chart, based on the values in the field added to this shelf. This allows you to see the performance over time. When a field is added to this shelf, a scrolling filter is automatically created that displays the data for each member.

Most of the time, a date field is used to create this type of analysis. When a date field is added to this shelf, you will see the **PAGE CONTROL**, shown in Figure 5-33.

Figure 5-33 Page control for a date field

This control creates an animated, step-by-step, filter that displays the data for each value in the field on the Pages shelf. Each chart can be displayed automatically or manually. In the date field shown in the figure, the chart would display data for each year.

A date field in the Pages shelf has the shortcut menu shown earlier in Figure 5-15. This lets you select a different date option like quarter or month to display the data by. The illustrated options on the page control are explained below.

① Displays the previous value in the field. You can also open the drop-down list and select a value to display data by, on the chart.
② Displays the next value in the field.
③ Each tick mark on the slider represents a value. Slide this button to select another value.
④ The first button rewinds the animation to the beginning. The middle button pauses the animation. The last button plays the animation.
⑤ Select one of these buttons (Slow, Normal, Fast), to determine the speed that the animation plays.
⑥ If checked, the **SHOW HISTORY** option will display values from any previous page, as faded marks on the chart.

  Clicking the button displays the panel shown in Figure 5-34. The options are used to customize how the history is displayed on the current page. All of the options on this panel, are not available for all chart types.

Figure 5-34 History customization options

A **PAGE** is the chart displayed for the dimension member. In Figure 5-33 shown earlier, the page displayed would be for the year 2013. When the chart for the year 2015 is displayed, the history displayed on the 2015 chart would be for 2014. The first page does not have history to display.

Exercise 5.15: Use The Pages Shelf

In this exercise you will learn how to use the Pages shelf to create a year filter with history.

1. Duplicate the E5.1 sheet ⇒ Rename it to E5.15 Year pages filter.

2. Add the Order Date field to the Pages shelf ⇒ Display the Filter dialog box ⇒ Select all of the years.

3. Select the **SLOW** option on the Filter control.

4. Click the Show History button ⇒ Display the Marks Format drop-down list ⇒ Click the More Colors option ⇒ Select the color red ⇒ Clear the Fade option, on the Show History window. I am using these options so that you can easily see the history data. On your own, you may not want to use such contrasting colors.

5. Select the year 2013 from the drop-down list on the Filter control, if it isn't already selected ⇒ Click the right arrow button to start the animation. The chart for 2016 should look like the one shown in Figure 5-35.

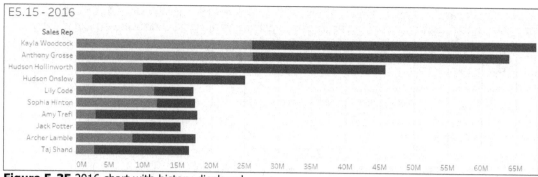

Figure 5-35 2016 chart with history displayed

When you click on a value (in the chart above, the values are the bars), you will see a tooltip, like the one shown in Figure 5-36. The options on the toolbar are explained below.

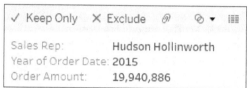

Figure 5-36 Tooltip

Selecting the KEEP ONLY option will only display the value(s) that you have selected on the chart.

The EXCLUDE option removes the selected value(s) from the chart.

The GROUP MEMBERS (paper clip) option is used to create a group.

The CREATE SET option is used to create a set.

The VIEW DATA option displays the View Data dialog box. It is used to view the summary data or rows of data that were used to create the value displayed on the chart. [See Viewing Data]

Grouping Data

Groups are created to combine dimension members to display them as one category. An example that comes to mind is combining members that are the same, but have a different value, like New York and NY.

Groups can also be created to combine dimension members (values). For example, the E5.13 chart displays data by territory. The Mid East and New England territories could be combined to create a group named North East, as that is how the states in these territories are often referred to. Other facts about groups are listed below.

- ☑ Groups can be used in a hierarchy.
- ☑ Groups can be used in a calculated field.
- ☑ A dimension can only be used in one group in the workbook.
- ☑ Groups are created to combine the values in a column into a separate field. This can be helpful because groups can be used to view data from a different perspective.
- ☑ Groups cannot be used to create other groups.

Exercise 5.16: Create A Group By Selecting Category Members

This exercise will show you how to create a group by selecting values displayed on a chart. While the field used in this exercise has the word "category" in it, you can use any field. For example, you can use the Customer Name or Shipped Via field to select specific customers or shipping options, to create a group.

1. Duplicate the E5.2 sheet ⇒ Rename it to `E5.16 Group by category members`.

2. In the Packaging Materials category, select the Dispenser - Bubble Wrap and Bubble Wrap members.

3. You should see the toolbar shown in Figure 5-37. Click the Group Members (paper clip) button shown in the figure. The Dispenser - Bubble Wrap and Bubble Wrap members can still be used as individual members. The other charts in the workbook that use these members will not be changed to the group that you just created.

Figure 5-37 Member toolbar

 The **GROUP MEMBERS** button is also on the Sheet tab toolbar, on the workspace.

You will see the following.

☑ The members and their values have been combined on the table, as illustrated in Figure 5-38.

☑ The **SUB CATEGORY (GROUP)** has been add to the Dimension section of the Data pane, as shown at the bottom of Figure 5-39.

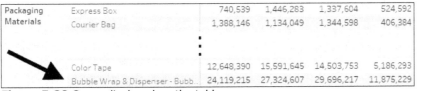

Figure 5-38 Group displayed on the table

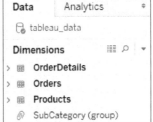

Figure 5-39 Sub category group in the Data pane

Create A Group By Selecting Marks On A Chart

This way of creating a group uses at least two dimensions on a chart to create a group.

Creating a group visually is helpful when the chart type does not have headers that can be selected, like you did in Exercise 5.16.

Figure 5-40 shows a scatter chart that has two dimensions (Territory and Sub Category).

The steps below explain how to create a group by selecting marks on a chart.

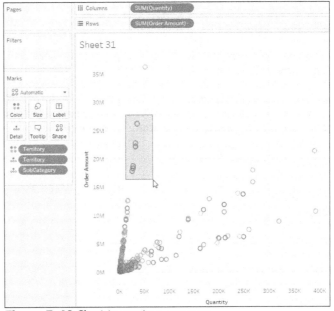

Figure 5-40 Chart to create a group on

1. On the chart, draw a box around the marks that you want to use to create a group for, as shown above in Figure 5-40.

2. On the toolbar shown in Figure 5-41, you can select **ALL DIMENSIONS**, which will create a group for the Sub Category and Territory members that are selected.

   Selecting one of the other options on the drop-down list, will only create a group for a specific dimension, which may be what you want.

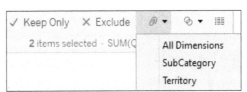

Figure 5-41 Tooltip for selected items on the chart

3. Once you select an option, the group will be created and displayed on the Data pane. You can rename or edit the group, as needed.

Exercise 5.17: Create A Group From The Data Pane

The Create Group dialog box provides more functionality then the Group Members button does, that you used in the previous exercise. Creating a group from the Data pane does not require a specific chart to be selected.

1. In the Data pane, right-click on the Territory field ⇒ Create ⇒ Group.

2. In the Field Name field, type North East.

3. Select the Mideast and New England members ⇒ Click the Group button.

   You should see the group shown in Figure 5-42. The name next to the paper clip is the alias name. You can change it here, or on the chart or by selecting the Edit Alias option on a shortcut menu.

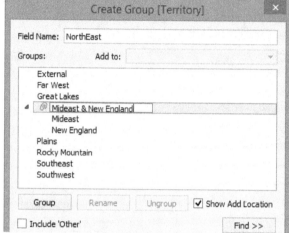

Figure 5-42 Create Group dialog box

4. Change the Alias name to North East ⇒ Click OK.

5. On a new sheet, add the North East group and State field to the Rows shelf.

6. Add the Order Amount field to the Columns shelf.

7. Select the Text table chart. Notice that the states in the Mideast and New England territories (shown in the E5.13 table) are now combined into the North East territory.

8. Add the Order Date field to the Columns shelf.

   The table should look like the one shown in Figure 5-43.

NorthEast	State	Order Date			
		2013	2014	2015	2016
External	PR	3,376,451	2,183,130	2,905,689	1,371,432
Far West	AK	3,619,528	5,105,584	4,196,407	1,799,986
	CA	10,865,514	11,848,976	14,908,784	5,806,610
	HI	383,482	156,693	374,973	774,608
		⋮			
North East	CT	1,616,296	1,488,617	1,916,559	568,265
	MA	2,876,467	4,411,562	4,269,650	1,592,047
	MD	3,058,136	3,459,551	2,525,560	1,354,046
	ME	1,753,965	2,917,005	2,681,154	1,615,574
	NH	978,527	1,099,576	2,673,691	754,965
	NJ	7,680,995	8,269,540	8,003,934	2,182,723
	NY	12,716,977	13,559,029	12,768,110	5,961,641
	PA	12,499,412	17,274,491	14,650,839	7,532,241
	VT	1,510,699	1,336,653	1,347,792	864,836

Figure 5-43 Table created from a group

9. Rename the sheet to E5.17 Table created using a group.

Understanding The Include Other Option

This option is available on the shortcut menu for a group that is used to create a chart, as shown in Figure 5-44. When applied, all of the other members are combined on the chart, into a group named "Other".

If this option is applied to the E5.17 chart, the chart would look like the one shown in Figure 5-45. All of the chart is not displayed in the figure.

NorthEast	State	Order Date			
		2013	2014	2015	2016
North East	CT	1,616,296	1,488,617	1,916,559	568,265
	MA	2,876,467	4,411,562	4,269,650	1,592,047
	MD	3,058,136	3,459,551	2,525,560	1,354,046
	ME	1,753,965	2,917,005	2,681,154	1,615,574
	NH	978,527	1,099,576	2,673,691	754,965
	NJ	7,680,995	8,269,540	8,003,934	2,182,723
	NY	12,716,977	13,559,029	12,768,110	5,961,641
	PA	12,499,412	17,274,491	14,650,839	7,532,241
	VT	1,510,699	1,336,653	1,347,792	864,836
Other	AK	3,619,528	5,105,584	4,196,407	1,799,986
	AL	5,777,202	5,078,780	6,253,981	3,975,946
	AR	3,397,027	3,678,066	3,022,145	1,595,199
	AZ	3,310,997	4,293,655	4,577,339	2,507,514
	CA	10,865,514	11,848,976	14,908,784	5,806,610

Figure 5-45 Include Other option applied to the E5.17 chart

Figure 5-44 Shortcut menu for a group field used to create a chart

Sets

Sets are created to use a subset of the data. A set is a field that is created, based on conditions. There are two types of sets that can be created, as explained below.

- ☑ A **CONSTANT SET** has dimension members that do not change. You select the members for the set. Members from more than one dimension can be used to create a set.
- ☑ A **COMPUTED SET** is dynamic because the members change, as the data changes. This is because a condition (like filter criteria) is created to determine which members should be included in the set. Examples of a computed set include, orders with an amount over $10,000 and Top 10 products based on units sold.

 Sets can only be created in Tableau Desktop and Tableau Public. They can be used and viewed in Tableau Online and Tableau Server.

Set Characteristics

Below are some features of sets.

- ☑ Once a set is created, a new section on the Data pane is created.
- ☑ A computed set is like a temporary table, as the values in the table can change.
- ☑ Sets have different icons, depending on how they are created.
- ☑ The same dimension can be used in more than one set.
- ☑ Two sets that use the same dimension can be combined.
- ☑ Using a set is a way to filter data.
- ☑ A set can be created from a filter.
- ☑ When a set is added to the Filters shelf, it displays an In/Out option. This option indicates whether the values fall in the set criteria or are outside of the set criteria.
- ☑ While sets are often added to the Filters shelf, they can also be added to the Rows and Columns shelves and the Marks card.
- ☑ Sets can be used like any other field.
- ☑ A set can be used to create a hierarchy.

☑ A set can be used to create a calculated field.

☑ When Actions are created, sets are automatically created.

☑ The options for creating a set are the same as the options for creating a group.

Exercise 5.18: Create A Constant Set

In this exercise, you will learn how to create a constant set for the Dispenser Products sub category, then add the set to a filter.

1. Duplicate the E5.2 sheet ⇒ Rename it to `E5.18 Constant set`.

2. Select the following sub categories on the chart: Clear Tape, Dispenser - Tape, Dispenser - Bubble Wrap, Color Tape and Bubble Wrap.

3. On the popup toolbar, select the **CREATE SET** option, shown in Figure 5-46.

Figure 5-46 Create Set toolbar option

4. On the Create Set dialog box, type `Dispenser Products` in the Name field, as shown in Figure 5-47.

    As shown in the figure, the set can be added to the Filters shelf.

    The other option is to drag the set from the Data pane to the Filters shelf.

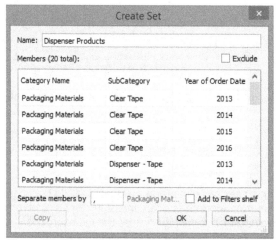

Figure 5-47 Create Set dialog box

5. Check the Add to Filters shelf option ⇒ Click OK.
    At the bottom of the Data pane, you should see the Sets section, with the set that you just created.

Understanding The Show In/Out Of Set Option

This option is on the shortcut menu for a set that is added to a shelf. When selected, it displays the dialog box shown in Figure 5-48.

Select the **IN** option when you only want to display records, on the chart, for the members in the set.

Select the **OUT** option to display members that are not in the set.

The options on the Condition and Top tabs are the same as the ones on the Filter dialog box.

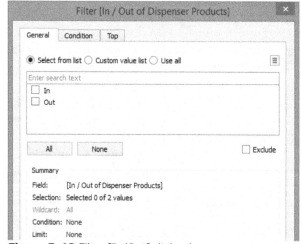

Figure 5-48 Filter [In/Out] dialog box

Exercise 5.19: Create A Computed (Dynamic) Set

In this exercise, you will learn how to create a set that displays customer order totals that are equal to or greater than 2 million.

Create The Dynamic Set

1. Right-click on the Customer Name field ⇒ Create ⇒ Create Set.

2. In the Name field, type Order Total >= 2 Million.

3. On the Condition tab, select the By field option ⇒ Open the first drop-down list and select the Order Amount field ⇒ Open the operators drop-down list and select >=.

4. In the next field type 2,000,000, as shown in Figure 5-49 ⇒ Click OK.

Figure 5-49 Filter criteria for a set

Create The Chart

1. On a new sheet, select the following fields: Customer Name, Order Date and Order Amount.

2. Select the Text tables chart. Notice that there are 663 rows displayed in the table.

3. Drag the set that you just created to the Filters shelf ⇒ Display the drop-down list for the set ⇒ Show In/Out of set ⇒ Select In. Notice that there are now 53 rows displayed in the table.

    If more rows are added to the table that have an order amount greater than 2 million, they will automatically be displayed in the table. This is what makes the set dynamic.

4. Rename the sheet to E5.19 Computed dynamic set.

Exercise 5.20: Create a Set From A Filter

If you have created a filter that you would like to use on more than one chart in the workbook, creating a set from the filter is an option. A set can be added to more than one chart in a workbook. The set that you will learn how to create in this exercise is based on a filter that has Top 10 criteria, for the Order Amount field. The set will then be added to a different chart.

1. Display the E5.9 sheet.

2. Open the drop-down list for the Sub Category filter ⇒ Create Set.

3. In the Name field, type Top 10 Order Amount For Sub Category Field.
    If you view the criteria on the Top tab, you will see that it is the same criteria that was shown earlier in Figure 5-25. You should see the Top 10 set at the bottom of the Data pane.

4. Duplicate the E5.2 sheet ⇒ Rename it to E5.20 Set created from a filter.

5. Drag the Top 10 set to the Filters shelf.

The chart shown in Figure 5-50 displays the top 10 sub categories, based on the total sales for the sub category.

Category Name	Sub Category	Order Date			
		2013≞	2014	2015	2016
Clothing	Jacket	11,838,591	13,371,035	12,501,359	5,505,267
	Slippers	21,636,463	23,973,307	24,858,649	9,682,260
	T-Shirt	27,132,392	31,705,923	26,858,588	13,127,490
Clothing Novelty	Novelty	8,493,622	10,204,366	8,793,880	3,631,925
Computer Novelty	USB Drive	13,351,569	15,291,372	16,411,297	6,905,534
	Mug	42,789,622	49,776,616	50,287,724	20,695,715
Packaging Materials	Shipping Carton	10,434,147	11,891,527	12,331,962	4,706,784
	Color Tape	12,648,390	15,591,645	14,503,753	5,186,293
	Bubble Wrap	21,174,354	23,765,985	25,925,243	9,882,621
Toys	Remote Control Car	7,773,048	11,104,167	10,069,900	3,896,522

Figure 5-50 Top 10 chart created using a set

Making Columns In A Table Wider
There may be times when you cannot see all of the data in a column. For example, in Figure 5-50 above, all of the first column heading is not visible. To make a column wider, place the mouse pointer in the table at the end of the column, as illustrated in Figure 5-51. Then drag the column to the right. When dragging the column, you will see a dashed vertical line, as shown in Figure 5-52.

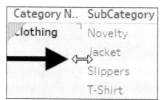

Figure 5-51 Mouse pointer in position to change the column width

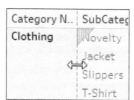

Figure 5-52 Column width being changed

Viewing Data

Earlier in this book you learned how to view data on the Data Source tab. If you have not noticed, you have not used the Data Source tab in a while. Some of the basic tasks that you learned how to do on the Data Source tab, like adding another data source to the workbook file and changing the fields data type can be done on a sheet tab.

While you can switch to the Data Source tab to view data, you can view the data used to create a chart. You may find this more suited to your needs because you will not have to view all of the rows of data or all of the fields in the data source, like you would on the Data Source tab. If the need arises to view data, the steps below show you how.

Tableau Public does not have all of the options that Tableau Desktop has on the View Data dialog box.

1. Click on the tab for the chart that you want to see the data for.

2. Analysis menu ⇒ View Data.

You will see the dialog box shown in Figure 5-53. The **SUMMARY TAB** displays the actual data displayed on the chart.

The **COPY** button is enabled when rows of data are selected on the dialog box. It is used to copy the selected rows to the clipboard, so that the data can be pasted into another application.

The **EXPORT ALL** button, exports the data to a .csv file.

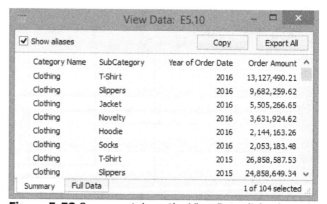

Figure 5-53 Summary tab on the View Data dialog box

The **FULL DATA TAB** shown in Figure 5-54, displays the fields and rows of data used to create the chart.

Check the **SHOW ALL FIELDS** option, if you want to see all of the fields in the data source.

Figure 5-54 Full Data tab on the View Data dialog box

View The Data For A Mark

You may want to only view the data for a portion of a chart, like a bar or slice on a chart. Having the option to view a subset of the data on the chart is helpful when something on the chart does not look quite right. The steps below show you how to view a subset of the data displayed on a chart.

1. Display the chart that you want to view data for.

2. On the chart, right-click on the mark that you want to view ⇒ View Data, as shown in Figure 5-55.

   As illustrated in the figure, more than one mark can be selected.

   You will see the View Data dialog box shown earlier in Figure 5-53.

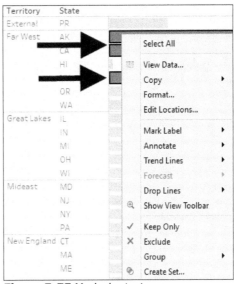

Figure 5-55 Mark shortcut menu

Exercise 5.21: Create A Bookmark File

This file type is used to share one sheet, in a workbook that has many sheets, with other people. By default, bookmark files are saved in the My Tableau Repository/Bookmarks folder, but you can save them in another location. Bookmark files save the following:

- ☑ Connection information.
- ☑ The data and metadata for the sheet.
- ☑ Calculated fields used on the sheet.

 A bookmark file cannot be created using **TABLEAU PUBLIC**. It also cannot be created for a dashboard or story.

While you can copy a sheet from one workbook to another workbook, creating a bookmark file is probably a better solution, as you will not have to remember which workbook has the sheet (chart) that you want to share.

1. Display the E5.15 sheet.

2. Window menu ⇒ Bookmark ⇒ Create Bookmark.

3. Navigate to the folder that you created for this book ⇒ Save the file as E5.21 Bookmark file.

Opening A Bookmark File

While a bookmark file is saved with its own file name, when you open it, it is opened inside of the workbook that you currently have open. If you do not want the bookmark file to be added to the workbook that you have open, close the workbook (not Tableau) before opening the bookmark file.

To open the bookmark file, File ⇒ Open ⇒ Navigate to the folder where the bookmark file is stored ⇒ Double-click on the bookmark file.

Exercise 5.22: Copy Sheets To A Different Workbook

In Chapter 2, you learned how to import one workbook into another workbook. The concept of copying sheets to a different workbook, is the same concept.

In this exercise you will copy sheets to a new workbook, that will be used in the next chapter.

> **TABLEAU PUBLIC** does not support copying sheets. Instead, complete the steps below.
> 1. Save the Chapter 5 workbook with the name in step 4 below.
> 2. Delete all of the tabs in the Chapter 6 workbook, except the ones in step 1 below.

1. Select the following sheets: E5.2, E5.4, E5.7, E5.8 and E5.9.

2. Right-click on one of the selected tabs ⇒ Copy.

3. File ⇒ New. When the new workbook is displayed, Data ⇒ Paste. You should see the five sheets in the new workbook.

4. Save the workbook in your folder, as Chapter 6 Calculations and parameters.

CREATING CALCULATED FIELDS

After reading this chapter and completing the exercises, you will know how to:

- ☑ Create calculated fields
- ☑ Use the ATTR, CONTAINS and DATEDIFF functions
- ☑ Create Ad-Hoc calculations
- ☑ Use the Quick Table Calculation options to display percent of total, running totals and YTD totals
- ☑ Create table calculations
- ☑ Drill down on total calculations
- ☑ Create parameters

CHAPTER 6

Calculations

As you have seen in the previous chapters, you can get a lot accomplished in Tableau by using the built-in aggregate functions, clicking, dropping and dragging. As a famous chef says, "Let's kick it up a notch". By that I mean, learning how to create calculated fields and parameters opens up another level of functionality that you can add to charts. If you have created formulas in a spreadsheet, you are already familiar with how calculations are created and used in Tableau.

All of the data that has been used so far to create charts, came from a data source. There will be times when data that you need to display, does not exist in a data source. Examples of data not stored in a data source are customer total order amounts per quarter, order processing time and line item total. Data, like the previous examples, that can be calculated, is usually not stored in a data source. This is why the data in a data source is often referred to as **RAW DATA**.

Types Of Calculations

There are several ways to create calculations, as explained below.

① **BASIC CALCULATIONS** This type includes aggregate calculations. Basic calculations are processed at the database level, which creates the query used to create charts.

② **TABLE CALCULATIONS** These calculations are processed against the records returned from the query. The result set from the query usually has fewer records then the data source has. In addition to using table calculation functions, **QUICK TABLE CALCULATIONS** (pre-built calculations) can be used.

③ **LEVEL OF DETAIL (LOD) CALCULATIONS** These calculations are processed at the database level. They calculate aggregations that are outside of the level of detail displayed on the chart. Level of detail expressions replace writing SQL, to control the granularity of data displayed on a chart.

Calculation Data Types

The following data types are supported in calculations.

☑ **STRING** Most of the time, this data type has text, but it can support numeric data.

☑ **NUMBER** The numeric values supported are numbers with decimal points and integers.

☑ **DATE AND DATE/TIME** These data types support the default date hierarchy that was covered in Chapter 5.

☑ **BOOLEAN** Stores the values true and false.

Aggregate Data

Fields in the Dimensions and Measures sections of the Data pane can be aggregated, as explained below.

Dimensions

The functions shown in Figure 6-1 are not automatically applied to fields in the Dimensions section that are added to a shelf. You have to add them manually.

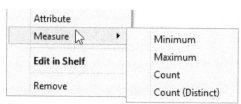

Figure 6-1 Dimension aggregate functions

Measures

As you have seen, when a field in the Measures section, of the Data pane, is added to a shelf, it is automatically assigned the SUM aggregate function.

You can accept this aggregate function or change it to a different function, as shown in Figure 6-2.

You can also remove the aggregate function by clicking on (the checked) **AGGREGATE MEASURES** option on the Analysis menu.

Removing the aggregate function is known as **DISAGGREGATING DATA**.

The **EDIT IN SHELF** option is used to edit the calculated field in the shelf.

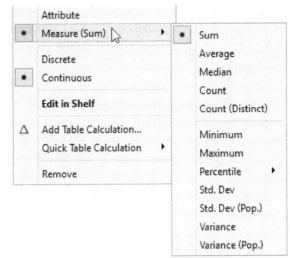

Figure 6-2 Measure aggregate functions

Attribute Option

As shown above in Figures 6-1 and 6-2, dimensions and measures have this option. When selected, this option defines the field as an Attribute, by applying the ATTR function to the field. If selected, the **ATTRIBUTE** option (which is the **ATTR FUNCTION**) returns the value of an expression if it only has one value for all of the rows in the group. If that is not the case, the Attribute option will display an asterisk (*). Null values are ignored.

> **What Is AGG?**
> When an aggregated measure is used in a calculation that is placed on a shelf, **AGG** will be displayed before the field name, as shown later in Figure 6-10, at the bottom of the Marks card. This is done automatically. It signifies that the field has a calculation which uses an aggregate function. What you will find is that the aggregation cannot be changed.

Calculated Fields

Calculated fields are fields that have data that is currently not stored in the data source. These fields are created on the fly, so to speak, because they are calculated each time the report is run or in the case of Tableau, each time the chart is refreshed. Calculations that are created using the Calculated Fields option are available to all sheets in the workbook. Calculated fields can also be created that are sheet specific.

Calculated Field Tips

- ☑ Calculated fields are created by using formulas. These formulas usually include at least one field from the data source and a function.
- ☑ Calculated fields can be created from the Columns or Rows shelves.
- ☑ Calculated fields are created for dimensions and measures.
- ☑ Calculated fields can be created from a field in the Data pane.
- ☑ Calculated fields can be created from the Analysis menu.
- ☑ If text is used in a formula, it has to be surrounded by double quotes.

Figure 6-3 shows a calculated field. It uses two fields from a data source. While both fields have brackets, they are only required when a field name has a space. I use brackets for all fields to maintain consistency.

Figure 6-3 Calculated field

Options For Creating A Calculated Field

There are two ways to create a calculated field: Use the Calculation Editor (also known as the Formula Editor) and create an Ad-Hoc calculation.

Calculation Editor

The window shown in Figure 6-4 is used to create a calculated field. It can be opened by using one of the options listed below. Clicking on the triangle illustrated in the figure, displays functions by category, that you can select to use to create a formula. The drop-down list on the right side of the window, lists the categories of functions. The default is All, which displays all of the functions. Using this window is optional. You can type the function that you need, right on the Calculation Editor.

How To Open The Calculation Editor

☑ Data pane ⇒ Right-click on any field on the pane ⇒ Create ⇒ Calculated field. If the formula that you create will use an existing field, right-click on the field and it will be added to the window, as shown in Figure 6-4.

☑ Data pane ⇒ Dimensions section drop-down list ⇒ Create Calculated Field.

☑ Analysis menu ⇒ Create Calculated Field.

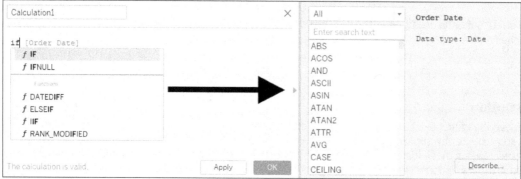

Figure 6-4 Calculation Editor

Calculation Editor Tips

☑ What you type in the **NAME FIELD**, is the name that will be displayed in the Data pane for the calculated field that you create.

☑ The **FORMULA BOX** is below the name field. It is where you type in the formula. As shown above in Figure 6-4, on the left, the formula box has an auto fill feature. It is enabled as you are typing the formula. You can select an option for the drop-down list or keep typing.

☑ When you create a formula, it will be displayed in various colors, as explained below.

  ☑ Fields are displayed in orange.

  ☑ Functions are displayed in blue.

  ☑ Parameters are displayed in purple.

  ☑ Comments are displayed in green.

☑ Fields can be dragged from the Data pane to the formula box.

While calculated fields can create numeric data, they can also be used to create text fields, boolean fields (true/false) and date fields. The options discussed below can be used to create formulas for calculated fields.

☑ **FIELDS** in the data source.

☑ **OPERATORS** [See Operators]

☑ **FUNCTIONS** for each data type, logical functions, conversion functions and more.

☑ **COMMENTS** used to create notes and documentation for the calculated field. [In the Data pane, right-click on the field ⇒ Default Properties ⇒ Comment]

☑ **PARAMETERS** are used to get data from the person viewing the report. The data will be used as a variable in the calculated field.

Operators

Operators are used for basic math formulas and comparison of text, numeric values and dates. Popular operators are listed below.

= equal to	> greater than	< less than	+ addition	* multiply
<> not equal to	>= greater than or equal to	<= less than or equal to	- subtraction	

Functions

Functions are pre-built formulas. There are functions for each data type, as well as logical and conversion functions. Some of these are shown in the figures at the end of this section. The biggest difference between creating formulas in a spreadsheet and in Tableau, is that an equal sign is not used at the beginning of a formula in Tableau. In addition to the categories of functions discussed below, there are also **PASS-THROUGH FUNCTIONS** (functions that send SQL expressions to the database) and functions that are only used for specific data sources. Below are the categories of functions in Tableau.

- ☑ **AGGREGATE FUNCTIONS** were covered in Chapter 4, Table, 4-1. The ATTR function is also an aggregate function.
- ☑ **STRING FUNCTIONS** are used to manipulate text data. Figure 6-5 shows some of the string functions.
- ☑ **NUMBER FUNCTIONS** are used to manipulate numeric data. Figure 6-6 shows some of the number functions.
- ☑ **DATE FUNCTIONS** is a popular function category because many reports and charts are date driven. You have already seen the YEAR and MONTH functions in use. Figure 6-7 shows some of the date functions.
- ☑ **LOGICAL FUNCTIONS** are used to test to see if data meets the criteria that you create. Based on the result of the test, an action will be taken. Figure 6-8 shows some of the logical functions.
- ☑ **TABLE CALCULATION FUNCTIONS** are used to customize table calculations. These functions are applied to the entire table.
- ☑ **TYPE CONVERSION FUNCTIONS** are used to change the data type for a field.
- ☑ **USER FUNCTIONS** are created to filter who can see which records on a chart. These functions are used when the charts are stored on Tableau Server.

Figure 6-5 String functions   **Figure 6-6** Number functions   **Figure 6-7** Date functions   **Figure 6-8** Logical functions

If...Then...Else Statements

This is one of the most used lines of programming code, probably the most popular Logical function. This statement is used to set different options, based on what you need to happen when the data is evaluated. The syntax is below.

If **EXPRESSION/CONDITION** Then **TRUE STATEMENT** Else **FALSE STATEMENT**

Parts Of The If Then Else Statement Explained

① The **EXPRESSION/CONDITION** must evaluate to true or false.
② The **TRUE STATEMENT** will execute if the Expression/Condition is true.
③ The **FALSE STATEMENT** will execute if the Expression/Condition is false.

The plain English translation of an If Then Else statement is: **IF** Choice A meets this condition, **THEN** do X, **ELSE** do Y.

Walk through the examples in Table 6-1 to gain a better understanding of If Then Else statements. Fill in the column on the right, based on the numbers in the Choice A column.

Choice A	What Does Field B=
26	
1	
25	

Table 6-1 If Then Else examples

If Choice A is greater than 25, then Field B = 100, else Field B = 0.
It may help to understand If...Then...Else statements if you think of them as a true or false test question. In the example above, the test question can be worded as "Is Choice A greater than 25?" There are two possible answers:

① Yes it is (True). If it is, Field B would be set to 100.
② No it isn't (False). If it isn't, Field B would be set to 0.

How Did You Do?

Table 6-2 contains the answers for the second column in Table 6-1. The third column in the table explains the answer.

Choice A	Field B=	Reason
26	100	The answer is 100 because 26 is greater than 25.
1	0	The answer is 0 because 1 is less than 25.
25	0	The answer is 0 because 25 is not greater than 25.

Table 6-2 Answers for Table 6-1

To complicate If statements even more, there can be multiple true and false statements in the same If Then Else statement. When this is the case, the additional statements have to be enclosed in parenthesis. If Then Else statements with multiple true and false statements are known as **NESTED IF STATEMENTS**.

Tableau also uses the **IIF STATEMENT**, which is a variation of the IF statement. It works the same as the If statement discussed above. It selects one of the two choices, depending on the evaluation of the expression. I know IIF as the Immediate IF statement. If you have used the If statement, you will be able to easily adapt to using the IIF statement, even though the syntax is different. For example, IIF statements do not use the words "Then" or "Else".

Exercise 6.1: Use The ATTR Function To Calculate The Order Amount By Territory

The calculation that you will create in this exercise will only display order amount totals for a specific territory.

1. In the Chapter 6 Calculations workbook that you created in Chapter 5, open the Calculation Editor ⇒ Type `Territory-Attr` as the file name.

2. Type the formula shown below ⇒ When done, you should see a message at the bottom of the editor that says that the calculation is valid.

```
If ATTR([Territory]) = "Plains" then Sum([Order Amount])
END
```

3. Click Apply ⇒ Click OK. In the Measures section, you will see the calculated field that you just created, as shown at the bottom of Figure 6-9.

   On a new sheet, add the Territory and State fields to the Rows shelf.

Figure 6-9 Calculated field

4. Data pane ⇒ Show the filter for the Territory and State fields.

5. Drag the Territory-Attr field to the Text button on the Marks card.

   The table should look like the one shown in Figure 6-10.

   Notice that the "Plains" territory is the only one that displays totals.

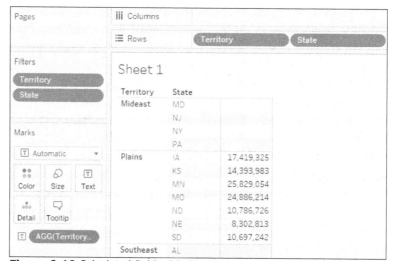

Figure 6-10 Calculated field added to the table

6. Rename the sheet to `E6.1 ATTR function`.

Exercise 6.2: Calculate The Line Item Total

In this exercise, you will learn how to create a formula that will calculate the total for each item ordered.

1. On the Calculation Editor, type `Line Item Total` as the field name.

2. Type the formula shown below. It should look like the one shown earlier in Figure 6-3 ⇒ Click OK.

   `[Quantity] * [Unit Price]`

3. On a new sheet add the Order ID, Customer Name and Product Name fields to the Rows shelf. When warned that 73595 members will be added, click the **ADD ALL MEMBERS** button. Later in this exercise, you will create a filter to reduce the number of rows.

4. On the shortcut menu for the Line Item Total field, select Default Properties ⇒ Number Format ⇒ Select Currency (Custom) ⇒ Change the Decimal places option to zero ⇒ Click OK.

5. Drag the Line Item Total field to the Text button on the Marks card.

6. Create a filter for the Order ID field to only display Order ID's 1 to 5.

7. Rename the sheet to `E6.2 Line item total calculation`.

   The chart should look like the one shown in Figure 6-11.

Order ID	Customer Name	Product Name	
1	Aakriti Byrraju	Ride on toy sedan car (Black)..	$2,300
2	Bala Dixit	Developer joke mug - old C dev..	$117
		USB food flash drive - chocolat..	$288
3	Tailspin Toys (Tomnolen, ..	Superhero action jacket (Blue).	$90
4	Tailspin Toys (Lakemore, OH)	Developer joke mug - old C dev..	$26
		Furry gorilla with big eyes slip..	$160
		Permanent marker black 5mm..	$288
5	Sara Huiting	Dinosaur battery-powered sli..	$96
		Large sized bubblewrap roll 5..	$480
		Plush shark slippers (Gray) L	$128

Figure 6-11 Line item total formula

Exercise 6.3: Combine String Field Values

In this exercise, you will learn how to create a calculated field that combines the contents of two string fields. This will allow the data in both fields to be displayed as one field.

1. On the Calculation Editor, type `Rep First and Last Name`, as the field name.

2. From the Data pane, drag the First Name field to the editor.

3. Press the space bar and type + " " +. There is a space between the quotes.

4. Drag the Last Name field to the end of the formula, as shown below ⇒ Click OK.

   `[FirstName] + " " + [LastName]`

5. Duplicate the E6.2 chart ⇒ Rename it `E6.3 Combine string fields`.

6. Drag the Rep First and Last Name field (it is below the Sales Reps table, in the Dimensions section on the Data pane), to the Rows shelf and place it after the Order ID field. The first three columns of the table should look like the ones shown in Figure 6-12.

Order ID ≟	Rep First and L..	Customer Name
1	Kayla Woodcock	Aakriti Byrraju
2	Anthony Grosse	Bala Dixit
3	Amy Trefl	Tailspin Toys (Tomnolen, ..

Figure 6-12 Combined calculated field

Exercise 6.4: Use The CONTAINS String Function

In this exercise you will learn how to create a formula that selects records that have the word "Novelty" in the Category Name field, in the Products table.

1. On the Data pane, right-click on the Category Name field ⇒ Create ⇒ Calculated Field.

2. Type Novelty Categories as the field name.

3. Create the formula shown below. Notice that the Novelty Categories calculated field has a boolean data type.

    CONTAINS([Category Name], "Novelty")

4. On a new sheet, add the following fields to the Rows shelf: Category Name and Product Name.

5. Add the Order Amount field to the Columns shelf ⇒ Change the chart type to a text table.

6. Add the Novelty Categories field to the Filters shelf ⇒

    Select the True option, shown in Figure 6-13 ⇒

    Click OK.

Figure 6-13 Filter options to only display records that have "Novelty" in the Category Name field

7. Rename the sheet to
    E6.4 CONTAINS string function.

    If you scroll down the table, you will see that each of the Category names has the word "Novelty", as shown in Figure 6-14.

Category Name	Product Name	
Clothing Novelty	Halloween skull mask (Gray) L	4,224,647
	Halloween skull mask (Gray) M	4,241,159
	Halloween skull mask (Gray) S	3,574,038
	Halloween skull mask (Gray) XL	3,885,218
	Halloween zombie mask (Light Brown) L	3,589,935
	Halloween zombie mask (Light Brown) M	4,487,315
	Halloween zombie mask (Light Brown) S	3,398,344
	Halloween zombie mask (Light Brown) ..	3,723,137
Computer Novelty	DBA joke mug - daaaaaa-ta (Black)	4,260,050

Figure 6-14 Table filtered by a calculated field

Date Functions

Table 6-3 explains some of the more popular date functions.

Function	What The Function Does . . .
Now	Uses the system date on your computer.
DateAdd	Increments a date field by intervals, including days, weeks, months and years.
DateDiff	Calculates the difference between the start and end date fields used in the formula.
Month	Extracts the month from a Date or Date/Time field and returns a whole number. This will calculate the month number (1-12).
Year	Extracts the year from a Date or Date/Time field and returns a whole number. This will calculate the year.

Table 6-3 Date functions explained

Exercise 6.5: Create A Date Formula To Calculate The Order Processing Time

In this exercise you will create a formula to calculate how long it is between the day an order is placed and the day the order was shipped. This is known as the order processing time. The result of this calculation can be used to let you know if the expected number of days orders need to be shipped in, is met. For example, if all orders need to be shipped in three days, any order with a number greater than three in the calculated field, indicates that the order was not shipped within the expected time frame. In Tableau Public, this exercise ran painfully slow for me, when creating it.

Create The Order Processing Time Calculated Field

1. Open the Calculation Editor ⇒ Name the field Order Processing Time.

2. Create the formula shown below.

    DATEDIFF('day',[Order Date], [Shipped Date])

3. Add the following fields to the Rows shelf: Order ID, Customer Name, Order Date, Shipped Date and Order Amount ⇒ Add all members of the Order ID field.

4. On the Rows shelf, display the shortcut menu for the Order Date field ⇒ Select the **EXACT DATE** option, then select the Discrete option, on the shortcut menu, if it is not already selected.

5. Repeat step 4 for the Shipped Date field.

6. On the Rows shelf, display the shortcut menu for the Order Amount field ⇒ Select Discrete.

 I have used the DATEDIFF function in several software packages. The function works as expected in some software packages and in others, not so much. When I added the Order Processing Time calculated field to the chart, it displayed the values in the last column, shown in Figure 6-15. Clearly, there is a problem with the order processing formula, in terms of how the DATEDIFF function processes data, because all of the order and shipped dates are the same. This means that the order processing time should be the same, for all of the rows shown in the figure. This is an example of paying attention to and understanding the data displayed on a visualization. My first thought was to change the value to Discrete. I did that, but it did not resolve the problem. After trying other options, I finally figured it out. The next step resolved the issued.

Order ID	Customer Name	Order Date	Shipped Date	Order Amount	
1	Aakriti Byrraju	01/01/2013	01/02/2013	23,153.23	1
2	Bala Dixit	01/01/2013	01/02/2013	110.48	2
3	Tailspin Toys (Tomnolen, ..	01/01/2013	01/02/2013	132.56	1
4	Tailspin Toys (Lakemore, ..	01/01/2013	01/02/2013	2,507.22	3
5	Sara Huiting	01/01/2013	01/02/2013	3,447.57	3
6	Alinne Matos	01/01/2013	01/02/2013	2,595.6	3
7	Wingtip Toys (Trumansbu..	01/01/2013	01/02/2013	10.12	4

Figure 6-15 Result of the DATEDIFF function formula

7. In the Data pane, display the shortcut menu for the Order Processing Time field ⇒ Select **CONVERT TO DIMENSION**.

8. Drag the Order Processing Time field (now in the Dimensions section on the Data pane) to the Text button on the Marks card. Now, all of the rows shown above in Figure 6-15 have the same order processing time, which is correct. If you display the row in the table for Order ID 270, you will see the values shown in Figure 6-16. This is much better <smile> ⇒ On the shortcut menu, select the Discrete option.

Order ID	Customer Name	Order Date	Shipped Date	Order Amount	
270	Svetlana Todorovic	01/03/2013	01/04/2013	680.09	1
271	Tailspin Toys (Howells, NE)	01/04/2013	01/07/2013	104.94	3
272	Wingtip Toys (Goodings G..	01/04/2013	01/07/2013	2,587.31	3
273	Tailspin Toys (Tunnelhill, ..	01/04/2013	01/07/2013	12,832.9	3
274	Seo-yun Paik	01/04/2013	01/07/2013	2,647.54	3
275	Tailspin Toys (Great Neck ..	01/04/2013	01/07/2013	265.16	3
276	Tailspin Toys (Airport Dri..	01/04/2013	01/07/2013	2,674.6	3
277	Wingtip Toys (Lucasville, ..	01/04/2013	01/07/2013	2,622.07	3
278	Leyla Siavashi	01/04/2013	01/07/2013	132.58	3
279	Kamala Nishad	01/05/2013	01/07/2013	8,019.18	2
280	Tailspin Toys (Fieldbrook, ..	01/05/2013	01/07/2013	76.02	2

Figure 6-16 Revised order processing time values

Ad-Hoc Calculations

This type of calculation is created and edited on a shelf. If you have created formulas in a spreadsheet, creating an ad-hoc calculation will be familiar. Unlike calculated fields, by default, ad-hoc calculations do not have a name. This means that they can only be used on the chart that they are created for. If you decide that you want to use an ad-hoc calculation for other charts in the workbook, drag the ad-hoc calculation to the Data pane. When prompted, type in a name for the calculation. There are three ways to create an ad-hoc calculation, as explained below.

☑ Double-click on a field on a shelf. The appearance of the field will change, as shown at the top of Figure 6-17.

☑ Double-click on an empty shelf or double-click on an empty part of a shelf to create a new calculation. You will see an empty field, as shown at the end of the Rows shelf, in Figure 6-17.

☑ Select the New Calculation option on a shelf drop-down list, as shown later in Figure 6-19.

Figure 6-17 New field ready to be created

 Ad-Hoc calculations can only be created from the Columns and Rows shelves and from the Marks card. Once a calculated field is created, or you drag an ad-hoc field to the Data pane, it is a good idea to format the numeric data for the new field (right-click on the field ⇒ Number Format), just like you would format numeric fields in the data source.

Once you understand functions and how to create formulas, you will probably find that ad-hoc calculations are the quickest way to create new fields of data. Like the Calculation Editor, when creating an ad-hoc calculation, the auto fill feature is enabled. What I like about this method of creating formulas, is that they can be saved and used in other charts, if they are dragged to the Data pane and given a name.

Exercise 6.6: Create Ad-Hoc Calculations

In this exercise you will use the ad-hoc method to create the line item total and full name calculations that you created earlier in this chapter, using he Calculation Editor. The goal is to demonstrate the differences between the two options for creating a calculation.

Create The Rep Name Ad-Hoc Calculation

1. On a new sheet, double-click in the Rows shelf.

2. In the pill, type the formula shown below, then press Enter. You should see a table that displays the sales rep's first and last names. Right now, the calculation can only be used on the sheet that it was created on, but that is about to change <smile>.

   `[FirstName] + " " + [LastName]`

3. Drag the pill in the Rows shelf to the Dimensions section of the Data pane. You will see the formula shown in Figure 6-18.

   Figure 6-18 Ad-hoc calculation

4. Rename the field to Rep Full Name. Notice that the name on the pill on the Rows shelf and on the table have been updated with the field name.

Another Way To Add A New Field To A Shelf
In the previous part of the exercise, you double-clicked to add a pill to a shelf. There is another way.
Hold the mouse pointer to the right of the shelf name ⇒ Display the shortcut menu shown in Figure 6-19 ⇒
Select **NEW CALCULATION**. The options that are displayed on the shortcut menu depend on whether or not the
shelf is empty.

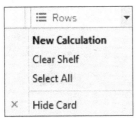
Figure 6-19 Rows shelf shortcut menu

Create The Line Item Ad-Hoc Calculation

In this part of the exercise, you will create a formula to calculate the line item total, like you did in Exercise 6.2.

1. Create the formula shown below on the Rows shelf.

   ```
   [Quantity] * [Unit Price]
   ```

2. Drag the calculation to the Data pane.

 Based on the calculation, the field will automatically be added to the correct section (dimensions or measures)
of the Data pane.

3. Rename the field to Item Total.

Add An Ad-Hoc Calculation To A Chart

In this part of the exercise, you will remove an existing field on a chart and replace it with an ad-hoc calculation.

1. Duplicate the E6.3 sheet ⇒ Rename it to E6.6 Ad-hoc calculation.

2. Remove the Rep First and Last Name field from the Rows shelf.

3. Add the Rep Full Name ad-hoc calculated field to the Rows shelf, after the Order ID field. The chart should look
   the same as the one on the E6.3 sheet.

Table Calculation Types

Just like calculated fields, this type of calculation uses a formula also. The difference is that the functions are built into
Tableau, just like the aggregated functions are. The difference between aggregated functions is that they often
calculate values across two or more rows of data. Table calculations are processed locally, like Quick Table calculations.

Table calculations are a way to transform the values from a measure used on a chart. This is based on the dimensions
in the level of detail. There are three types of Table Calculations that can be created, as explained below.

☑ **QUICK TABLE CALCULATION** The options shown in Figure 6-20 create totals, differences and growth
calculations. They are available for numeric fields on the Columns, Rows, Pages and Filters shelves. They are
also available on the Marks card. Depending on the shelf that you select the Quick Table Calculation option
from, determines the options that are available. These functions are used to change the values displayed.
They do not require you to manually type the formula. Because these functions are applied to values
displayed on the chart, they are processed locally, instead of being processed at the database level, like
calculated fields are. (1)

☑ **ADD TABLE CALCULATION** This option is used to create a table calculation using the options shown in
Figure 6-21. The options shown are calculations that can be applied to a measure, to change the measures
values. (1)

☑ **APPLY TO TOTALS** This option, shown in Figure 6-22, is available from the Filters shelf. It is used to add totals by using a table calculation filter to apply the totals. This means that you can select/decide when a table calculation filter should be applied to the totals. This option is available for a calculated field that is added to the Filters shelf. The table or chart must already have totals displayed.

(1) This calculation option is available for numeric fields on the Filters, Columns and Rows shelves, as well as the Marks card.

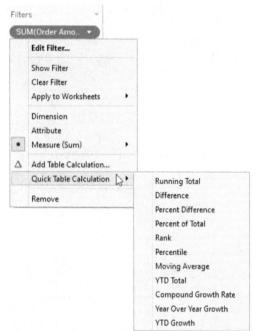

Figure 6-20 Quick Table Calculation options

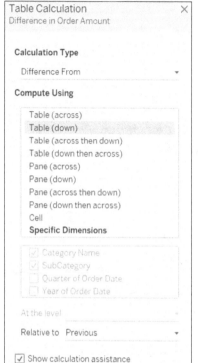

Figure 6-21 Add Table Calculation options

Figure 6-22 Apply to Totals option

Understanding Data Granularity

Data granularity refers to the level of detail displayed on a chart. Granularity is created using dimension fields. For example, Exercise 5.8 displayed data at the quarter level. Data displayed at the quarter level has a higher granularity, then data displayed at the year level. The higher the granularity, the more rows or columns will be displayed on the table.

Quick Table Calculations

Figure 6-23 shows the Quick Table Calculation options. These are built-in functions.

The exercises in this section will show you how to use the following functions: Running Total, Percent of Total and YTD Total. (YTD stands for Year to Date).

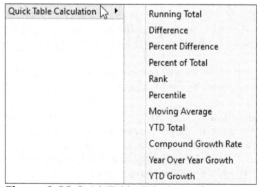

Figure 6-23 Quick Table Calculation functions

Exercise 6.7: Create A Running Total Calculation

This exercise will show you how to display a running total of the Order Amount.

1. Rename a new sheet to `E6.7 Running Total`.

2. Add the Order Date field to the Rows shelf ⇒ Click the plus sign in front of the field name, to display the quarters on the table.

3. Display the shortcut menu for the Order Amount field ⇒ Default Properties ⇒ Number Format ⇒ Number (Custom) ⇒ Change the Decimal places field to zero.

4. Add the Order Amount field to the end of the Rows shelf ⇒ On the shortcut menu, select Discrete.

5. Add the **MEASURE NAMES** field to the Columns shelf ⇒ On the shortcut menu, select **EDIT ALIASES** ⇒ Click in the Value (Alias) column for the No Measure Value member ⇒ Change the alias to `Running Total`, as shown in Figure 6-24.

Member	Has Alias	Value (Alias)
No Measure Value		Running Total
Number of Records		Number of Records
Order Amount		Order Amount
Quantity		Quantity
Unit Price		Unit Price

Edit Aliases [Measure Names]

Figure 6-24 Alias name changed

6. Add the Measure Names field to the Filters shelf ⇒ Clear all of the options except the Order Amount field.

7. Drag the Order Amount field to the Text button ⇒ Display the shortcut menu ⇒ Quick Table Calculation ⇒ Running Total. The table should look like the one shown in Figure 6-25.

Year of Order Date	Quarter of Order Date	Order Amount	Running Total
2013	Q1	37,560,393	37,560,393
	Q2	81,696,577	119,256,970
	Q3	52,376,261	171,633,232
	Q4	52,370,003	224,003,234
2014	Q1	59,909,955	283,913,189
	Q2	77,756,622	361,669,811
	Q3	55,470,616	417,140,427
	Q4	66,981,085	484,121,512
2015	Q1	69,065,123	553,186,636
	Q2	68,386,935	621,573,571
	Q3	45,791,788	667,365,359
	Q4	73,453,781	740,819,139
2016	Q1	72,690,797	813,509,936
	Q2	36,834,409	850,344,345

Figure 6-25 Table with a running total column

Exercise 6.8: Create A Percent Of Total Calculation

The Percent of Total function will display percents, which represents the value, instead of displaying the actual values.

1. Add the Category Name field to the Rows shelf ⇒ Add the Order Date field to the Columns shelf.

2. Drag the Order Amount field to the Text button.

   The table should look like the one shown in Figure 6-26.

	Order Date			
Category Name	2013	2014	2015	2016
Clothing	69,894,950	79,710,520	74,699,978	32,512,363
Clothing Novelty	8,493,622	10,204,366	8,793,880	3,631,925
Computer Novelty	57,175,659	65,974,019	67,551,728	28,055,842
Novelty Items				4,273,287
Packaging Materials	68,381,599	79,274,515	79,804,491	31,702,229
Toys	20,057,404	24,954,859	25,847,550	9,349,560

Figure 6-26 Table before the Quick Table Calculation is applied

3. On the shortcut menu for the Order Amount field on the Marks card, select Quick Table Calculation ⇒ Percent of Total.

    The table should look like the one shown in Figure 6-27.

Category Name	Order Date			
	2013	2014	2015	2016
Clothing	27.22%	31.04%	29.09%	12.66%
Clothing Novelty	27.29%	32.79%	28.25%	11.67%
Computer Novelty.	26.14%	30.16%	30.88%	12.83%
Novelty Items				100.00%
Packaging Materials	26.39%	30.59%	30.79%	12.23%
Toys	25.01%	31.11%	32.23%	11.66%

Figure 6-27 Percent of Total Quick Table Calculation applied to the table

4. Rename the sheet to `E6.8 Percent of total calculation`.

Figure 6-28 shows the Order Amount field on the Marks card. Notice the triangle, illustrated in the figure. It indicates that a table calculation is applied to the measure.

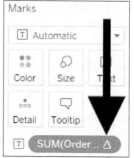

Figure 6-28 Order Amount field on the Marks card

Apply A Quick Table Calculation To A Chart

Most of the time, Quick Table calculations are applied to tables, but they can be applied to a chart. The steps below show you how to apply a Quick Table Calculation to a chart.

1. Duplicate the E6.8 sheet.

2. Change the chart type to Horizontal bars.

3. Display the shortcut menu for the Order Amount field ⇒ Clear Table Calculation. The chart should look like the one shown in Figure 6-29.

Figure 6-29 Horizontal bar chart before the Quick Table calculation is applied

4. Reapply the Quick Table Calculation Percent of Total option to the Order Amount field. The chart should look like the one shown in Figure 6-30.

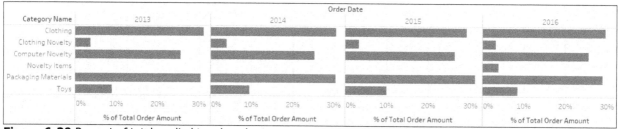

Figure 6-30 Percent of total applied to a bar chart

Exercise 6.9: Create A YTD Total Calculation

Creating this total uses the same steps as creating a running total. Instead of selecting the Quick Table Running Total option, select the YTD Total option. In Exercise 6.7, you changed the alias name of the Order Amount field used on the Measure Names field on the Columns shelf. The alias name is used throughout the workbook. So if you needed to use the Order Amount field and display it with a different name, you would have to duplicate the Order Amount field and create a different alias name. That is what you will learn how to do in this exercise.

1. Rename a new sheet to E6.9 YTD total.

2. Duplicate the Order Amount field in the Data pane ⇒ Scroll down and rename the duplicated field to YTD Order Amount.

3. Add the Order Date field to the Rows shelf ⇒ Click the plus sign to display the quarters.

4. Add the Order Amount field to the Rows shelf ⇒ On the shortcut menu, select Discrete.

5. Add the Measure Names field to the Columns shelf ⇒ Modify the filter for this field, to use the YTD Order Amount field.

6. Drag the YTD Order Amount field to the Text button ⇒ On the shortcut menu ⇒ Quick Table Calculation ⇒ Select the YTD Total option.

7. On the table, right-click on the Running Total column heading ⇒ Edit Alias ⇒ Type YTD Total.

   The table should look like the one shown in Figure 6-31.

   Notice that the YTD total is reset for each year.

Year of Ord..	Quarter of ..	Order Amount	YTD Total
2013	Q1	37,560,393	37,560,393
	Q2	81,696,577	119,256,970
	Q3	52,376,261	171,633,232
	Q4	52,370,003	224,003,234
2014	Q1	59,909,955	59,909,955
	Q2	77,756,622	137,666,577
	Q3	55,470,616	193,137,193
	Q4	66,981,085	260,118,278
2015	Q1	69,065,123	69,065,123
	Q2	68,386,935	137,452,058
	Q3	45,791,788	183,243,846
	Q4	73,453,781	256,697,627
2016	Q1	72,690,797	72,690,797
	Q2	36,834,409	109,525,206

Figure 6-31 Table with a YTD column

Table Calculations

The Quick Table calculations that you learned how to use in the previous section can be created using a calculated field. Table calculations are created using a measure field on the chart. Like Quick Table calculations, in Table calculations, the calculation is used to transform the measures value. They can be used to transform values to show running totals, percent of totals and rankings, among other options.

I suspect that most of the time, you will used the Quick Table calculation option, but I wanted to show you how the Table Calculation option works. What you will notice is that table calculations update the chart in real time. This can be helpful, as this type of calculation is often used to answer "What-If" questions.

Exercise 6.10: Use The Add Table Calculation Option

This exercise will show you how to use the Table Calculation window to create a scenario that will display the difference between the current order amount value and the previous order amount value, displayed on the chart.

1. Duplicate the E5.4 sheet ⇒ Rename it to E6.10 Add Table Calculation.

2. On the shortcut menu for the Order Amount field, on the Rows shelf ⇒ **ADD TABLE CALCULATION** option.

    The options in the **CALCULATION TYPE** drop-down list, shown in Figure 6-32, are used to select the type of calculation that you want to create.

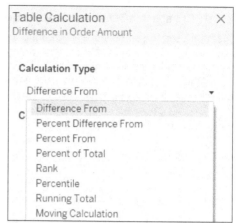

Figure 6-32 Calculation Type options

3. Select the **DIFFERENCE FROM** option, if it is not already selected.

The options in the **COMPUTE USING** list change, depending on the Calculation Type that is selected and the number of dimensions used to create the chart. Each time you select a different option from this list, parts of the chart will be highlighted. The highlighting displays the direction and scope of the calculation. The first word in each option is the **SCOPE** (what part of the chart to include in the calculation). The words in parenthesis are the direction.

4. Select the default **TABLE (ACROSS)** Compute Using option ⇒ Click the X in the upper right corner of the window, to close it.

    The chart should look like the one shown in Figure 6-33. Notice in the lower right corner, that there is a message that says there is one null value. This is because the "previous" Relative To option was selected. Because the first value on the chart does not have a previous value that it can be compared to, the result is a null value, which is correct.

    Also notice that the Order Amount field on the Rows shelf has the same triangle symbol that Quick Calculations have.

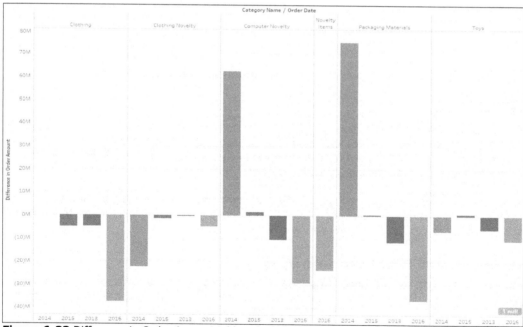

Figure 6-33 Difference in Order Amount table calculation

Modifying A Table Calculation

There are three ways to edit a table calculation (from options on the fields shortcut menu, shown in Figure 6-34), as listed below.

① **EDIT IN SHELF** This option displays the calculation on the shelf, as shown in Figure 6-35. You can type in the changes.

② Use the **COMPUTE USING** options, shown in Figure 6-34 and the **RELATIVE TO** options.

③ **EDIT TABLE CALCULATION** This option opens the Table Calculation dialog box, shown earlier in Figure 6-32.

Figure 6-34 Measure shortcut menu

Rows   ([Order Amount])) - LOOKUP(ZN(SUM([Order Amount])), -1)

Figure 6-35 Edit in shelf option enabled

Adding Totals

The **TOTALS** option on the Analysis menu has the options shown in Figure 6-36. They are used to add totals and sub totals to tables.

The **ROW TOTALS TO LEFT OPTION**, displays the grand total column before the columns that have the data that will be totaled.

The **COLUMN TOTALS TO TOP** option, displays the grand total row at the top of the table, as shown in Figure 6-37, instead of at the bottom, as shown later in Figure 6-38.

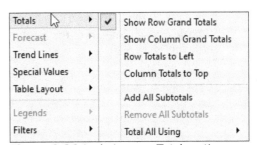

Figure 6-36 Analysis menu Totals options

| Category Name | SubCategory | Order Date | | | | |
		2013	2014	2015	2016	Grand Total
Grand Total		140,088,511	162,086,065	160,270,095	70,011,569	532,456,240
Clothing	Socks	4,335,075	4,495,791	4,996,531	2,053,183	15,880,580
	Hoodie	4,952,430	6,164,464	5,484,850	2,144,163	18,745,907
	Jacket	11,838,591	13,371,035	12,501,359	5,505,267	43,216,252

Figure 6-37 Column totals displayed at the top of the table

Exercise 6.11: Add Grand Totals To A Table

This may be one of the most used built-in options for adding totals. This exercise will show you how to add totals to rows and columns.

1. Duplicate the E5.7 sheet ⇒ Rename it to E6.11 Grand totals.

2. Analysis menu ⇒ Totals ⇒ Show Row Grand Totals. The last column in the table displays the totals for each row.

3. Analysis menu ⇒ Totals ⇒ Show Column Grand Totals.

    The last row in the table displays totals for each column, as shown in Figure 6-38.

Category Name	Sub Category	2013	2014	2015	2016	Grand Total
Clothing	Socks	4,335,075	4,495,791	4,996,531	2,053,183	15,880,580
	Hoodie	4,952,430	6,164,464	5,484,850	2,144,163	18,745,907
	Jacket	11,838,591	13,371,035	12,501,359	5,505,267	43,216,252
	T-Shirt	27,132,392	31,705,923	26,858,588	13,127,490	98,824,393
Computer Novelty	Office Misc	1,034,469	906,032	852,707	454,593	3,247,801
	USB Drive	13,351,569	15,291,372	16,411,297	6,905,534	51,959,771
Novelty Items	Chocolate Candy				4,273,287	4,273,287
Packaging Materials	Courier Bag	1,388,146	1,134,049	1,344,598	406,384	4,273,178
	Clear Tape	1,986,887	2,267,366	1,839,724	994,931	7,088,908
	Marker	2,838,609	2,979,492	3,140,076	1,300,790	10,258,967
	Dispenser - Bubble Wrap	2,944,861	3,558,623	3,770,974	1,992,608	12,267,065
	Dispenser - Tape	3,060,142	3,580,497	3,732,085	1,431,793	11,804,517
	Bag	4,001,479	4,630,355	4,091,852	1,657,199	14,380,885
	Shipping Carton	10,434,147	11,891,527	12,331,962	4,706,784	39,364,420
	Color Tape	12,648,390	15,591,645	14,503,753	5,186,293	47,930,082
	Bubble Wrap	21,174,354	23,765,985	25,925,243	9,882,621	80,748,203
Toys	Truck	1,590,014	1,070,485	1,556,512	445,171	4,662,182
	Car	7,603,910	8,577,258	10,858,083	3,646,956	30,686,207
	Remote Control Car	7,773,048	11,104,167	10,069,900	3,896,522	32,843,637
Grand Total		140,088,511	162,086,065	160,270,095	70,011,569	532,456,240

(column header above: Order Date)

Figure 6-38 Table with row and column grand totals

 The reason that the values in the year columns are in ascending order, is because the E5.7 exercise table was sorted that way.

Drill Down On Grand Total Calculations

Grand total columns can be used to drill down on the data in the table. There are two ways to do this, as explained below. When either drill-down option is used, the table will display the data by quarter. This includes sub totals, if the table has them.

① Right-click on the Grant Total column heading and select Drill down, as shown in Figure 6-39.

② Hold the mouse pointer over the column heading to display the tooltip, then click the **DRILL DOWN** button, shown in Figure 6-40.

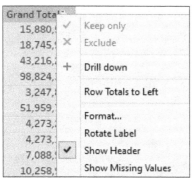

Figure 6-40 Column heading tooltip

Figure 6-39 Grand Total column heading shortcut menu

Exercise 6.12: Add Subtotals To A Table

Subtotal values are automatically created for each group on the table. The table used in the previous exercise only has one group.

1. Duplicate the E5.7 sheet ⇒ Rename it to E6.12 Subtotals.

2. Analysis menu ⇒ Totals ⇒ Add All Subtotals.

The top of the table should look like the one shown in Figure 6-41.

Category N..	Sub Category	Order Date			
		2013≜	2014	2015	2016
Clothing	Socks	4,335,075	4,495,791	4,996,531	2,053,183
	Hoodie	4,952,430	6,164,464	5,484,850	2,144,163
	Jacket	11,838,591	13,371,035	12,501,359	5,505,267
	T-Shirt	27,132,392	31,705,923	26,858,588	13,127,490
	Total	48,258,487	55,737,213	49,841,329	22,830,104
Computer Novelty	Office Misc	1,034,469	906,032	852,707	454,593
	USB Drive	13,351,569	15,291,372	16,411,297	6,905,534
	Total	14,386,037	16,197,404	17,264,004	7,360,127
Novelty Items	Chocolate Candy				4,273,287
	Total				4,273,287

Figure 6-41 Subtotals added to a table

If the Territory field was added to the beginning of the Rows shelf, in the E6.12 table and row grand totals were added, the table shown above in Figure 6-41 would look like the one shown in Figure 6-42.

Territory	Category N..	Sub Category	Order Date			
			2013≜	2014	2015	2016
External	Clothing	Socks	117,463	4,242	22,306	9,700
		Hoodie	161,996	23,446	26,132	20,336
		Jacket	148,554	173,938	156,254	22,738
		T-Shirt	600,309	386,413	345,629	112,367
		Total	1,028,322	588,039	550,321	165,141
	⋮					
	Novelty Items	Chocolate Candy				63,488
		Total				63,488
	Packaging Materials	Courier Bag	7,011	7,299	4,504	
		Clear Tape	8,615	200	9,872	4,444
	⋮					
		Total	326,168	156,445	215,876	62,472
Far West	Clothing	Socks	407,172	386,155	513,405	206,306
		Hoodie	515,538	1,000,730	675,304	190,985

Figure 6-42 Table with subtotals and grand totals

Adding Percents

The options on the shortcut menu shown in Figure 6-43 are used to add percents to a chart.

The **PERCENTAGE OF** options are on the Analysis menu.

There is often a need when analyzing data to see what percent a value is, in addition to, or instead of viewing the actual data values.

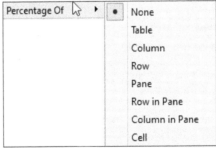

Figure 6-43 Percentage Of options

Exercise 6.13: Rank Customer Order Totals By State In 2016

In this exercise, you will learn how to use the RANK function to display states in order based on the total order amount for 2016.

1. Rename a new sheet to `E6.13 Rank states`.

2. Right-click on the Order Amount field ⇒ Create ⇒ Calculated Field ⇒ Type `Rank States`, as the field name.

3. Create the formula shown below.

```
RANK(Sum([Order Amount]))
```

4. Add the State field to the Rows shelf ⇒ Add the Rank States field to the Columns shelf.

5. Drag the Order Date field to the Filters shelf ⇒ Select Years ⇒ Click Next ⇒ Select the year 2016.

6. Drag the Order Amount field to the Tooltip button.

7. On the toolbar, click the Sort descending and Show Mark Labels buttons. The label displayed is the states rank number. The chart should look like the one shown in Figure 6-44.

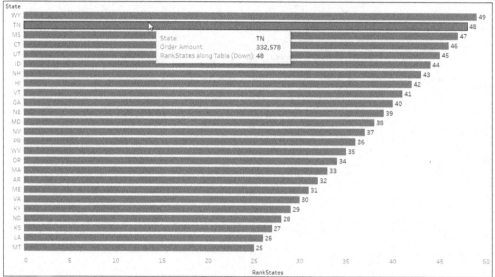

Figure 6-44 RANK function used to create a chart

If the Territory field was used as a filter, you could view states in a specific territory, as shown in Figure 6-45.

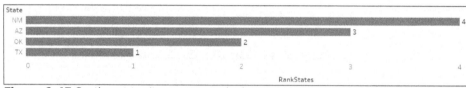

Figure 6-45 Southwest territory states ranked

What Is A Parameter?

A parameter is used to select the value for a filter or calculated field. They are created so that the person viewing the chart can select values that they need, to be able to see another view of the data. Parameters can also be used with reference lines and bins. Parameters make the chart or dashboard interactive. Parameters are like variables because they are used to store a value.

Parameters can be created using one of the following options. Once a parameter is created, the Parameters section is added to the bottom of the Data pane.

☑ Use the Create shortcut menu option on a field in the Data pane.
☑ Use the Create Parameter option on the Dimensions section shortcut menu.

Types Of Parameters

There are two types of parameters that can be created, as explained below.

① **BASIC PARAMETERS** This type of parameter is the one that has been discussed so far. These parameters are limited, in that they can only be used to select one value. Probably, the best known basic parameter is one that lets the person viewing the chart, select a different Top N value.

In Chapter 5 Exercise 5.8, you learned how to create a filter that only displayed data if the sub category has a total order amount greater than 3 million dollars. The parameter would replace the constant (hard coded) value of 3 million dollars. This will let the person viewing the chart select the value that they want to use in the filter.

② **ADVANCED PARAMETERS** These parameters have more flexibility then basic parameters. That is because an advanced parameter can be created to select a different field to display on a chart. An example that comes to mind is creating a parameter that is used to select a field to sort on, as the way to display data.

Exercise 6.14: Create A Parameter For A Top N Filter

In this exercise you will modify the E5.9 chart, so that the N value can be selected for the Sub Category filter.

1. Duplicate the E5.9 sheet ⇒ Rename it to `E6.14 Top N filter parameter`.

2. Open the Filter dialog box for the Sub Category filter ⇒ On the General tab, click the **ALL BUTTON**, so that all sub categories are included.

3. On the Top tab, open the drop-down list for the field with the number 10 in it and select **CREATE A NEW PARAMETER**, as shown in Figure 6-46.

Figure 6-46 Option to create a parameter

4. In the Name field, type `Top N Parameter`.

5. Change the Maximum value to 10.

   The options shown in Figure 6-47 will allow any value from 1 to 10 to be selected, as the N value.

   The **SET FROM PARAMETER** option is enabled when the workbook has more than one parameter.

   The **SET FROM FIELD** option is used to select a field that has the values needed to create a list of values for the parameter.

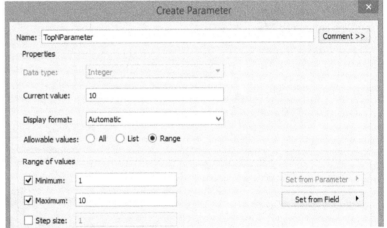

Figure 6-47 Top N parameter options

The options shown in Figure 6-48 are used when you want to select specific values or use one value and display a different value on the parameter.

The **PASTE FROM CLIPBOARD** option will use data that you have copied to the clipboard to create the list of values for the parameters.

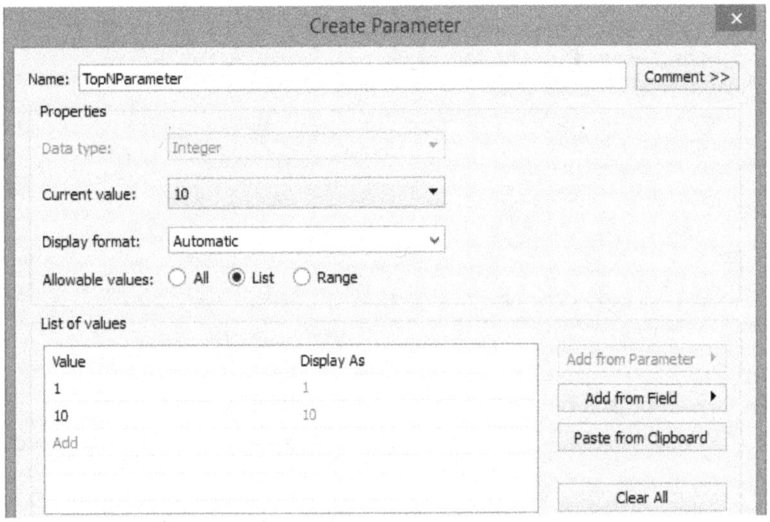

Figure 6-48 Parameter list options

6. Click OK. The Top tab should display the name of the parameter that you just created ⇒ Click OK.

Because the parameter uses numeric values, it is displayed as a slider, as shown in Figure 6-49. Yes, I thought the same thing that you are thinking now. Why can't a drop-down list or radio buttons be used for a parameter?

The only option is to use the **TYPE IN** option on the parameters shortcut menu. As its name implies, you have to type the value in.

Figure 6-49 Top N parameter

Exercise 6.15: Create A Parameter For A Calculated Field

In this exercise you will learn how to create a parameter that allows the user to select a percent that will be used in a calculated field, to forecast future sales, based on the current sales. This scenario allows for What-If analysis.

Create The Parameter

This parameter will allow specific percents from 5% to 25% to be selected.

1. Rename a new sheet to E6.15 Calculated field parameter.

2. From the Dimensions section drop-down list, open the Create Parameter dialog box.

3. In the Name field, type Select Percent. The **FLOAT** data type is the best option for percent values.

4. In the Current value field, type .05.

5. Open the Display format drop-down list and select the options illustrated in Figure 6-50.

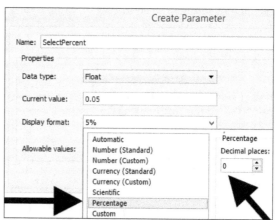

Figure 6-50 Percent options for the parameter field

6. Select the Allowable Values **RANGE OPTION** ⇒ Select the Range of Values options, shown at the bottom of Figure 6-51 ⇒ Click OK.

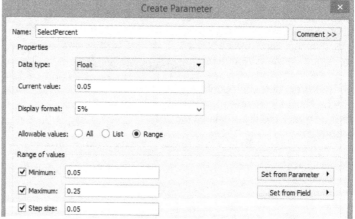

Figure 6-51 Parameter options for a percent value

Create The Calculated Field
The calculated field will use the parameter field that was created in the previous section of this exercise.

1. Create a calculated field named `Sales Forecast`.

2. Create the formula shown below.

```
[Order Amount] * (1 + [SelectPercent])
```

Create The Chart
1. Add the Order Amount and Sales Forecast fields to the Rows shelf.

2. Add the Category Name field to the Columns shelf.

3. Add the Order Date field to the Filters shelf ⇒ Select Years ⇒ Click Next ⇒ Select the year 2015. On your own, you would select the previous year. I did not do that in this exercise because the data set does not have a full year of data for 2016.

4. On the Data pane, display the shortcut menu for the Select Percent parameter ⇒ Show Parameter Control.

5. Change the chart type to Side-by-side bars. The chart and parameter should look like the ones shown in Figure 6-52.

When you click on the arrow buttons below the parameter, the percent will change and the chart will reflect the forecast value, based on the percent that is selected.

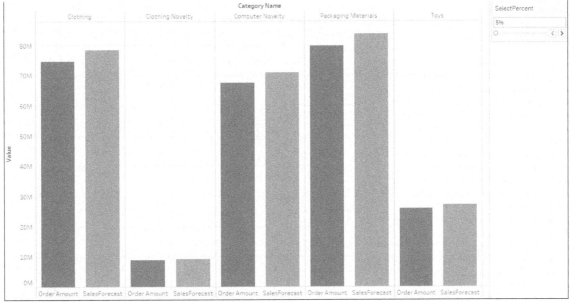

Figure 6-52 Chart with a parameter used in a calculation

Overview

After reading this chapter and completing the exercises you will be able to create the following types of charts: Heat map, Symbol map, Tree map, Circle view, Dual line, Area and more.

CHAPTER 7

Overview

This chapter picks up where Chapter 4 left off, in terms of creating charts. The charts created in that chapter are considered basic charts. Many of the chart types covered in this chapter are considered "advanced" because they require more steps to complete, then the charts in Chapter 4 did. As needed, you may find it helpful to review the chart type descriptions in Chapter 4. As you will see, some charts have the word "map" as part of the chart name, even though the data is not displayed on a geographical map.

Exercise 7.1: Create A Heat Map

1. Save the Chapter 6 Calculations and Parameters workbook as `Chapter 7 Advanced Charts`.

2. Delete all of the sheets except E6.8 and E6.11.

3. Duplicate the E6.11 sheet ⇒ Rename it to `E7.1 Heat map`.

4. Remove the Sub Category field from the Filters shelf.

5. From the Show Me pane, select the Heat maps chart.

6. Make the Year columns wider.

7. Drag the Order Amount field to the Color button.

8. Click the Color button ⇒ Click the Edit Colors button ⇒ Open the Palette drop-down list and select one of the color schemes that has the word "diverging" at the end of its name.

    The chart should look like the one shown in Figure 7-1.

Category Name	SubCategory	Order Date			
		2013	2014	2015	2016
Clothing	Hoodie	■	■	■	▪
	Jacket	■	■	■	■
	Slippers	■	■		■
	Socks	■	▪	■	▪
	T-Shirt		■		■
Clothing Novelty	Novelty	■	■	■	▪
Computer Novelty	Mug	■	■	■	■
	Office Misc	·	·	·	·
	USB Drive	■	■	■	■

Figure 7-1 Heat map

Geography Maps

Tableau has online and offline background maps. Internet access is required to load charts that have geographical maps. If you do not have internet access, offline maps can be used, because Tableau comes with three background maps. The background maps are explained below. (Map ⇒ Background Maps, displays the options).

- ☑ **NONE** displays data between longitude and latitude axes.
- ☑ **OFFLINE** stores the images in a cache file in Internet Explorer. This option is only available in Tableau Desktop.
- ☑ **TABLEAU** connects to Tableau's background map. This is the default background map.

 If you have added a Map box map to the workbook, it will be displayed on the Background Maps menu.

Exercise 7.2: Create A Symbol Map

1. Rename a new sheet as `E7.2 Symbol map`.

2. Double-click on the State field. You will see that the **LONGITUDE FIELD** is automatically added to the Columns shelf and the **LATITUDE FIELD** is added to the Rows shelf. The symbol map is automatically selected.

 Double-clicking on the Country or City field automatically adds the Longitude and Latitude fields to the Columns shelf.

3. Drag the City field to the map ⇒ Drag the Order Amount field to the map.

If you want to display a different symbol, use the **CIRCLE MAP**, instead of the Symbol map.

4. Drag the Territory field to the Color button.

In the upper left corner of the map, you should see the toolbar shown in Figure 7-2. If not, hold the mouse pointer over the map. Clicking the + (plus) and - (minus) buttons will zoom in and out on the map. The **PAN** button shown in the figure is used to move the map around on the canvas.

Figure 7-2 Symbol map

The options shown in Figure 7-3 are used to create the **FILLED MAP** shown in the figure. I don't know if I did something wrong, but using the City field like I did in Exercise 7.2, did not work when I created the Filled map.

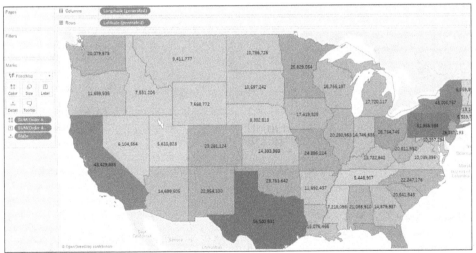

Figure 7-3 Filled map

Exercise 7.3: Create A Tree Map Chart

In this exercise you will create a tree map that displays hierarchical data by state. On your own, you could modify the tree map, that will be created in this exercise, to display the data by territory, state and city.

1. Rename a new sheet as E7.3 Tree map.

2. Double-click on the State field ⇒ Double-click on the Order Amount field.

3. Select the Tree maps chart.

4. Drag the Territory field to the Color button. The colors represent the different territories. The chart should look like the one shown in Figure 7-4.

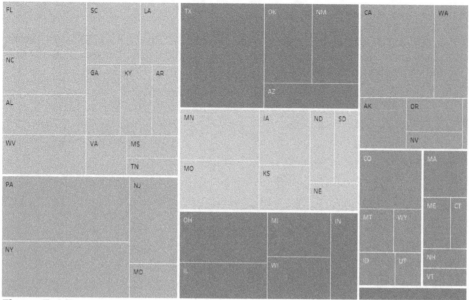

Figure 7-4 Tree map chart

Exercise 7.4: Create A Circle View Chart

This exercise will show you how to create a chart that will display/show how sales (order amounts) are distributed between the categories.

1. Rename a new sheet as E7.4 Circle view chart.

2. Add the Category Name and Sub Category fields to the Columns shelf.

3. Add the Order Amount field to the Rows shelf.

4. Drag the Product Name field to the Detail button.

5. Select the Circle views chart.

6. Make the columns wider. On this chart, I found using the labels at the bottom of the chart the easiest way to resize the columns. It can be time consuming to get the column widths the way that you want them because the columns cannot be sized individually. The other option is to rotate category labels.

7. Right-click on a label at the bottom of the chart ⇒ **ROTATE LABEL.** The chart should look like the one shown in Figure 7-5.

Exercise 7.5: Create A Side By Side Circle Chart

In this exercise you will learn how to create a chart that displays how sales (order amounts) are distributed by the categories, over several years, by territory.

1. Rename a new sheet as E7.5 Side by side circle chart.

2. Add the Order Date and Category Name fields to the Columns shelf.

3. Add the Order Amount field to the Rows shelf.

4. Select the Side-by-side circles chart.

5. Drag the Category Name field to the Color button.

6. Drag the Territory field to the Shape button.

7. Move the Category Name field to the end of the Columns shelf. I don't understand why the fields get swapped, when this chart type is selected.

8. Open the Marks card drop-down list and change the shape to Circle. The chart should look like the one shown in Figure 7-6.

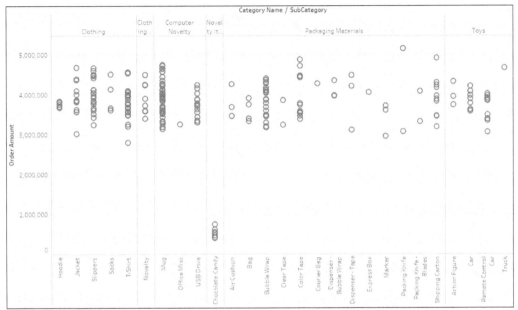

Figure 7-5 Circle view chart

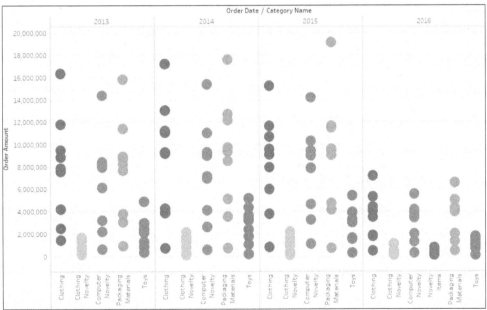

Figure 7-6 Side-by-side circle chart

Exercise 7.6: Create A Dual Line Chart

The chart that you will create in this exercise will display order amounts and sales costs by year and quarter.

1. Rename a new sheet as E7.6 Dual line chart.

2. On the Data pane, select the Financial Data data set.

3. Add the Order Date field to the Columns shelf.

4. Add the Order Amount and Sales Costs fields to the Rows shelf.

5. Select the Dual lines chart.

6. Click the button in front of the Order Date field. The data should now be displayed by quarter.

7. Open the shortcut menu for the quarter Order Date field and select Discrete. This will display data for each quarter that has data. The chart should look like the one shown in Figure 7-7.

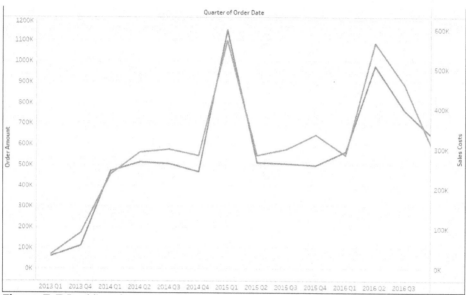

Figure 7-7 Dual line chart

Exercise 7.7: Create A Discrete Area Chart

The area chart that you will learn how to create in this exercise will display the totals by year and quarter.

1. Rename a new sheet as E7.7 Discrete area chart.

2. On the Data pane, select the Orders data set.

3. Select the Order Date and Order Amount fields ⇒ Select the Area (discrete) chart.

4. Click the plus sign on the Order Date field on the Columns shelf.

5. Drag the Category Name field to the Color button. The chart should look like the one shown in Figure 7-8.

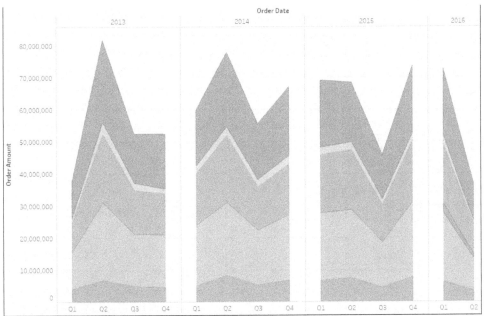

Figure 7-8 Discrete area chart

Exercise 7.8: Create A Combination Chart

This exercise will show you how to create a chart that displays the territory data as a bar chart and the order totals as a line chart. This chart type is different from the Dual Combination chart that you will create in the next exercise because it does not require a date field.

1. Rename a new sheet as E7.8 Combination chart.

2. Add the Territory field to the Columns shelf ⇒ Add the Order Amount field to the Rows shelf.

3. Sort the Territory field in ascending order by the Order Amount field.

4. Drag the Territory field to the Color button.

5. Drag the Quantity field to the Rows shelf ⇒
    On the drop-down list for the Quantity field,
    select **DUAL AXIS** ⇒
    Then select **MARK TYPE** ⇒ Line, as shown in Figure 7-9.

Figure 7-9 Mark Type options

6. Change the Mark Type for the Order Amount field to Bar.

7. Click on the line on the chart ⇒ Click the Size button on the Marks card ⇒ Move the slider to the right, to make the line on the chart wider.

8. Hide the legend.

9. Drag the Order Amount field to the Label button. The chart should look like the one shown in Figure 7-10.

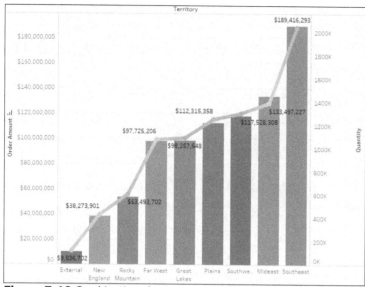

Figure 7-10 Combination chart

Exercise 7.9: Create A Dual Combination Chart

In the previous exercise, you learned that a dual combination chart requires a date field. The chart that you will learn how to create in this exercise will display order amounts and quantity, by quarter.

1. Rename a new sheet as E7.9 Dual combination chart.

2. Select the Order Date, Order Amount and Quantity fields ⇒ Select the Dual combination chart.

3. Click the button in front of the Order Date field to display quarters ⇒ Change the field to Discrete.

4. Right-click on a date at the bottom of the chart ⇒ Rotate Label.

    The chart should look like the one shown in Figure 7-11.

    Like the combination chart that you created in the previous exercise, a dual combination chart has the Mark Type options.

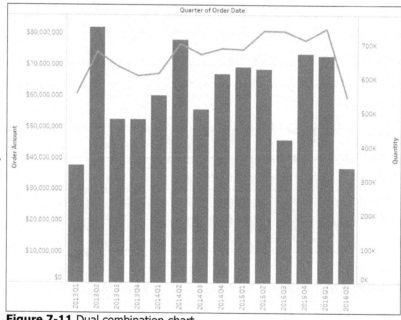

Figure 7-11 Dual combination chart

Exercise 7.10: Create A Scatter Plot Chart

The scatter chart that you will learn how to create in this exercise will display the quantity and unit price, by territory.

1. Rename a new sheet as E7.10 Scatter chart.

2. Select the following fields: State, Territory, Quantity and Unit Price.

3. Select the Scatter Plots chart.

    The chart and legend should look like the ones shown in Figure 7-12.

    The CTRL, Shift and B keys will make the symbols larger.

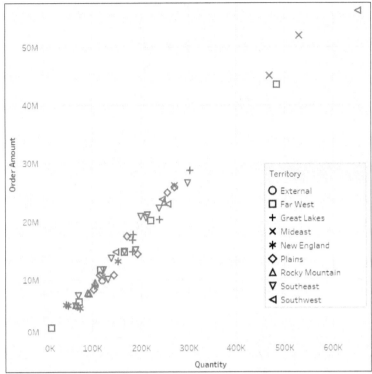

Figure 7-12 Scatter plot chart

Changing The Shape Of The Symbols Displayed On The Chart

If you wanted to change the shapes displayed on the chart, click the Shape button the Marks card or hold the mouse pointer over the upper right corner of the legend to display the shortcut menu, then select **EDIT SHAPE**.

You will see the Edit Shape dialog box. Open the Select Shape Palette drop-down list to display the other shape options, shown in Figure 7-13.

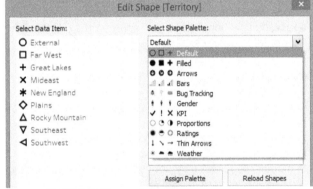

Figure 7-13 Edit Shape dialog box

Exercise 7.11: Create A Box And Whisker Plot Chart

By far, this is the most technical chart covered in this book. This chart type is often used when the distribution of data needs to be displayed statistically. Another popular use for this chart type is to display stock data, because stocks have four values: Open, high, low and closing price.

In this exercise, you will create a chart that displays the order totals by territory.

1. Rename a new sheet as E7.11 Box and whisker chart.

2. Add the Territory field to the Columns shelf ⇒ Add the Order Amount field to the Rows shelf.

3. Drag the State field to the Detail button.

4. Select the Box-and-Whisker plots chart. The chart should look like the one shown in Figure 7-14. On the chart, each territory has its own set of values.

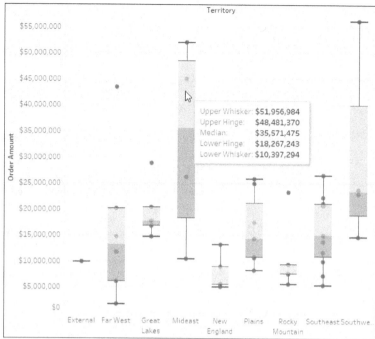

Figure 7-14 Box and Whisker plot chart

Understanding A Box And Whisker Chart

This section explains the parts of the chart.

The **BOX(ES)** display the distance between the upper and lower quartiles (also known as the inter-quartile range).

The **WHISKERS** (the horizontal lines) represent the Q1, Q3, lowest and highest quartiles. In the figure, you will see four horizontal lines for each box.

Tooltip Values

This section explains the options on the tooltip.

The Median, Q1, and Q3 values divide the data set into four equal parts.

The **MEDIAN VALUE** represents the middle (or 50% of) the count of numbers (values). The important thing to remember is that the median values may not be displayed in the middle of the box.

Q1 Represents 25% of the lower hinge (quartiles) values.

Q2 Represents 75% of the higher hinge (quartiles) values.

The lower and upper whisker options represent the minimum and maximum values.

CHAPTER 8

DASHBOARDS AND STORIES

Overview

After reading this chapter and completing the exercises you will be able to create basic dashboards, actions and stories.

Overview

If you made it to this chapter, you have come a long way from when you first opened Tableau. This chapter covers the tools that bring together everything that you have learned so far. These tools are dashboards and stories. They are used to display two or more worksheets (aka sheets) or dashboards in one view. These tools are used when you want to share the charts with other people or to create presentations.

Dashboards

While a chart provides a single view of the data, a dashboard provides the ability to see multiple views of the data on one screen. This gives you the ability to provide a bigger picture of the data. A dashboard can be created using any charts in the workbook, even if the charts have different data sources. For example, all of the exercises in Chapter 7, except E7.6, used the Orders Dataset. The E7.6 chart uses the Financial Data data set. The E7.6 chart can be added to the same dashboard that uses the E7.2 chart.

Dashboard Workspace

Figure 8-1 shows the dashboard workspace. Many of the options on the menus and toolbar are not available for dashboards or stories, for that matter, that are available for charts. The options and sections on the dashboard workspace are explained below.

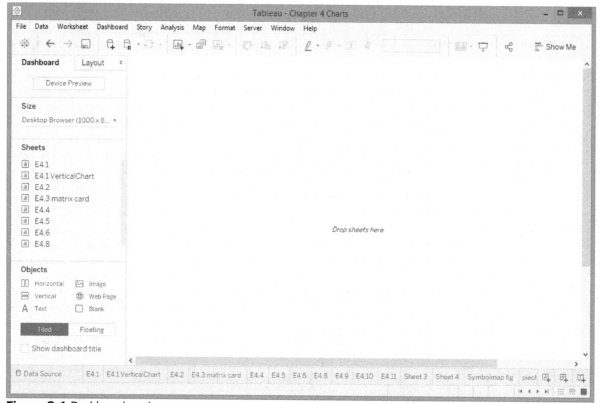

Figure 8-1 Dashboard workspace

Dashboard Pane

The **DEVICE PREVIEW BUTTON** has the options shown in Figure 8-2. They are used to select the layout for the device and model that the dashboard will be displayed on.

Figure 8-2 Device preview options

The options on the **SIZE** drop-down list, shown in Figure 8-3, are used to select the size that the dashboard will be viewed in. The first drop-down list (with the Fixed size option), also has the following options. The **AUTOMATIC** option will resize the dashboard as needed to display on the selected device. The **RANGE** option displays the window shown in Figure 8-4. The options are used to select the minimum and maximum size, width and height of the dashboard area.

Figure 8-3 Size options

Figure 8-4 Range options

The **SHEETS** section displays all of the sheets in the workbook that can be used to create a dashboard. As shown earlier in Figure 8-1, some sheets have a name that describes the chart and others do not.

When it comes time to create a dashboard, having descriptive sheet names is helpful. Otherwise, unless you have a photographic memory, you will have to keep flipping back and forth to the sheet pages to know which chart(s) to add. The sheets have the shortcut menu shown in Figure 8-5.

Figure 8-5 Sheet shortcut menu

The options in the **OBJECTS SECTION** of the Dashboard pane are used to add content to a dashboard and group items displayed on the dashboard. The options are explained below.

The **HORIZONTAL** and **VERTICAL OPTIONS** and are layout containers. Charts and other objects including filters, are added to the containers. Using containers is a way to keep objects together and makes it easier to align and resize objects. Select the horizontal option to display charts side by side. This container resizes the width of the objects. The vertical option stacks the charts and resizes the height of the objects in the container.

The **TEXT** option is used to add text to the dashboard. Examples include comments or instructions about the charts displayed on the dashboard.

The **IMAGE** option is used to add an image to the dashboard. This is helpful if you want to add a company logo to the dashboard.

The **WEB PAGE** option is used to display a web page on the dashboard.

The **BLANK** option is used to add white space to the dashboard, usually between containers.

Objects on the dashboard can be **TILED** (do not overlap) or **FLOATING** (can be placed anywhere on the dashboard, including being layered on top of other objects).

If checked, the **SHOW DASHBOARD TITLE** option will display the default title for the dashboard, which you can change.

Dashboard Menu

Except for the first option, the options shown in Figure 8-6 are only available when a dashboard sheet is displayed. Many of the options are the same as the ones on the Worksheet menu.

The **DEVICE LAYOUTS** option is used to add another layout to the dashboard. The layout options are Desktop, Tablet and Phone. These layout options are used to modify the dashboard so that it is displayed correctly for the selected device layout.

Figure 8-6 Dashboard menu

Exercise 8.1: Create A Sales By State And Category Dashboard

In addition to creating a dashboard, this exercise will also show you how to prepare sheets as needed, to be added to a dashboard.

Prepare The Sheets For The Dashboard

From time to time, you may find that you need to make changes to the charts that were created, so that they work the way you need them to when they are used to create a dashboard.

1. Save the Chapter 7 Advanced Charts workbook as `Chapter 8 Dashboards and Stories.`

2. Delete all of the sheets except, E6.8, E6.11, E7.1, E7.2, E7.8 and E7.9.

3. Select the E6.8 sheet ⇒ Delete the Order Amount field on the Marks card ⇒ Drag the Order Amount field to the Text button.

4. Select the E7.8 sheet ⇒ Create a filter using the Category Name field ⇒ If prompted, select all of the filter categories ⇒ Show the filter.

5. Rename the sheets listed below.
    Rename the E6.8 sheet to `Sales by year.`
    Rename the E6.11 sheet to `Sales by sub category.`
    Rename the E7.1 sheet to `Sales by category.`
    Rename the E7.2 sheet to `Sales by state.`
    Rename the E7.8 sheet to `Sales by territory.`
    Rename the E7.9 sheet to `Sales by quarter.`

6. Duplicate the Sales by state chart ⇒ Rename it to `Sales map by state.` The copy of the map will be used in another exercise that does not need the filter that will be applied to it, in this exercise.

Create The Dashboard

1. Click the **NEW DASHBOARD** button at the bottom of the workspace (or Dashboard menu ⇒ New Dashboard) ⇒ Rename the dashboard to `E8.1 Sales by state & category.`

2. On the Dashboard pane, click the Device Preview button ⇒ Change the device type to Desktop, by clicking either arrow button.

3. Open the Size drop-down list ⇒ Select the Automatic option.

4. Drag the Sales by state sheet to the canvas.

5. Drag the Sales by territory sheet to the canvas. You will see a gray box. This box indicates where the chart will be placed ⇒ As needed, drag the mouse until the gray box is to the right of the map, as shown in Figure 8-7, then release the mouse button. The dashboard should look like the one shown in Figure 8-8. As you can see, the charts on the dashboard take up a lot of space.

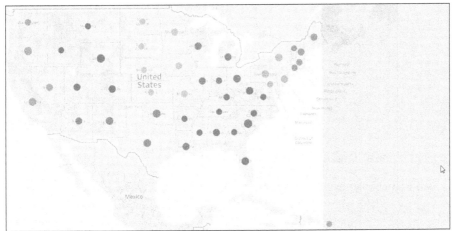

Figure 8-7 Position where the second chart will be placed

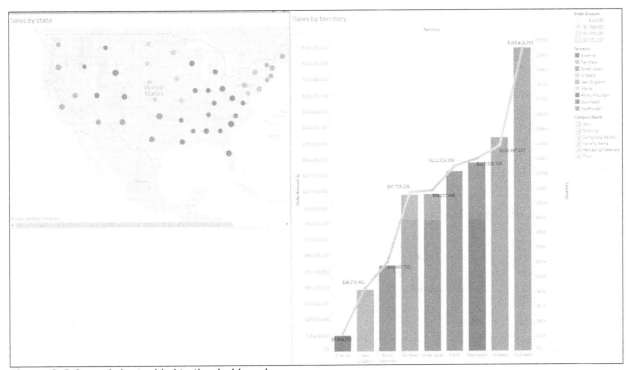

Figure 8-8 Second chart added to the dashboard

6. Add the Sales by year chart to the dashboard, below the map.

Customize The Dashboard

In this part of the exercise, you will learn how to make changes to the dashboard. The legends are not needed. The map would look better if it only displayed the United States, as no other part of the map has data. Currently, the filter will only be applied to the Sales by territory chart. It would be better if the filter was also applied to the map.

1. Click the down arrow button on the Order Amount legend, as shown in Figure 8-9 ⇒ Select Remove from Dashboard.

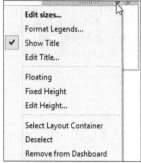

Figure 8-9 Legend shortcut menu

2.   Remove the Territory legend.

3.   Select the right side of the maps frame and make the frame smaller.

4.   Use the Pan option on the map so that only the United States portion of the map is displayed.

5.   Make the Sales by territory chart smaller.

6.   Right-click on a blank space in the Category Name filter ⇒ Apply to Worksheets ⇒ Selected Worksheets.

The Selected Worksheets option displays the dialog box shown in Figure 8-10. When a filter is applied to a worksheet, the filter is connected to the sheet, every place that it is used in the workbook.

If the same sheet is used in another dashboard, but does not need the filter, create a copy of the sheet before the filter is added to it. You did this in the first section of this exercise.

If the dashboard displayed more sheets, they would be listed on this dialog box.

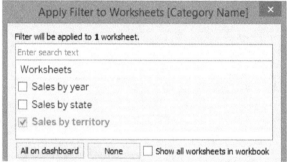

Figure 8-10 Apply Filter to Worksheets dialog box

7.   Select the Sales by year worksheet ⇒ Click OK. This will apply the filter to the table below the map.

8.   Press the F7 key to display the dashboard in presentation mode ⇒ Clear some of the options on the filter. The values on the chart and table will change, but the values on the map will not change. That is what should happen in this exercise because the filter was not applied to the map ⇒ Press the F7 key or the ESC (escape) key to return to the dashboard workspace.

Container Shortcut Menu

If you right-click on a blank space in a container that has a chart, you will see the shortcut menu shown in Figure 8-11. Some of the options are explained below.

The **GO TO SHEET** option is used to view the sheet for the chart in the container. This is helpful if you have hidden the sheet tab at the bottom of the workspace. It is common to hide sheets and often dashboards if the workbook has a story that uses all of these items.

The **FIT** options shown in the figure, are used to select how the chart is displayed in the container.

When selected, the **USE AS FILTER** option will use one chart to filter data on other charts, on the dashboard.

Figure 8-11 Container shortcut menu

Exercise 8.2: Use Two Filters In A Dashboard

In this exercise you will create a dashboard that uses two filters. The first filter will control the values displayed in the second filter. You will also learn how to use containers.

Modify The Sales By Sub Category Chart

Currently, this table has a filter for the Sub Category field. In this part of the exercise, you will create a filter for the Category Name field, then link the Sub Category filter to it. This will force the Sub Category filter to only display values that are for the selected categories.

 | The steps in this exercise that link the filter fields can also be done from a dashboard sheet. |

1. Display the Sales by sub category chart.

2. Drag the Category Name field to the top of the Filters shelf. All of the categories should be selected on the Filter dialog box ⇒ Click OK ⇒ Show the filter.

3. Show the Sub Category filter ⇒
    On the right side of the chart, display the shortcut menu for the Sub Category filter ⇒
    Select the **MULTIPLE VALUES (DROP DOWN)** option ⇒ Select the **ONLY RELEVANT VALUES** option.

Create The Dashboard

In this part of the exercise you will add three charts to the dashboard sheet.

1. Add a Dashboard sheet ⇒ Rename it to E8.2 Filter on 2 fields.

2. On the Dashboard pane, change the size to Automatic.

3. Drag the Vertical container object to the canvas.

4. Drag the Sales by territory sheet to the canvas and place it in the vertical container object.

5. Delete the filter for the chart. (Select the **REMOVE FROM DASHBOARD** option on the filters shortcut menu).

6. Drag the Sales by sub category sheet to the canvas and place it below the chart already on the canvas.

7. Make both charts smaller.

8. Drag the Sales by category chart to the canvas and place it to the right of the charts, already on the canvas ⇒ Remove the Order Amount legend, that has the gray boxes.

9.   Open the shortcut menu for the Category Name filter ⇒ Apply to Worksheets ⇒ Selected Worksheets ⇒ Click the **ALL ON DASHBOARD** button ⇒ Click OK.

Test the dashboard by selecting different combinations of Category Name and Sub Category filter options. Notice that the Sub Category values change, depending on the Category Name(s) that are selected. You will also see that each of the charts displays data based on your selections. The dashboard should look like the one shown in Figure 8-12.

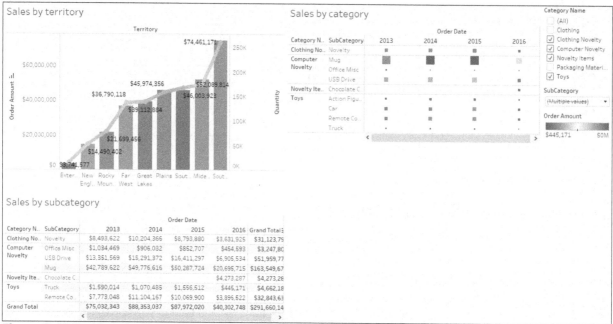

Figure 8-12 Dashboard with two linked filters

Layout Pane

The options in the **SELECTED ITEM** section, shown in Figure 8-13, are used to select an exact location (position) and size for the selected object.

The **OBJECTS** section displays all of the items on the dashboard. The items displayed have shortcut menu's. Tiled and floating objects are displayed in a hierarchy, in this section. The icons in front of each item, represent the type of item it is. The horizontal and vertical entries let you know what type of container the objects below it are stored in. Tiled objects cannot be reordered. Floating objects can be reordered from this tab, by dragging them to another location.

Objects Shortcut Menu

Each object has it's own shortcut menu, as shown below. These shortcut menus are also available when the Dashboard pane is displayed, but I find it easier to access them from the Layout tab.

The shortcut menu for a chart is similar to the one shown earlier in Figure 8-11.
The shortcut menu for a filter is shown in Figure 8-14.
The shortcut menu for a legend is shown in Figure 8-15.
The shortcut menu for a container is shown in Figure 8-16.

The **DISTRIBUTE EVENLY** option, on the Container shortcut menu is helpful when there are two or more charts in the same container. Use this option to evenly space out the objects in the container. For example, Figure 8-17 shows three charts. The bar chart in the middle is not fully displayed. Applying this option, redisplays the charts, as shown in Figure 8-18.

Figure 8-13 Layout pane

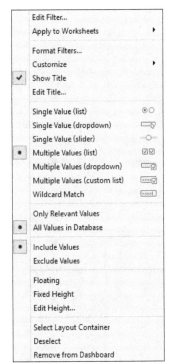

Figure 8-14 Filter shortcut menu

Figure 8-15 Legend shortcut menu

Figure 8-16 Container shortcut menu

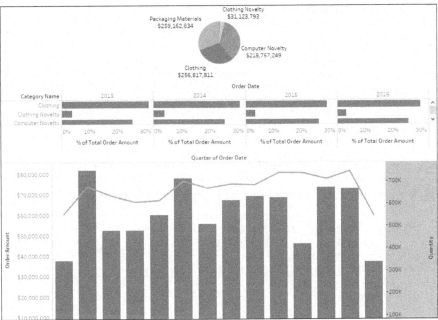

Figure 8-17 Three charts displayed in a container

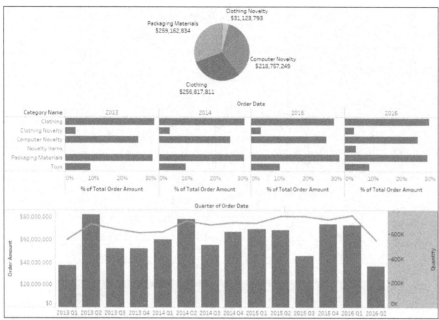

Figure 8-18 Distribute evenly option applied to the container

What Are Actions?

Actions are used to add interaction between sheets in the same workbook. Dashboards and stories are considered sheets. The three types of actions that can be created are shown at the bottom of Figure 8-19, on the **ADD ACTIONS** button. (Dashboard menu ⇒ Actions, opens this dialog box) The options are explained below.

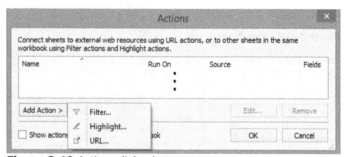

The **FILTER** option uses one chart to filter other charts on the dashboard, by selecting options on the dialog box, shown later in Figure 8-22. The options let you select which other charts to apply the filter to. The filter options can also be used to link to another sheet in the workbook.

Figure 8-19 Actions dialog box

If you want one chart to filter all of the other charts on the dashboard, an easier way to create the filter action is to select the Use as Filter option on the shortcut menu, shown earlier in Figure 8-11, on the chart that you want to use as the filter. Doing this will automatically create an action which will be added to the Actions dialog box.

The **HIGHLIGHT** option is used to add a background color (highlight) to a part of a chart, using the options shown in Figure 8-20.

The **URL** option is used to create a link to a web site, using the options shown in Figure 8-21.

Figure 8-20 Add Highlight Action dialog box

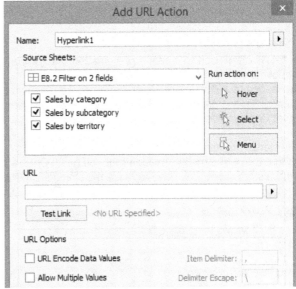

Figure 8-21 Add URL Action dialog box

Exercise 8.3: Create A Link To Another Dashboard

In this exercise, you will use the Filter action to link to another dashboard. The process is the same for linking to a sheet in the workbook.

1. Duplicate the E8.2 dashboard ⇒ Rename it to `E8.3 Link to another dashboard`.

2. Remove the Sales by territory chart from the dashboard.

3. On the Actions dialog box, click the Add Action button ⇒ Filter.

4. In the Name field type `Link to E8.1 Dashboard`.

5. Select the options shown in Figure 8-22 ⇒ In the **RUN ACTION ON** section, click the Select button ⇒ Click OK twice.

   To link to another dashboard or sheet, creating filter criteria is not a requirement.

   The **SELECT** Run action on option, shown in the figure, will trigger the action (displaying the Target sheet) when you click on a value in the Sales by category chart. In the heat map chart, the values are the squares in the year columns.

   If you wanted to link to a sheet instead of a dashboard, in the **TARGET SHEETS** drop-down list, select the sheet, instead of a dashboard.

Figure 8-22 Filter action options to link to another dashboard

6.   Test the action by clicking on a square on the Sales by category chart. You should see the E8.1 dashboard.

Creating Stories

This tool is often used to create a presentation or to display data in a structured, sequential way or in a specific order. Dashboards and sheets can be used to create a story. A story is another type of sheet, similar to dashboard sheets. When added to a story, each sheet or dashboard is known as a **STORY POINT**. Think of story points as slides on a PowerPoint presentation or pages in a book. As you will see, each story point can have a caption that explains the content displayed on the story point.

While stories are easy to create, it is a good idea to review the sheets and dashboards that you want to use, to make sure that they have the information that you need. Once a sheet or dashboard is added to a story, it can't be changed from the story sheet. You have to make the changes on the worksheet.

Story Workspace

Figure 8-23 shows the story workspace.

As you can see, it looks similar to the dashboard workspace.

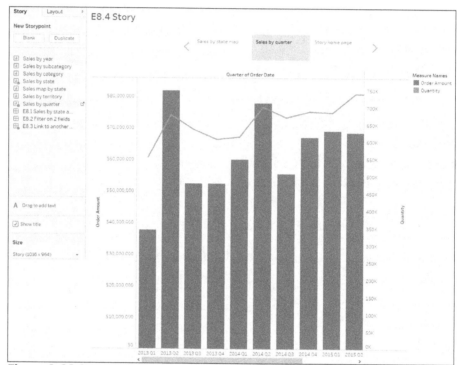

Figure 8-23 Story workspace

Story Pane

The options on this pane are explained below.

New Story Point Options

The **BLANK** button is used to create a story point using a worksheet or dashboard.

The **DUPLICATE** button is used to create a story point using an existing story point.

The next section lists all of the sheets and dashboards in the workbook.

The **DRAG TO ADD TEXT** option is used to add a floating text box to the story point.

The **SIZE** option works the same as it does for a dashboard.

The **NAVIGATION BUTTONS** are at the top of the canvas. Each chart or dashboard added to the story has its own box. You can change the caption that is displayed in each gray box, by double-clicking on the box and typing in what you want.

Layout Pane

Figure 8-24 shows the options that are available to customize the story pages. The options are explained below.

The **CAPTION BOXES** option is the default navigation option, shown above in Figure 8-23.

The **NUMBERS** option is shown in Figure 8-24.

The **DOTS** option displays the story points, as shown in Figure 8-25.

The **SHOW ARROWS** option displays the arrow before and after the caption box or number boxes. In addition to clicking on a gray box, the arrows are another way to display the previous or next story point.

The **TOOLBAR** shown above the story points, in Figure 8-24, has the following options, from left to right.

- ☑ **DELETE** the story point that is displayed.
- ☑ **REVERT** redisplay the chart to the way it was before a change (like selecting a filter option) was made to how the data is displayed.
- ☑ **UPDATE** apply updates to the story point that is displayed.
- ☑ **SAVE AS NEW** is enabled when a chart object (like a specific filter value), has been selected. When this button is clicked, the story point (chart) that is displayed is duplicated. The new story point displays the chart with the change currently applied.

Figure 8-24 Layout pane options

Figure 8-25 Dots story point navigation layout

Story Menu

Except for the first option, the options shown in Figure 8-26 are only available when a story sheet is selected. Many of the options are the same as the ones on the Worksheet menu.

The **SHOW BACK/FORWARD BUTTONS** option displays/hides the navigation arrows next to the story points.

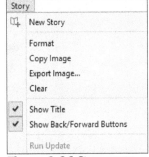

Figure 8-26 Story menu

Exercise 8.4: Create A Story

In this exercise you will create a story that uses two charts and one dashboard.

1. Add a Story sheet ⇒ Rename it to E8.4 Story.

2. Drag the Sales by state chart to the canvas.

3. Click in the gray caption box ⇒ Type Sales by state map.

4. On the Story pane, click the Blank button ⇒ Drag the Sales by quarter chart to the canvas ⇒ Change the caption to Sales by quarter.

5. Add the E8.3 dashboard to the story ⇒ Change the caption to `Story Home Page`. The second page of the story should look like the one shown earlier in Figure 8-23.

Changing The Order Of The Story Pages

You may have the need to change the order that the story pages are displayed in.

When that is the case, drag the caption or number box in the navigator, in the direction that you want it moved to. The triangles illustrated in Figure 8-27, indicate the new location for the page.

Figure 8-27 Triangles indicating the new location for the page

 If the navigator is using numbers, the pages are automatically renumbered when you reorder them. For example, if you move the second page to the fourth position, the current third and fourth pages will be renumbered as 2 and 3, and the second page will be renumbered to 4.

6. Move the Story Home Page sheet to the beginning of the story. You can press the F7 key to view the story in presentation mode.

Resize Captions

If you find that the text that you entered is too large for the default caption size, you can resize the box. Keep in mind that all caption boxes are resized at the same time.

To make the caption boxes wider, place the mouse pointer on the left or right side border and drag the mouse to make the box wider.

To resize the caption box horizontally and vertically, place the mouse pointer on the lower right corner of the box and drag the mouse button, up or down.

INDEX

.csv files, 2-3, 2-13
.txt file type, 2-13, 2-14

A

actions option, 4-4, 8-10
add a new data source button, 4-9
add data to pivot option, 3-16
add table calculations, 4-11, 6-11, 6-16
add to context option, 5-14
add to sheet option, 4-18
adding totals, 6-17
ad-hoc calculations, 6-10
aggregate functions, 4-20, 6-5
aggregate measures option, 4-5, 6-3
aggregated data, 3-8, 6-2
aggregation default property, 4-19
aggregations, 4-20
aliases option, 2-8, 6-13
all values in database option, 5-11
analysis menu, 4-5
analytics pane, 4-36
apply filter to worksheets dialog box, 8-6
apply to totals option, 6-12
apply to worksheets, 5-7
area chart (continuous), 4-22
area chart (discrete), 4-22, 7-6
assume referential integrity option, 2-12
attr function, 6-3, 6-6
attribute option, 6-3
auto updates, 4-5
automatically update button, 2-14
average function, 4-21

B

background maps, 4-7
bar chart, 4-15
blending data, 3-26
bookmark option, 2-12
bookmarks (.tbm) file, 1-10, 1-14, 5-23
boolean data type, 2-2
box and whisker chart, 4-23, 7-9
bullet chart, 4-23

C

calculated fields, 6-3
calculation editor, 6-4
calculation types, 6-2
canvas section, 2-7
caption boxes, 8-13
cardinality, 3-19
cell size option, 4-8
change data source location (data source tab), 2-16
change data source location (sheet tab), 2-16
change the data type, 2-9, 2-15
change the field reference, 2-21
chart types, 4-21

circle views chart, 4-22, 7-4
clear option, 4-4
clear sheet button, 4-9
clipboard data saved dialog box, 2-22
color button (marks card), 4-26, 4-27
color default property, 4-19
color option, 4-15
columns shelf, 4-10
combination chart, 7-7
combine string field values, 6-7
combined field option, 4-24
computed set, 5-19, 5-21
computed sorting, 5-2
connect pane, 1-12
connect to a pdf file, 2-18
connect to data option, 2-4
connect to sql server database, 2-16
connection options, 2-7
connections section (data source tab), 2-5
constant set, 5-19, 5-20
container shortcut menu, 8-6
contains function, 6-8
context filters, 5-14
continuous date, 4-12
continuous option, 4-11, 4-13
convert to continuous, 4-18
convert to dimension option, 4-18, 6-9
convert to discrete, 4-18
convert to measure, 4-18
convert to union option, 3-21
copy/paste formatting option, 4-15
copy/paste option, 4-15
count (distinct) function, 4-21
count function, 4-21
create bins option, 2-8, 4-23
create calculated field option, 4-6
create folders, 4-35
create group dialog box, 5-18
create option, 4-18
create set, 5-7
create user filter, 4-8
crosstab to excel option, 4-4
cube data, 2-8
custom sort order, 5-3
custom split, 2-10
customize (filter option), 5-11, 5-12
cycle fields, 4-6

D

dashboard menu, 8-4
dashboards, 8-2
data blending, 3-27
data cleansing options, 3-7
data extract (.tde) file, 1-10, 3-11, 3-14
data granularity, 6-12
data interpreter, 3-6
data menu options (data source tab), 2-11
data menu options (sheet tab), 4-3

data pane, 4-17
data sharing options, 1-11
data source (.tds) file, 1-10, 3-26
data source tab toolbar, 2-13
data source tab workspace, 2-5
data types, 2-2
date add function, 6-8
date data type, 2-2
date diff function, 6-8, 6-9
date field hierarchy, 5-9
date functions, 6-5, 6-8
date part, 4-12
date properties option, 4-17
date time data type, 2-2, 2-9
default number format dialog box, 4-20
default properties options, 4-19
default repository location, 2-11
default sort order, 5-4
describe option (data source tab), 2-8
describe option (sheet tab), 4-19
describe sheet option, 4-5
detail button (marks card), 4-26
device layouts option, 8-4
device preview button, 8-2
difference from option, 6-16
dimension field shortcut menu, 2-21
dimensions, 4-12
dimensions section shortcut menu, 4-18
direct connection, 1-9
discrete date, 4-12
discrete option, 4-11, 4-14
distribute evenly option, 8-8
drill down, 6-18
driver requirements (access & excel), 2-15
dual combination chart, 4-22, 7-8
dual lines chart, 4-22, 7-5
duplicate as crosstab, 4-5
duplicate button, 4-9
duplicate data source, 2-11

E

edit aliases, 4-11
edit calculated fields option, 4-6
edit colors (legend), 4-33
edit comment dialog box, 4-19
edit data source filters, 2-12
edit filter, 5-10
edit filter action dialog box, 8-11
edit in shelf option, 4-11
edit relationships, 4-3
edit title (filter option), 5-11
enable automatic product updates, 2-13
exact date option, 4-11, 6-9
exclude option (pages shelf), 5-16
exclude values option, 5-11
export (worksheet option), 4-4
export data from a sheet tab, 2-23
export data to csv, 2-12, 2-23
export image dialog box, 4-4
export option, 4-15
export packaged workbook, 4-3
extract connection, 1-9, 2-7, 3-11, 3-12, 3-14
extract data, 3-14

extract transform load (etl), 1-9

F

field reference, 2-21
field shortcut menu options, 4-18
file menu options (data source tab), 2-10
file menu options (sheet tab), 4-3
file types, 1-10
filled map chart, 4-21, 7-3
film strip view, 4-35
filter action, 8-10
filter dialog box, 3-13
filter option, 4-11
filter shortcut menu options, 5-10
filters (sheet tab), 5-6
filters option, 4-6
filters option (data source tab), 2-7, 3-11
filters shelf, 5-6
fit button, 4-9
fix axes button, 4-9
folder structures, 1-13
folders option, 4-18
forecast option, 4-6
format menu, 4-8
format option, 4-11
frequency table chart, 4-23
functions, 4-20, 6-5

G

gantt chart, 4-23
generate field names automatically option, 3-21
generated fields, 4-19
geographic data type, 2-2
geographic role, 2-9, 4-17
grid section, 2-7
group by option, 4-18
group members (pages shelf), 5-16
group members button, 4-9
grouping data, 5-16

H

heat map chart, 4-21, 7-2
hide card option, 5-11
hierarchy for a date field, 5-9
hierarchy option, 4-18, 5-5
highlight action, 8-10
highlight background color, 4-27
highlight button, 4-9
highlight table chart, 4-21, 4-27
highlighters option, 4-6
histogram chart, 4-23
horizontal bars chart, 4-22

I

if statement, 6-5
iif statement, 6-6
import workbook option, 2-10, 2-23
include in tooltip option, 4-11
include other (group option), 5-19
include values option, 5-11

J

join null values to null values, 2-12
joins, 3-19
json file type, 1-9, 2-13

L

label button (marks card), 4-26, 4-28
latitude generated field, 4-19, 7-2
layout pane (dashboards), 8-8
layout pane (stories), 8-13
left pane (data source tab), 2-5
level of detail (lod) calculations, 6-2
lines chart (continuous), 4-22, 4-30
lines chart (discrete), 4-22, 4-31
live connection, 1-9, 2-7, 3-11, 3-12
logical functions, 6-5
longitude generated field, 4-19, 7-2

M

map menu, 4-7
map source (.tms) file, 1-10
maps, 7-2
marks card, 4-25
maximum function, 4-21
measure names generated field, 4-19, 4-22, 4-32, 6-13
measure values generated field, 4-19, 4-22, 4-32
measures, 4-13
median function, 4-21
merge mismatched fields, 2-10
metadata grid, 2-8
minimum function, 4-21
month function, 6-8
multiple values (filter option), 5-11, 5-13, 8-7
my tableau repository, 1-10, 1-13

N

named ranges, 3-5
navigation bar, 4-14
navigation buttons, 8-12
new custom sql option, 2-6
new data source button (sheet tab), 2-4
new data source option (data source tab), 2-11
new story point options, 8-12
new union option, 2-6, 3-22
new worksheet button, 4-9
now function, 6-8
null values, 3-9
number formation default property, 4-19
number functions, 6-5
number of records calculated field, 4-6, 4-19
numerical data type, 2-2

O

objects shortcut menu, 8-8
odbc, 1-9, 2-18
olap cube, 2-8
one-to-many relationship, 3-18
one-to-one relationship, 3-18
only relevant values option, 5-11, 8-7
order of operations, 3-11, 3-27
other databases (odbc) option, 2-18

P

packaged data source (.tdsx) file, 1-10, 3-26
packaged workbooks (.twbx) file, 1-10, 2-10, 4-3
packed bubbles chart, 4-23
page control, 5-14
pages shelf, 5-14
parameter top n filter, 6-21
parameters, 6-20
parameters option, 4-6
parameters section (data pane), 4-19
paste data as connection, 2-10
paste data as data source, 2-11, 2-22
paste option, 4-3
path button (marks card), 4-26
pause auto updates button (data source tab), 2-14
pause auto updates button (sheet tab), 4-9
pdf file data source, 2-18
percent of total calculation, 6-13
percentage of option, 4-6, 6-19
percentile function, 4-21
percents (adding), 6-19
pie chart, 4-22, 4-28
pill, 3-9, 4-14
pinning a workbook, 1-15
pivot data, 3-16
pivot option, 2-10
preference (.tps) file, 1-10, 1-14
presentation mode, 4-8
print to pdf option, 4-3
properties option, 4-17
publish data source, 2-12

Q

quick filter, 5-10
quick table calculations, 4-11, 6-2, 6-11, 6-12, 6-14

R

range of values option, 5-11
rank function, 6-19
refresh (data) option, 3-12
refresh all extracts, 4-3
refresh data source, 2-11
refresh thumbnail, 4-34
remove filter, 5-10
remove option, 4-11
rename a data set, 3-24
rename column heading, 4-32
rename data source dialog box, 2-22
replace a relational data source, 2-19
replace data source option, 4-4
replace reference, 4-19
repository location, 2-10
revert to saved option, 4-3
rows shelf, 4-10
run update button, 4-9
run update option, 4-5
running total, 6-13

S

save to tableau public options, 2-10
saved data sources, 1-13
saving data sources, 2-24
saving workbooks, 2-24
scatter chart, 4-22, 7-8
server menu options (data source tab), 2-12
server menu options (sheet tab), 4-8
sets, 5-19
sets section (data pane), 4-19
settings and performance options, 2-13
shape button (marks card), 4-26
shape default property, 4-19
shape symbols (charts), 7-9
share workbook with others button, 4-9
sheet tab toolbar, 4-9
sheet tab workspace, 4-2
show film strip button, 4-29
show filter option (data pane), 4-18
show filter option (sheet tab), 4-11, 5-10, 5-11
show highlighter option, 4-11
show history option, 5-15
show in/out of set option, 5-20
show mark labels option, 4-5
show me button, 4-21
show missing values option, 4-11
show sheet sorter button, 4-29, 4-34
show status bar, 2-12
show tabs button, 4-29
show/hide cards button, 4-9
side-by-side bar chart, 4-22, 4-29
side-by-side circles chart, 4-22, 7-4
single value (filter option), 5-11
size button (marks card), 4-26, 4-28
slicing filters, 5-13
sort default property, 4-19
sort measure names (ascending/descending) buttons, 4-9
sort option, 4-11
sort using the legend, 5-3
sorting data, 5-2
special values option, 4-6
split data, 3-10
split data (custom), 2-10
split option, 2-10
sql server database connection, 2-16
stack marks, 4-5
stacked bars chart, 4-22, 4-30
star schema, 3-22
start page, 1-11
status bar (sheet tab), 4-29
std dev (pop) function, 4-21
std dev function, 4-21
stories, 8-12
story menu, 8-13
string data type, 2-2
string functions, 6-5
structured query language (sql), 1-9
sum function, 4-21, 6-6
swap rows and columns, 4-6, 4-9, 4-16
symbol map chart, 4-21, 7-21

T

table calculation functions, 6-5
table calculations, 6-2, 6-11, 6-15
table layout option, 4-6
tableau desktop, 1-5
tableau desktop public app, 1-6, 1-8
tableau online, 1-6
tableau public option (data source tab), 2-12
tableau public option (sheet tab), 4-8
tableau reader, 1-6
tableau software editions, 1-5
text button (marks card), 4-26
text file types, 2-13
text table chart, 4-21, 4-24
thumbnail shortcut menu, 4-34
toolbar (data source tab), 2-13
toolbar (sheet tab), 4-9
toolbar (story points), 8-13
tooltip button (marks card), 4-26
tooltip option, 4-4
top 10 filter criteria, 5-10, 6-21
total using default property, 4-19
totals options, 4-6
transform option, 4-18
tree maps chart, 4-22, 7-3
trend lines options, 4-6
truncated date, 4-12
type conversion functions, 6-5

U

union, 1-10, 2-6, 3-22
unsaved workbook, 2-22
update now button, 2-14
url action, 2-13, 8-10
use separate legends option, 4-33
user functions, 6-5
using folders option, 4-35

V

variance (pop) function, 4-21
variance function, 4-21
view data dialog box, 2-6, 2-23, 5-16, 5-22

W

window menu options (data source tab), 2-12
window menu options (sheet tab), 4-8
workbooks (.twb) file, 1-10
workbooks from earlier versions, 1-19
worksheet menu options, 4-4

Y

year function, 6-8
ytd total option, 6-15

www.ingramcontent.com/pod-product-compliance
Lightning Source LLC
LaVergne TN
LVHW060141070326
832902LV00018B/2886